A
WORD
OR
TWO
ABOUT
LEARNING DISABILITIES

A WORD OR TWO

ABOUT

LEARNING DISABILITIES

By

Doreen Kronick

1973

© Academic Therapy Publications
San Rafael, California 94901

Academic Therapy Publications
P.O. Box 899
1539 Fourth Street
San Rafael, California 94901

Books, tests, and materials
for and about the learning disabled

International Standard
Book Number: 0-87879-070-5

Library of Congress
Catalog Card Number: 73-88788

Cover Design: James H. Wallace

First printing: 1973
Second printing: 1976

This book was set in IBM Century
8 point and 10 point medium
and medium italic type.
Chapter titles were set in
Varityper 20 point Univers
extra bold extended;
section headings were set in
IBM Univers 10 point bold.
The paper used was 60 pound
Arbor for the text;
10 point CIS for the cover.

Printed in the
United States of America

Contents

PART ONE
Social-Psychological Implications
of Learning Disabilities for Child and Family

   11   Chapter 1:   Shock and Denial
   35   Chapter 2:   Isolation and Alienation
   51   Chapter 3:   Why Did It Have to Happen To Me?
   59   Chapter 4:   Guilt, Bargaining and Magic, Depression and Mourning
   65   Chapter 5:   Apathy, Group Identification, Myths, Secondary Gain, Professional Mixed Messages
   81   Chapter 6:   Developing a Realistic Self-Concept

PART TWO
The Socialization Process

  101   Chapter 7:   The Communication Components of Time, Space, and Relatedness
  123   Chapter 8:   Parents' Attitudes Are Important
  133   Chapter 9:   Dealing With Behavior

PART THREE
The Family in the Community

  157   Chapter 10:   Relating to the Professional
  165   Chapter 11:   Person to Person — *Betty Lou Kratoville*
  178   Chapter 12:   Telling It Like It Is! — *Betty Lou Kratoville*
  183   Chapter 13:   Maximizing the School Experience

PART FOUR
Recreation and Camping for the Learning Disabled

  197   Chapter 14:   For Recreation Administrators and Leaders
  207   Chapter 15:   A Parent's Guide to Camping
  215   Chapter 16:   For Directors of Nonspecialized Camps
  233   Chapter 17:   Establishing a Special Camp
  245   Chapter 18:   Program Ideas and Games

Sorrow may be fated,
but to survive it and grow
is an achievement all its own.
—Robert Coles

To Noah who taught me all I know, but most of all, courage.

To Ed, Margie, and Sam whose knowledge made our lives liveable, and whose honesty and support of parents taught me what professionalism is all about.

To Eleanor whose interest and help made the difference.

To Gene who started me in a new career.

To Stan who made it all possible.

To Joe who shared the pain and triumphs and supported the desire to write.

To John who has made writing a pleasure.

To the fraternity of dedicated parents and professionals who have changed the lot of the learning disabled from despair to hope and whose valued friendship has deepened my life.

To Adam because he is too delightful to be omitted.

To Sarah who can't wait to spend the royalties.

Part One

Social-Psychological Implications of Learning Disabilities for Child and Family

Chapter 1:

Shock and Denial

LEARNING DISABILITIES were unknown for most of our civilized history. They have been described and worked with, in our current terms of reference, for thirty to forty years. S. Orton, A. Strauss, and H. Werner delineated the phenomenon and devised remedial procedures in the 1930s and 1940s. Nonetheless, the vast majority of learning-disabled* children in North America languished undiscovered and unassisted until the social action of parents initiated massive changes in the 1960s and 1970s. Robert Coles, in his book *Children of Crisis*, refers to "an enabling historical moment,"[1] and indeed, that phrase appropriately describes the phenomenon I have observed. Parents from the Yukon to California, from Quebec to Florida, seemed to arrive independently at a decision to seek one another and band together to effect mutual support and change. Perhaps someday a sociologist will study the factors leading to the formation of associations concerned with the l.d. child in that period of history. It would be fascinating to learn why parents of the l.d. child who had remained subdued in the past, immobilized by fear, guilt, and shame, should (without realizing that others were involved in the same process), now find the courage to fight for reform at the risk of exposure, rejection, and reaction. I was one of three who founded the Ontario Association for Children with Learning Disabilities in November 1963. Two of the founders were unaware that there were other groups working toward the same goal, and one had heard of a group in New York. After we were formed, we learned that identical groups were scattered throughout the U.S.A.

Perhaps, because this is the period in North American history when lesser-status groups, such as the blacks, women, and homosexuals, have been clamoring for acceptance and equality, the parents of the learning disabled found the strength to press for their children's rights. Likelier still, these

---

*Henceforth referred to as l.d.

parents were spurred to formation and activism by the same subtle changes in our society which prompted lower-status groups to expose their true conditions and demand change.

If, indeed, someone does study the l.d. movement, he should examine the next phase, wherein the current generation of parents is producing, once again, fewer individuals who are dedicated enough to man the legislative and educational efforts of the volunteer associations. Generally speaking, today's parents of the l.d. child seem more dependent and, once again, apathetic. Possibly, our first difficult thrust was the most exciting, and parents may view the ongoing efforts as less rewarding. This may partially explain their reduced involvement.

Regardless of the current apathy, the volunteer movement remains an outstanding model of grass-roots social action. Parents of all social classes and professionals have combined their efforts to effect impressive changes in the first five to ten years of its existence. It is easy to forget that as recently as the early 1960s few professionals or lay persons in North America knew what learning disabilities were. The universities did not teach the diagnosis or treatment of the disability, and the consequence of this dearth of information was that l.d. children received no help. The services presently being offered to the learning disabled in U.S.A. and Canada number in the thousands. Certainly they vary in quality and fall far short of serving all children who require their help. We are just embarking on services for the preschool child, the adolescent, and the adult, and have a long way to travel. However, as those persons who carry on the thrust continue the arduous process of ensuring our children's rights to success, it is important not to forget the courageous beginning efforts. Our children will need convincing spokesmen and forceful intervention for many years to come, and we can learn much from the initiators who telescoped a lifetime of change into a mere few years. It is to these remarkable and deeply human people that I dedicate this book, as well as to my patient and understanding family.

The beginning efforts of volunteer associations were directed toward obtaining community diagnostic and remedial services, and this is as it should be. I feel confident that the dynamics of assessment have now become so exciting to the professionals in this field that refinements in diagnoses will occur without further outside encouragement. Similarly, we have focused with sophisticated precision on the academic disorders of the l.d. child, and a flood of theories and materials directed toward relieving these disorders have resulted. I welcome the developments in remediation because, without question, academic problems are central to the dysfunction of the learning disabled. Nonetheless, as our knowledge of learning disabilities is deepening with the passage of time, it is becoming apparent to an increasing number of professionals and parents that we must be concerned with the whole child, his adjustment to family, neighborhood, and larger community—how he relates to others, how others relate to him, and how he spends his time.

THE NATURAL PLACE to start is with the family. We cannot place total responsibility for the child's adjustment onto the methods the school adopts or fails to adopt, or, for that matter, on any one facet of the child's life. Much of his environment occurs outside of the school, within the family structure and larger community. This makes it important to begin looking at the family's reactions to having a learning-disabled member, the way the family relates to the community, the community to it, and the effects on the developing child and family constellation.

My qualifications for documenting the reactions of child and family emerge primarily from nine years of exposure to such children and their families. It began when I cofounded the first volunteer association concerned with the l.d. in Canada. From that point in time to this, thousands of families in crisis sought me out, by letter, by telephone, and by personal visit—Canadians, Americans, and eventually persons from many parts of the world. In the past four years I have lectured extensively in North America, which afforded me the opportunity to meet a cross section of families of the learning disabled, geographically, financially, and racially. This section chronicles their feelings and consequent behavior as I have observed them and as they have related them to me. This does not pretend to be research, and I readily concede the possibility that my observations could be colored by my perceptions. It has been suggested that my observations relate only the middle-class experience and feelings. This is not so, since the reactions that I catalogue here do not relate to any specific financial status of the many families I have met. The only selective process operant was that the parents I met had to be sufficiently confident or interested to attend a school or other meeting where I was present, or contact me through other means.

One has to assume that l.d. children, being born randomly to a cross section of the population in U.S.A. and Canada, find themselves in a percentage of families who are as mentally healthy as any group of families, selected by chance. L. F. Kurlander and Dorothy Colodny comment, "It must be noted that the incidence of parents with their own neurotic disturbance seems less in this population (since causality is partly external) although by the time we see them, these parents too are very upset."[2] Other than children who exhibit learning disabilities from severe environmental deprivation, there is no documentation, to my knowledge, to support a direct etiological relationship between child-rearing practices and learning disabilities in children. In fact, there is much evidence that contraindicates this assumption. Before the birth of the l.d. child, one can assume that there was nothing unusual which would distinguish this family from their neighbors. Therefore, the process of describing the reactions of the family is essentially a description of the reactions of healthy people to a particular set of stresses. We should be concerned only when one of the stages is prolonged or exaggerated.

Since there is no prototype parent of the l.d. child, families bring every conceivable combination of attributes and past experiences to the situation. Therefore, although many of the stages through which they pass in the process of adjusting to the disability will be shared by other families with l.d. children, their reactions to those stages will be as different as one set of parents is from another. Some families discover that a learning-disabled member is the catalyst for family solidarity and deep moral growth, others find the situation to be profoundly disintegrative, and many feel that there are elements of additional closeness *and* divisiveness in the experience. Some of the stages I describe in this section, such as shock, denial, isolation, anger, magic, guilt, and depression seem to be fairly universal to families with l.d. children, although they vary markedly in intensity and duration, and the methods used in coping with these stages also vary. Some of the other behaviors that I will be delineating, such as parent polarization, believing in myths, scapegoating, and pecking order are not practised by every family but are sufficiently prevalent to bear mention.

Someday perhaps a clinician may wish to pursue the questions of why some parents or children never progress beyond denial or self pity, some become paralyzed into apathy and dependence, some become unduly aggressive, and some seemingly ordinary people exhibit remarkable growth, channelling their feelings into successful, constructive efforts to effect changes for children. I will describe the feelings and experiences, hypothesizing a bit, and leave to persons better qualified than I the task of determining why individuals react diversely to similar problems.

The majority of studies of human development have focused on the intact organism in a typical environment. We know relatively little about how the development of the neurologically different child creates a diverse set of factors, an altered response to his environment, thus altering the environmental response to him. Up to the present time we have responded to and treated his reactions basically in the same manner as we treat persons who have followed normal developmental expectations. Using normal development as our term of reference, we have created assumptions about his differences. This causes us to consider the behaviors he demonstrates as being deviant, rather than being normal in terms of his particular constitutional factors and environment, even though they may be maladaptive to our society. There are important implications in the way such assumptions affect our attitudes and treatment techniques.

AS MY INTEREST in the social-psychological implications of learning disabilities developed in recent years, I have sought relevant literature. My thinking has been moulded and deepened by a number of writers, most notably: Beatrice A. Wright, Physical Disability—A Psychological Approach; Erving Goffman, *Stigma*; Elisabeth Kubler-Ross, *On Death and Dying*; Bernard T. Hall, *The Silent Language*; Joel R. Davitz et al., *The Communication of Emotional Meaning*; and L. F. Kurlander and Dorothy Colodny, "Pseudoneurosis in the Neurologically Handicapped Child."[3]

I was fascinated to note that the stages that Elisabeth Kubler-Ross describes as being those experienced by dying persons are the same stages experienced by handicapped children and their parents, upon discovering and coming to terms with a handicap. This leads me to suppose that, in all likelihood, people in our culture probably react to diverse stresses of a severe nature by passing through the prescribed stages of shock, denial, isolation, anger, guilt, bargaining, depression, acceptance, and hope. Regardless of whether or not one can generalize reactions to stress, discovering that one has parented a less able child can be equated with dying in that one's expectation for the child's attainment, success, and recognition for achievements have been killed, so we suffer feelings of deep loss. It is understandable, therefore, that our reactions are similar to those of persons facing death. We even lose the pleasure of anticipating that our son or daughter will develop an enjoyment of that which the world has to offer, since much of it is based upon accurate and selective perception. One mother commented, "When my son was first diagnosed as mildly retarded, my initial reaction was that he'll never be able to enjoy good music or books, and I grieved. He now is an intelligent l.d. adult and the only one of my children to enjoy classical music, but he rarely reads."

In most countries there are clearly defined concepts of class so that parents expect their children to undertake jobs commensurate with their social class. Selection of schools may be very much based upon the class in which the family finds itself, and it is expected that the child will acquire as extensive an education as others in his social strata. In U.S.A. and Canada, the end result may not differ markedly from the countries in which there is less expectation of interclass mobility. In other words, a high proportion of North American factory worker's sons may eventually become factory workers, and professional's children become professionals, but the expectations, in our culture, of the young child's attainment tend to be high. The great American dream is that every child will become President, and with the emergence of women's lib, that may be the dream that parents have for their daughters, as well! Thus, when we learn that we have a l.d. child, our feeling is that the child has lost the supposed American opportunity for the ultimate in attainment.

Shock

When we first discover that our child is learning disabled, our initial reaction is shock. We are so overwhelmed by the shattering news that we erect a protective barrier, only processing elements of the situation which we can handle at that time. This is the reason that many parents are too "socked in" to absorb and remember much of the initial diagnosis and need the details reexplained at a later date, or supplied to them in writing after they have heard them verbally.

Denial

One of the ways we cope with profound shock is by denial. Elisabeth Kubler-Ross comments, "Denial functions as a buffer after unexpected shocking news, allows the patient to collect himself and, with time, mobilize other, less radical defenses."[4] The manifestation of denial can be troublesome to professionals, friends, and relatives of the family, particularly if it is prolonged. Family acquaintances are faced with the dilemma of whether to "go along" with the denial or try to force reality onto the parents. It is vitally important for professionals to appreciate that parents and child must spend some time in the denial stage, just as they must spend some time feeling alienated, angry, depressed, and going through the process of bargaining. It is only when denial becomes prolonged that professional intervention is indicated. Many healthy parents and children will progress from stage to stage within a reasonable period of time, yet retain vestiges of earlier stages. Thus, we can be realistic and accept our child's strengths and limitations, yet nourish a small hope that we will awaken one day to find that it has all been a bad dream, that our child is "normal." This acceptance and nonacceptance on different levels of our consciousness often results in sending mixed messages to the child. Consider the family in which the mother has set herself up as a parent who accepts the handicap, encouraging her child to consider his difficulties in realistic career planning, yet eagerly provides him with material on universities that are prepared to enroll l.d. youth.

It is particularly easy to deny the l.d. in one's offspring because of the uneven picture of development such children typically present. Although the child may be significantly retarded in one aspect of his development, he obviously functions in an intelligent manner in other ways. Furthermore, the range of development for the young child is so broad that parents can control their concerns about a developmental lag by referring to histories of children of their acquaintance who were equally slow to speak, walk, or read, yet emerged as totally "normal" people. It is relatively simple for the parent of the l.d. to find reasons for the child's deficiencies. This is illustrated by the mother of the kindergarten child in the movie, *Early Recognition of Learning Disabilities*,[5] who explains away her daughter's inability to handle crayons by stating that she is an overly clean mother who did not give her daughter crayons lest she write on the walls. In a similar fashion, we tend to explain away our child's clumsiness by the fact that we have not allowed him enough practice because we impatiently perform the task for him, or that his father does not throw balls to him. We rationalize his poor language skills with the excuse that we are such verbal people that he has limited opportunities to verbalize, or that we meet all his needs so that he has no need to talk. A prevalent parental response is that "Johnny is just like I was when I was a child." The assumption here is that since the parent reached functional adulthood, despite a similar developmental pattern, the child will as well. Whereas this assumption may bear much truth, it neglects to allow for such questions as: Is the child's dysfunction more severe than his parent's was; are the demands upon him greater or different; what inner resources does he bring to the problem; and what price did the parent pay to achieve ultimate success?

Parents of children suffering from disabilities of a more serious nature than l.d. sometimes deny their child's disability by clinging to the idea that their child is learning disabled. Since many exceptionalities are accompanied by concomitant learning problems and much behavior that overlaps with learning disabilities, it is not difficult to comprehend the ease with which such parents continue to support this myth. They travel from professional to professional, from service to service, seeking the professional who will treat only the learning problem. They attempt to enroll their child in services designed specifically for the l.d., and eventually they find a professional or a service that will go along with their pretense. Unfortunately, the child's acceptance into the program, even if it is only a recreation program for the l.d., further reinforces the parent's insistence that the child is learning disabled. The tragedy of such cases is that the child does not receive the most appropriate services, and the parents' expectations and goals for their offspring are unrealistic. Some parents who employ this form of denial become paranoid-like in their behavior. "No one is interested, no one wants to help me or my child." They, of course, invite this rejection by their continued seeking of inappropriate services.

Larry did not develop speech until age five. He exhibits serious problems of comprehension and motor coordination. Following his year in kindergarten, the principal placed him in a l.d. class. His mother commenced to inform all with whom she came in contact that because Larry had not talked until age five, he had a five-year maturation lag and would develop intellectually, ad infinitum, until he graduated from the university. When he was discharged from the l.d. class, three years hence, because his comprehension was so poor, she stated that Larry had failed to produce because he was too friendly with his teacher.

Although the mother is a lab technician by training and the father a physician, Larry was not taken to a neurologist until age nine. He diagnosed Larry as being profoundly brain damaged, which the mother dismissed. She rationalized that her son disliked the electroencephalogram, squirmed during the test so that the results had to be discounted. In her firm conviction that Larry could accomplish anything, the mother enrolled him in a tutorial clinic during school hours. She woke him at 6:00 AM daily so that he could practice at the piano and do his optometric exercises before breakfast. After school he received his daily dose of tutoring by mother: language therapy, French lessons, Hebrew and piano lessons—and on the weekends, Sunday school. His parents are so anxious that he be "normal" that they magnify and generalize each small gain that he makes. Last summer he attended a summer school which has a clearly stated policy of serving dyslexics only. When I queried the director of the school, his reason for accepting Larry for enrollment was to show his staff the difference between dyslexic and brain-injured children. However, the fact that he was accepted confirms his parent's conviction that he is relatively unimpaired and highly intelligent.

Although shopping from professional to professional is a manifestation of the denial stage and a seeking of a diagnosis that the parents can accept, it also is a seeking of help and hope. Parents need direction and support. They seek a professional who will treat them as intact, intelligent persons, not totally responsible for their child's problem. It is important that they feel that the information on their child has been shared fully with them and that they are being included in the planning of a therapeutic approach. We cannot predict with accuracy the extent to which a learning disability is reversible; nonetheless, even if, in a professional's opinion, the disability is relatively irreversible, in the childhood years parents still need the element of hope.

Temara Dembo states:

> The struggle for hope just described is not limited to parents of
> severely handicapped children. Whenever a person suffers from a
> threatening loss of greatest importance to him, he struggles for

hope. In a situation of despair a person, to succeed in gaining hope, tries and usually is able to make a step that he would usually reject; he exchanges the dictum of probability, which guides us in everyday life, for the dictum of possibility.[6]

Further in the article Dembo states:

Here, if only in passing, let us mention that the client needs hope, not only to diminish his suffering, but also to be able to take care of his handicapped child and to engage, without undue strain, in other everyday activities. It is hope that saves him from paralizing despair and depression. The content of this hope is that the child will improve; the parent does not demand support of the hope of complete recovery.[7]

The parents need to feel that they are involved in efforts to alleviate the disability, to pacify their guilt. To these ends they should be referred to programs in school and community that might benefit the child and instructed in the particulars of a therapeutic home life. If there are no suitable services in the community, the diagnostician must explain to the parents the type of services which might benefit the child if they were available, and describe how groups of parents in other communities have succeeded in encouraging their communities to initiate services. Additionally, the diagnostician may be able to orient local services to ways whereby they can begin to meet the needs of the l.d. child and his family. There is a general practitioner in Ottawa, Ontario, who devotes one afternoon weekly to meeting with the staff of schools wherein his l.d. patients are enrolled. He shares his ideas on possible ways to effect learning and growth of his young patients. When the family can cling to the prospect of improvement, the likelihood that they linger unduly in the denial stage is reduced.

Outsider's Denial

One of the ways mothers structure the disability, its extent and implications, is through verbalization. However, they often are thwarted in their efforts to talk through this new dimension in their lives because of the denial of friends, relatives, and neighbors. These "outsiders" demonstrate denial by being uncomfortable with such discussion; they avoid initiating the topic and tend to change the subject of conversation when it is initiated by the mother. They adopt this attitude because of the acute discomfort we experience in our society when dealing with problems that seem to have irreversible and tragic components, such as terminal illness, death, disability, and retarded intellect. We worship the body beautiful and the keen mind, pretending that less is nonexistent.

When we discuss the denial mechanisms of relatives and other outsiders, we must take into account their own expectations of the child and consequent disappointment, their own fear that they or their child might become, or be found to be l.d. at some point in time, and the stigma of having a less than perfect child as a member of the greater family. To this we add ignorance. The exceptionality, learning disabilities, is difficult to comprehend, contrasting considerably to everyone's previous orientation to exceptionalities. In other words, when today's generation of adults were schoolchildren, if a classmate could not handle school work, once defects in sight and hearing were ruled out, the assumption was that the child was "stupid." Similarly, strange behavior signified mental illness. Now we tell our unbelieving family and acquaintances that the child is neither retarded nor psychotic, yet exhibits considerable problems in learning and, on occasion, handles himself inappropriately. Consequently, the typical response of outsiders is denial or stereotyping. "There's nothing the matter with this kid," they state, "he just needs some discipline." Or, "He's a perfectly normal child; it's you, his parents who are talking him into a disability and he's fulfilling your wishes." When the child is fed this message he desperately attempts to handle himself "normally." He tries hard to produce what he thinks is normal behavior, and the harder he tries, the more anxious he becomes. As he becomes increasingly anxious to conform, the energies that could be utilized to process the intricacies of his current social situation are diverted to anxiety, so he is even less likely to process his environment adequately, with the consequent reduced likelihood of appropriate behavior. The process is self-defeating.

Outsiders' propensity to view normalcy and handicap as clearly defined absolutes has the result that, if they do not insist that the child is normal, they are likely to assume that indeed he is retarded or "crazy," and they *expect him to act the part*! Thus, I have seen some l.d. children fulfill these expectations by acting the "clown" or "dummy," and they internalize some of these askewed expectations. They begin to think that everything they do is stupid or crazy.

The difficulty that child and family encounter with outsider's denial mechanisms is that every friend, relative, and acquaintance will perceive and comprehend the disability differently, and they will exhibit varying tolerances when confronted with it. This ranges from studied avoidance of child and family to acute discomfort whenever the topic is mentioned. The opposite extreme occurs when ready advice is proferred to child and parents with solutions that will solve all their problems. Both child and parents feel compelled to play each person's game, to "go along," to a considerable extent, with their various forms of denial or misconception. With each new acquaintance, the child is unsure whether he will be perceived as "just a child," "retarded," or "sick," and which role he is supposed to play. This reduces the opportunities he has to act as himself and have others respond to the real child, with consequent reduced opportunities to discover who he really is, to develop a self-image. Few outsiders perceive the l.d. as it really is, and this handicaps the child and parents as they progress past the denial stage, because they are not able to share their feelings, problems, and concerns with realistic outsiders. This phenomenon also contributes to the family's feelings of isolation and alienation. Outsider's discomfort, denial, and avoidance is interpreted as, "No one understands, no one cares," or, as many parents have stated to me, "You certainly learn who your friends are!" Ironically, the more deeply an outsider cares about the child, the greater is the likelihood that he will experience difficulty encountering the problem and that the parents will misinterpret this avoidance as disinterest.

Father's Denial

A common complaint of mothers of the l.d. is the father's denial of the child's disability. Frequently, the l.d. child is a boy and often the first born. This was to be the child who would achieve everything that his father achieved and succeed wherever his father had failed. This would be the perfect child that would be his immortality. Robert Coles, in *Children of Crisis* discusses how God and various utopias have disappointed us so that we seek our immortality in our children. Whereas both fathers and mothers tend to perceive their children as extensions of themselves, a flawed son seems to be a greater blow to the father. It undermines his feelings of intactness, his perceived capacity to produce a whole child and destroys his short- and long-term dreams, be they little league ball or upward mobility.

Regardless of the blurring of sex roles in our time, some stereotyped role expectation still occurs. The male, in our culture, is expected to respond to stresses with strength. In order to appear the strong male, the father is prevented from reacting to his grievous disappointment with grief, which likely is an emotion he should be able to acknowledge, as a steppingstone to adjustment. He is less likely to employ his wife's method of structuring the disability for herself by talking about it, because that more typically is female behavior. If the stress has served to divide husband and wife, rather than bring them together, the husband may not even find the environment sufficiently receptive for him to discuss his feelings and disappointments with his wife.

He is absent from his home many hours a day, so is not constantly faced with his child's problems and often manages to become involved in a variety of outside activities in order to maintain his distance from an unpleasant home situation. Although his wife bemoans his lack of involvement, she may, without realizing what she is doing, actually discourage his involvement with the child. "The moment you get near that child," she complains, "you say or do the wrong thing. I'm the one who reads the books about l.d. and goes to meetings," she continues, "while you remain ignorant."

In order to impress him with the gravity of the situation, she screams and shouts, and the more she does this, the greater the likelihood is that he will retreat. Typically, mothers of all children tend to be more concerned than fathers that their children's well-being might be in jeopardy, while fathers are more inclined to expose their children to verbal and physical rough and tumble. Thus the conflict of protection and care versus exposure generally is a mother-father conflict in the rearing of any child, but is accentuated in the families where a child is learning disabled. The mother is readier to protect her less adept and vulnerable offspring and likelier to consider normal demands and banter as injurious. She may contrive togetherness for father and child, devising activities that are unappealing to both parties. "Why don't you play ball with Johnny this afternoon," she urges. So a reluctant Johnny, who never catches the ball, and an even more reluctant and embarrassed father, move to the front lawn where an inept game of ball, doomed to failure from its inception, is staged for the neighborhood. Some mothers can continue to play the "I'm the martyr game" only if the father continues to remain uninvolved. Whereas they berate his uninvolvement, they unconsciously encourage its continuation. Some fathers defend their detached attitude by claiming that both parents cannot function hysterically, that one should retain a sense of proportion. Perhaps that attitude has some merit!

Although some fathers deny their child's disability with vigor, stoutly claiming that he is "all boy," they still may supply their child with numerous messages about his inadequacy. "You clumsy idiot, can't you hit the nail with the hammer?"; or, "Two and two are four, any fool knows that!"; or, "Come on, come on, hurry up, how come you're always so slow?"

The father's denial has to be assaulted in a number of ways, since each father is reached in a different manner. The first step is to help the mother feel empathy with the father's denial. She needs to realize that not only does his denial prevent the father from establishing a relationship with his offspring on the level that the child can contribute, but it prevents him from enjoying his son or daughter and appreciating what the child has to offer. The mother may require a number of lessons on how to communicate frankly with her husband and how to include him in decision making and planning. The father's role should not be relegated to meting out punishment for a day's misdemeanors or to be a sounding board for the woes of his harassed wife on his return from work. He should have an important role in planning home management, medical management, education, and recreation. Whenever possible, appointments with diagnosticians and educators should be arranged at a time when he is free to participate. When he tells his wife that she should go to talk to Johnny's teacher about the difficulty he's having, she can counter with, "When are you free, so we can visit the teacher together? I'd like to have you along." Regardless of the unsophisticated state of the father's knowledge, he should share in conferences and planning. He may not know the jargon but he may know his own child!

We mothers should allow our husbands to develop a relationship with our offspring without manipulating the situation or being concerned that our child will be traumatized or exposed to danger. We should allow our husband to suggest the activities that he most would enjoy doing with his child. There is no proof that ball throwing is any better than fishing, stamp collecting, taking trips, or what-have-you. Some fathers are not ball throwers or whatever else their wives may suppose constitutes the model father of the l.d. child. Let them find their own level, and do not expect remediation to accrue from the shared experience; be pleased to settle for camaraderie.

The second rule of thumb is: if the mother is concerned about how her husband talks to the child, or is afraid that he will allow him to venture outside without a hat, or permit the child to climb trees, then she should disappear, make herself scarce when they begin to interact. Mothers can be reassured that human youngsters, even the l.d., are hardy beings who will neither die of frostbite, starvation, or fatigue on the camping trip, or be unduly upset by their father's manner. The child will quickly adjust to his father's method of relating and respond to the love rather than the specific words.

Attendance at meetings of the volunteer association can be tremendously therapeutic for the father. I have known fathers who previously would not talk about their l.d. child finally come to discuss their youngster for the first time with other parents at meetings. If the husband will not attend open meetings, the mother should consider arranging to have meetings held at her house. She then can invite her husband to join the others for coffee and eventually involve him in an association project.

Schools and clinics may have to insist upon involvement of the father or threaten to exclude the child from a much-needed service. Some fathers require counseling with a group of fathers or with their wife. A particularly sad phenomenon is the father who has parented more than one l.d. child, thereby experiencing a repeated shattering of expectations. He may need considerable understanding and help. Surmounting the emotional and physical stresses of the l.d. family member challenges the resources of the most

intact family. When the parents are divided, the likelihood of effective management and healthy survival for all family members is considerably reduced.

Adopted Children

A significantly high percentage of l.d. children are adopted. We do not
know why this occurs, although several theories have been postulated. Therefore, the reactions of the adopted l.d. child and his parents merits mention.
Persons who have been unable to conceive or bear their own progeny often
carry feelings of inadequacy, of being less than all man or all woman, and
the discovery of a defect in the child seems to be a confirmation of their
inadequacy. After all, they may reason, what does an imperfect adult deserve
but an imperfect child? Consequently, their feelings of denial, guilt, anger,
and envy are no less acute than those of parents who conceived and bore a
learning-disabled child. Their attitudes seem to be related to their feelings
about sterility, adoption, and the child's antecedents. The adopted child is
likely to harbor fears that if he does not meet his adopted parents' expectations, they may reject or desert him, as may have been the case with his
natural parents.

The Child's Denial

Typically, the prenatal, perinatal, and postnatal histories of l.d. children
are not remarkable, and the parents generally have no cause to be concerned
that their child is damaged or different. This generally holds true for the
early preschool years as well, when any problems in functioning are so commonplace that they evoke no grave concern. Consequently, the child is
thought to be normal, and it is expected that he will achieve all that a normal person achieves, which will make his parents proud of his accomplishments. He incorporates into his value system the attributes that society
places upon individuals of his sex and subculture, and he assumes that he
has the expected attributes.

He learns from an early age that his family and society place less value
on the less functional individual. If you feel that your family does not have
such a value system, try to recall how frequently, in the course of a month,
you have commented casually about someone, "He's not too bright, so what
can you expect from him?"; or, "She's really a nut,"; or, "Why did you bring
that stupid kid home?" Even if the child's family suspects, or learns in his
preschool years that he has a learning disability, they tend to keep this information from him, furthering his expectations of his own normalcy, his
values of the prestige of normalcy, and the undesirability of a learning disability. Then he attends school and discovers that his life has been a decep-

tion. His parents have deceived him and he has deceived others by leading them to assume that he was "normal." He discovers that he cannot meet the demands made of his peers in the classroom, the gym, and the schoolyard, and he harbors anxieties that he never will attain his birthright of being an independent, productive adult. After all, if one fails grade one, how can he possibly anticipate being able to master increasingly complex demands? He may find himself excluded from the fraternity of the childhood group because he possesses too few of the skills to work, play, or converse with them. Their interests and customs may be more than he can master.

Educators deny his disability because they continue to make demands of him that he cannot meet, and they punish him for nonattainment. His parents still do not discuss his disability with him. Actually, at the same time that he is discovering that he is a less able person, his parents are having their earlier suspicions confirmed. They had hoped that when he started school, not only would all their nagging fears prove unfounded, but that indeed, he would excel. They are so overcome by their own devastation upon discovering his inability to cope, that they have little energy to devote to the child's feelings. They tend not to recognize, and may even resent and punish behavior that is an expression of his fears, his confusion, and concern about his newly discovered handicap. "You have your nerve behaving so badly! It's as if we don't have enough headaches already, with your problems in school!"

Parents play the game, "As long as we don't discuss the disability with the child we can pretend that it doesn't exist," and "as long as we hide from the unpleasant aspects of the disability, we need not face them." The child hastily learns that discussion of the disability is taboo. I asked forty sets of parents why they had not discussed the disability with their child, and the usual response was, "He already knows that he is different." Of course he knows that he is different, but he does not know *what* is the matter with him, and has developed many anxieties that he may be much worse than he actually is. Eight-year-old Jimmie told me that children who do not read never learn to read, and ten-year-old Cliff told me that people who do not read are "mental." Noah used to wonder whether he had a brain tumor like the actors on the "Ben Casey" show, and whether he, too, would die. The other rationale expressed by the parents was, "He has never asked what is the matter with him." Certainly he has never asked, because he clearly comprehends his parent's need to play the denial game. He quickly learns that discussion of his "problem" is taboo. "It must be even more shameful than sex," he reasons, "because we are allowed to discuss sex behind closed doors, but this topic must never be mentioned." However, whenever his parents have a private discussion with other adults, he may think that they are discussing his "craziness." Elisabeth Kubler-Ross comments:

> We make rounds and talk about many trivialities or the wonderful weather outside and the sensitive patient will play the game and talk about next spring, even if he is quite aware that there will be no next spring for him. These doctors, then, when asked, will tell us that their patients do not want to know the truth, that they never ask for it, and that they believe all is well. The doctors are, in fact, greatly relieved that they are not confronted and are often quite aware that they provoked this response in their patients . . . . those doctors who need denial themselves will find it in their patients and . . . those who can talk about terminal illness will find their patients better able to face and acknowledge it. Their need of denial is in direct proportion with the doctor's need for denial.[8]

As long as the child remains in contact with reality he cannot escape his experiences, so he must face them. However, many parents cannot cope with their feelings if they acknowledge what is happening to their offspring, so, in self-protection, they deny his reality. "The kids don't like me," he states. "Sure they like you," the parents reply. Or, "The teacher picks on on me," he complains. "That can't be so," we deny, "all teachers like all children equally well." Whether or not all the children dislike him or the teacher really picks on him, is not the central issue. The relevant factor, in these instances, is that this is what he feels is occurring, and we are denying him the opportunity to express his concerns and solicit our sympathy and support. Furthermore, we are denying his perceptions, and if, indeed, he did perceive the situation accurately, we may cause him to doubt his ability to assess his environment and may even teach him to perceive in a somewhat distorted fashion. In Chapter 6 I discuss the difficulty the l.d. child experiences in processing his social environment with accuracy; therefore, if we do suppress accurate perception, when it does occur, the consequences can be appreciable.

What is involved in the l.d. child accepting his disability? If the child accepts its existence, he then must accept its limitations upon his achievement. He must face the fear, however unfounded, that he may never achieve complete mastery over himself or his environment, which is the human goal. Finally, if he accepts the disability, he then must live with the concomitant guilt accompanying a disability. Bernard Schoenberg et al., state:

> During these preschool years, the child begins to struggle with particular conflicts growing out of his development. It is typical that he feels fear of retaliation from the parents for his intense

sexual and aggressive impulses toward them or towards siblings. These fears may be completely repressed, only to reappear as night terrors, tics, phobias, obsessions, or compulsions. When misfortunes or illness befall the preschooler, he often identifies these as just punishment for his vivid fantasies and wishful misdeeds. For a child with a serious or fatal illness guilt is often as common as fear. Since the child at this age cannot logically comprehend the causes of disease, he may understand his regressive illness as deserved punishment for real or imagined wrong doing. As if to confirm his punishment fantasy, hospitalization takes him from his parents, and he is subjected to numerous painful tests and therapies.[9]

The authors further state that the response to serious illness of the child ages six to ten is "not dissimilar from that already described for the preschooler."[10]

Of course the l.d. child does not have to face the prospect of dying, yet he is cognizant of the serious limitations with which he has been saddled, which he likely views as a punishment for unacceptable thoughts and deeds. He receives confirmation of this from the numerous assessments to which he is subjected, including the e.e.g. wires attached to his skull, yet explanations of the reasons for these probings rarely are forthcoming.

Beatrice A. Wright discusses our cultural belief in cause and effect and the inculcation of that belief at an early age in our young.[11] Such familiar statements as, "If you don't clean your teeth you'll have cavities, if you go to bed on time you'll be well rested, if you eat the wrong foods you'll become ill," and so on, teach our children at an early age that bad actions result in bad consequences. Our cause-effect thought process dates back at least to biblical times where consequences were clearly defined, such as "a tooth for a tooth," or turning to salt if one looked at a forbidden city (Sodom and Gomorrah). It hardly is surprising then, that the child will equate his disability with some wrongdoing. His thinking may be as unrealistic as that of his parents when they, too, attempt to assign blame for the disability. Thus, to accept the disability is to accept the concomitant guilt, and to deny it is to relieve oneself of a crushing burden.

Parents and children bring all their past experiences, their singular constitution, and their unique coping skills to this new experience, handling the new stress with attributes that they have brought to the situation. Elisabeth Kubler-Ross states, "People who use denial as a main defense will use denial much more extensively than others. Patients who faced past stressful situations with open confrontation will do similarly in the present situation."[12]

Inherent in the process of accepting oneself and one's limitations is the necessity of determining the specific areas in which one can succeed. One must ascertain the level of attainment at which one can realistically seek and experience the satisfaction of success. Beatrice A. Wright states, "Usually people set their aspirations near the top of their abilities. After success, goals are usually raised; after failure they are usually lowered. In other words, the level of aspiration operates as a protective mechanism so that most persons, whatever their abilities, experience success much of the time."[13]

It is most unfortunate that l.d. children rarely are allowed the opportunities to find their own levels academically, behaviorally, and socially; consequently, they experience failure much of the time. Their good degree of intelligence, normal appearance, and intact capabilities deter parents, educators, other children and adults from considering them truly disabled. When normal demands are made of them and they do not succeed, disappointment and punishment are the results. Parents and educators tend not to reward the child for genuine progress, regardless of how meritorious it may be in terms of the individual youngster, because it falls short of age expectations. Our educational thrust for the l.d. child has been that of normalcy, which I support. However, I do think that we should examine the implications for self-image and adjustment when we expose the child to a situation in which he is "low man on the totem pole" and experiences failures dozens of times a day, for thirteen years of his life. We permit him to be faced with daily demands that he cannot possibly meet: reading assignments given to the illiterate; competitive athletics to the uncoordinated; threading, sewing, and reading patterns to the visually and spatially disorganized; and speed tests for the youngster who can barely hold a pencil. We expect the child with the ability to sit quietly for a maximum of five minutes to complete two hours of seat work. The child's only alternative in these situations is to resort to diversionary tactics, excuses, and pretense.

Currently, the trend is to keep the child in the "regular" classroom, or, alternatively, to use the special class as a transitional placement until he can be returned to the "normal" stream. The result is competition with more functional children, and the harder the child tries to compete, the more frustrated and inferior he feels. Beatrice A. Wright points out that idolizing normal standards augments the severity of the disability by emphasizing the shortcomings of the person. The wrongdoing responsible for the disability becomes correspondingly accentuated and guilt prospers. The child learns that he must suppress behaviorisms associated with the disability, such as hyperactivity, impulsivity, repetition, inflexibility, and easy frustration because they are considered socially unacceptable and because his parents fear that these behaviors make him stand out as different and devalued. Consequently, the l.d. child finds it virtually impossible to extract any redeeming features of a healthy nature from his disability so that the only avenue left to him is denial.

Sibling's Denial

A typical reaction of a child to a handicapped brother or sister is that of denial. The child may have had dreams of a popular older brother who would fill the house with his boy friends, share interests and hobbies with his younger sibling, and be a source of pride in school and neighborhood. If the l.d. child is younger than his brother or sister, the older children may have imagined him as a plaything, a source of fun, companionship, an object to be parented. Undoubtedly all children fall short of living up to their brother's and sister's dreams of the ideal sibling, but l.d. children tend to disappoint them more completely. They are low-prestige people at school, clumsy athletically, inept in current childhood interests and conversations, sometimes social isolates, a source of embarrassment with their uncertain behavior, and self-concerned so that they are less likely to perceive when to reward their sibling for something considered meritorious by children.

The brother or sister frequently finds himself in the uncomfortable position of having to explain his sibling's behavior or lack of achievement. He may be pressed into the role of "looking out" for his sibling, protecting him at school and caring for him after the age when such care is required for more functional children. Some parents insist that the l.d. child be included in all social activities of his brother or sister and some deny the nondisabled sibling the opportunity to accelerate academically.

Parents typically devote an undue amount of time and energy to the needful child, paying less attention to their more functional children whose needs are not as obvious. The l.d. child's ineptitude and hence dependence, and his therapeutic and remedial procedures, lay heavy claims on the parent's time. Parents are forever alert to intercede in sudden instances of inappropriate behavior or to their child needing them at any time of day or night, and their other children sense this preoccupation. In addition, at some stages, many parents become oversolicitous and overprotective of their disabled child, needlessly performing self-help chores such as cutting food, dressing the youngster, and exempting him from household chores. They tend to be inconsistent in assuring that the demands they make are carried out, and they may allow the l.d. child to behave in a manner that would be unacceptable in other children. Justifiable or not, such behavior is excused on the basis of the disability. Thus, although the l.d. child may be the less favored of a parent's offspring, he appears to his brothers and sisters to be the recipient of special attention and favoritism. Even if the parents extend themselves in their efforts to devote a fair division of time to all their children, the nondisabled youngsters still sense their parent's often-present anxiety. The shortage of services, constant fear that the child will be denied normal educational opportunities, fear of exclusion, and uncertain future, make a degree of anxiety unavoidable. A group of siblings complained that their parents allowed themselves to become angry, frustrated, or impatient with the l.d. family member, yet they expected their nondisabled children always to behave in an understanding manner with their l.d. brother or sister. Since the l.d. child seems more normal than otherwise, it is particularly difficult for his siblings to accept the preferential treatment he receives.

Competition and hostility are emotions universal to siblings. Consequently, when a child learns that his brother or sister is learning disabled, the common reaction is guilt, an impression that his unacceptable feelings towards his sibling have caused this terrible thing to occur. Consider the plight of the youngest child in the family who is "replaced" by a younger sibling who is learning disabled. The new family member not only usurps his role as "baby" but continues to receive the extra attention and care long after his older sibling feels he should. This may precipitate intense feelings of rivalry. Nine-year-old Vicki remarked, "Gee mom, it seems like every day you go someplace with, do something for, make something for, or buy something for Steve." When the reasons for this were explained to Vicky, she exclaimed, "I should be so lucky as to have problems!" Indeed, the siblings may conclude that the only way to command parental attention is to have a learning disability.

Since some learning disabilities seem to run in families, it is appropriate to discuss the reactions of the l.d. child to his l.d. sibling. If the l.d. child has difficulty coming to terms with his disability, he may resent his sibling who is a constant reminder of his own defects. He might be angry and impatient with the handicapped behavior of his brother or sister since it reminds the outside world of his and his sibling's difference from others, and this hinders his efforts to "pass." This is somewhat analagous to the reactions of some children whose parents are foreign born. The children are ashamed of their parents' mannerisms which they feel will remind people of the national identification. The l.d. child will feel just as competitive with, and resentful of, his l.d. sibling as do nondisabled children of their brothers and sisters.

Sandy is an intelligent fourteen-year-old girl with problems in language retrieval and mathematics. She is easily frustrated and requires frequent encouragement in order to function academically. She is socially adept and has the nuances of dress, conversation, and other amenities down to a fine science. Sandy has been extremely irritated by her nineteen-year-old brother because, in addition to his appreciable learning and coordination problems, his social skills are unpolished. Her most frequent comment has been, "There's nothing the matter with him except that he feels sorry for himself! If he only tried, he'd do fine." She seeks assurance when she periodically asserts, "I'm not like him!" Fortunately, in recent months, Sandy has matured and gained confidence. Pity and empathy are replacing the scorn she exhibited previously.

Sibling's reactions will depend upon their age, maturity, place in the family, relationship to their disabled sibling, what they and their parents bring to the situation, and the honesty and manner in which the parents communicate the problem to them. Bernard Schoenberg et al., state, "Much depends upon how they are included, as part of the family, in the adaption to the crisis. Older children and adolescents can comprehend fairly completely the full implications of the illness, and the parents can be frank in sharing information and answering questions. For younger children with less mature conceptual capacities, too much and too complete an explanation will confuse instead of clarify."[14]

Thus we find that the siblings, by reason of guilt, envy, shame, and overidentification may deny the existence of the disability. It is vitally important for the parents and professionals to recognize that the added stresses of the l.d. child in the family and consequent degree of family disintegration have considerable effect on the siblings, regardless of how functional they appear. It is essential that their needs, concerns, and feelings not be ignored, denied or minimized, particularly during periods of acute stress.

Dealing with Sibling's Feelings

The first requisite of dealing with sibling's feelings is to examine our relationship with our l.d. child. One cannot completely alter the fact that l.d. children do demand an undue amount of parental time and attention. However, if the parent is living and breathing learning disabilities day and night, he is overdoing it. He needs some new interests and change of scenery for his sake and the sake of all the family members. If he is overprotecting or indulging his l.d. child, he should ask himself whose needs he is meeting by this, his or the child's. If he is being inconsistent, he should be made aware that l.d. children live in a disordered world. They have less control over themselves or their environment than their more intact peers. This lack of control terrifies them, which is the reason that some l.d. children rigidly organize some aspects of their functioning in an effort to create order out of chaos. It is for this reason, too, that they need a consistent approach from adults. They need to be certain that when an adult makes a demand that he can be depended upon to carry it out, that he will control the child and his environment. The youngster probably will test the adult to determine how firm the controls are, and the adult must prove that he will provide consistency, that he will not back down at the first sign of resistance. Furthermore, preferential treatment creates anxiety. The child fears that he must be very ill in order to merit such treatment. If the parents demand that he shoulder his share of household duties and be reprimanded for naughty behavior—just as his brothers and sisters are—he will begin to feel that perhaps he is not so different after all. When Judy returned from the hospital after major surgery, her brothers no longer slapped her, and everyone in the family was solicitous of her. Despite the unusually kind treatment, Judy's behavior became "bitchier" and more demanding. Finally her doctor suggested that the family return to their normal patterns of interaction. The reinstatement of normal demands and exposure to hazards such as slaps from brothers assured Judy that perhaps she wasn't terribly ill, after all, and with the reduced anxieties, once again she became a pleasant little girl. In *They Too Can Succeed* there are several suggestions on how parents can simplify their lives to allow more time for all of their children or devote the extra time that the l.d. child needs for special help, at an hour when it will not affect his brothers and sisters.[15]

One of the methods which proves helpful in dealing with sibling resentment is to have the parent verbalize what he thinks the child is feeling. "I think you resent the time I spend with John and the concern I have for him." (Be sympathetic, not accusatory.) Even if the child denies his resentment, he will feel better that you have acknowledged it. Share with him some of your concerns about his sibling *without* making them his concerns. In another situation you might remark, "I'll bet you wish that John would fill the house with friends his age and that you and he could share interests in common." Or, "Does the fact that Mark has trouble at school ever make you feel ashamed?" If we expose the emotions, we convey to our child that they are not shameful or bad. He will feel freer to discuss his concerns and disappointments with us, and we can afford him the dignity of our empathy, and the respect that his stresses are as important as ours and as those of his l.d. siblings. By bringing his feelings into the open, the family members often find that they can alter their way of functioning to create more positive family relationships. The Monroe County Association for Children with Learning Disabilities has a sibling discussion group to learn about learning disabilities and air feelings.

IN SUMMARY, the parents, siblings, and others who are involved with the l.d. child tend to respond to the shock of discovery of the disability with denial until they can mobilize other defenses. This stage must be recognized as a normal reaction for which allowances must be made, and it is discarded within a reasonable period of time by most families. However, the difference between denial and hope must be recognized. While denial should be replaced by more realistic attitudes, hope is a constant. Professionals must recognize this need to hope, and they must supply families with techniques to effect improvement or refer them to services directed towards this goal. Denial can be expressed in degrees, from absolute rejection of the idea that there is any problem, to inappropriate management of the disability, such as subjecting the child to endless years of remediation, or continuing pursuit of "longshot" therapeutic approaches through adolescence and into adulthood. Prolonged denial can lead to endless searching and seriously interfere with the parent's capacity to be helpful to the child or plan a realistic program for him.

Chapter 2:

Isolation and Alienation

It is a strange feeling to go
nameless up and down
the streets of other men's minds.

—Norman Cook

IF TWENTIETH CENTURY MAN is alienated from the beliefs and structures of family and society which formerly served to secure his finite and infinite world, freeing him to develop his individual relationship to that world, then the l.d. child is alienated from the alienated. He is different and devalued—an alien in the family and subculture, and he is often excluded from the general culture. The development of identity requires a secure base, a comfortable position as an accepted member of the group. When the base has disintegrated and the l.d. are not even allowed a foothold on its crumbling foundations, where will they stand in order to become? How can they develop a philosophy of life toward which they can behave with integrity, if much of what they do is discounted?

The parents and the l.d. child himself feel that few outsiders understand them or want to associate with and befriend them. If you venture into a playground where the l.d. child is playing, observe the other children's reactions to him. In many instances they seem to sense the subtle differences he projects, though he certainly is not overtly different, and they avoid him. Perhaps he handles his body clumsily, not knowing what to do with his arms or hands, or perhaps he talks about things that are not related to the situation, and he is shunned and given the message that he is unacceptable. The l.d. child is not necessarily rejected by peers because he does poorly in school or is in a special class, unless his school behavior is inappropriate, or he is several grades behind, or totally unable to handle the academic work. Academic accomplishment is not necessarily a high priority value of most children; on the contrary, the child who excels scholastically frequently finds that his academic excellence and good relationship with teachers contribute negatively to social success. It is the subtle inappropriateness of the mannerisms of some of the l.d. that single them out as being different.

In a three-year study of attitudes toward the handicapped, Gerd Jansen and Otto Esser found that the younger the children being tested, the more pronounced their aversion was to the handicap. "Rejection is the spontaneous reaction," the authors stated. "As children grow into society's system of norms, they also grow into pity."[1] They found that children dislike slightly handicapped youngsters more than gravely handicapped ones. They feel that healthy children first think of a child with a minor defect as an equal, but then are disappointed and angered when they find that he cannot keep up. By contrast, a child on crutches or in a wheel chair is so "different" that the healthy child feels no sense of identification.

When an adult meets a child for the first time, a similar interaction almost invariably occurs. In an effort to produce casual conversation the adult queries, "What's your name? How old are you? What grade are you in?" By the time he has reached the answer to the third question, an atypical component has been introduced into the conversation. Most l.d. children are uncomfortable with the question of grade, and provide a confused response. However, even when the occasional child is able to explain, with great aplomb, that he is receiving special education and why, or provide a sophisticated explanation of the reason he is behind in school, he has branded himself as being different. Since the adult was prepared only to engage in a casual encounter, giving as much energy to the interaction as one puts forth when declaring, "It's a nice day today," he terminates the conversation, and, once again, the child receives the message of being grossly different. Adults who do not know the child will remark, "Why don't you watch where you're going," or become impatient with the child who expresses himself poorly or seems slow to comprehend.

Friends and neighbors will extend hospitality less frequently to the disruptive or hyperactive child and his family. They feel uncomfortable in the presence of a "different" child and are unprepared to undergo the inconvenience of a visitor who requires special handling. Time and again, friends of families with a learning-disabled child have recounted to me their discomfort when the l.d. child examines all the rooms in their house, looks in their closets or whatever he does that the housewife considers a violation of her ground rules or privacy. They do not know how to handle the situation, whether to limit the child or speak to the parent. Consequently they avoid future discomfort by proferring no further invitations.

They discourage their children from playing with the l.d. child. They want their children to learn from their friends, be motivated and stimulated by them, and achieve high social status by associating with high status children. The l.d. child fails in providing these attributes. They feel that if their child befriends one who is l.d., he will be devalued by association. They discourage l.d. friendships because of unfamiliarity with and fear of differences in our culture. The l.d. child and his family perceive this reduced social intercourse as rejection. Some adopt the attitude, "If you won't accept us, we'll manage without you." Then their pride prohibits them from requesting much needed relief and assistance.

The family, of course, must assume some responsibility in this context. If their child is unable to handle himself acceptably, he should not be included in social visits, except for visiting relatives and friends who accept his behavior. These visits should be used to coach him in appropriate visiting behavior. Even if he is hyperactive, he can learn the acceptable and unacceptable times and places to release energy. If the parent has been lax with limits and unable to control the youngster, then he is not ready to be imposed on others. He also needs to learn that behavior such as examining the rooms in a house, touching objects, and jumping on furniture, although acceptable in his house, may not be acceptable in other persons' homes. However, even after the child has learned to be courteous and correct, the stigma of being negatively different may be sufficiently powerful to reduce the number of social invitations.

It helps a little if the parents view the situation in this light: First, a person's house is his castle, and visitors are welcome only if they do not violate territorial rights. These vary from rigid to permissive, but must be perceived by visitors and adhered to. (You know how you are welcome to putter in some people's kitchens, yet create anxiety if you attempt to assist another hostess, how you are expected to remove your shoes when entering some homes, whereas dirt will not bother another hostess.)

Second, people are prepared to extend only a portion of themselves to a social occasion. If an element is interjected that demands more of them emotionally or physically than they are prepared to give, they will avoid the added demands in the future.

Alienation from Educators

Nowhere does the child feel more alone than he does in school. To his knowledge, all his schoolmates can beat the system, and he stands out as being the only child who cannot meet expectations. He recognizes that educators are unprepared to accept his disability as being bonafide so that they persist in penalizing its manifestations. "Sloppy assignment! Doesn't care enough to write more neatly." He receives a twenty-five mark spelling penalty on each test, even though the teacher has been informed that he cannot remember the order of the letters in the words. His assignments are marked all wrong, even though he has the right answers hidden amongst the garbled verbiage. Teachers often will make no concessions to the disability, perceiving each requested concession as preferential treatment. However, they are often prepared to make considerable allowances for the obviously handicapped child, the blind, the deaf, and orthopedically handicapped.

Parents can deal with the overt manifestations of punishment and rejection that the l.d. child experiences from a succession of teachers, if the child is not too ashamed to mention them to his parents, or if he does not view them as just punishment for being bad-thus-disabled. I have known of l.d. children being spanked on bare buttocks with yardsticks, pinched each time they performed incorrectly, compelled to hold their completed assignment in front of their classmates so that they could see how sloppy it was, or asked to read to the class when the teacher was aware of their illiteracy. These assaults on their dignity were so clear that the parents, if not rendered impotent by fear of repercussions, could complain, though complaint only warned the teacher to resort to less obvious forms of scapegoating. The blatancy of such treatment means that it almost carries its own catharsis, that it is such tangible punishment that the child and parent can direct their hostility to the teacher's act, but this in no way makes it any more acceptable.

Nonetheless, it is the subtle forms of punishment and rejection which, in the long haul, may be the most undermining—the impatience with the child, the ignoring of an upraised hand, the reaction, "Oh, it's just you!" These experiences are so tenuous that the child cannot be absolutely certain that devaluation is not always implied, and so amorphous that he cannot describe them to his parents. The most corrosive aspect of this is that, in a similar fashion to blacks and other devalued groups in our culture, we all pretend that the devaluation does not occur. Thus we allow the child no accepted opportunities to vent his reactions or share his experiences. We have to ask ourselves what happens to children who are faced with an overdose of disrespect, assaults on their dignity, and punishment. The trauma of the overdoses may not be as damaging as the necessity to suffer them in silence.

Alice Thompson, Ph.D., in a letter to me, referred to the devaluation of the l.d. child in our schools:

> An urgent matter is the current tendency to consider brighter children more valuable or worthy than duller ones. Most teachers are infected with the notion that it is more important to develop the best in bright children than the best in duller ones. Since l.d. children are often mistaken for dull, they are often discounted, too. It is not part of a democratic principle to assume that bright people are "better" than duller ones, or worth more, or more im-

portant. But it is obvious that many teachers do not think it worth their while to elicit the best of which the duller are capable. They tend to disregard, if not actually to show contempt for, those who do not learn quickly. Since life is surely valued most for its feeling components, its satisfaction and happiness, we cannot suppose that the subjective experience of the less capable is of less importance than that of others. And there is no evidence to suggest that the plodders and the uneven learners make little contribution to the society. It is a vicious and insidious situation.[2]

Naturally, the learning disability itself alienates the child from the school program. Leon Eisenberg states:

At the same time it must be recognized that the reading difficulty is in itself a potent source of emotional distress. Embarrassed by fumbling recitations before his peers, cajoled, implored or bullied by his parents and his teachers to do what he cannot, the retarded reader is first disturbed and finally despondent about himself. His ineptness in reading penalizes him in all subjects and leads to his misidentification as a dullard. With class exercises conducted in what for him is a foreign language, he turns to other diversions, only to be chastised for disruptive behavior.[3]

Parents feel alienated from educators. Rarely are parents included in the critical educational decisions which affect their child's entire future. Some school boards refuse to recognize outside assessments, deciding on the child's placement and handling procedures solely on the basis of their own assessment, disregarding the possibility of error. Too few become involved in what happens to the child outside school hours, regardless of how critical this may be for his improvement.

More devastating yet is the attitude that the l.d. child is in the normal educational stream on sufferance. The parents receive the subtle message that they and their child had better behave or he will be removed to the classes for the educable mentally retarded. Since our schools tolerate a minimal deviation rate, which the l.d. child almost always exceeds, the child's and parent's fear of exclusion is reality based and profound. Many parents do not acquire the impression that they and the school are on the same team, with the child's welfare as their primary objective.

Neil was in an aphasic class for two years and returned to the "normal" stream in grade three. In early autumn of grade four his teacher had him arrive early at school every morning and noon for a week, and he remained behind at recess and after school hours, as well. His task was to spend this time looking at an arithmetic answer to determine his error. This made Neil upset and disorganized so that he began to take the wrong books home for homework, and he felt even more upset and pressured as he consequently became behind in his homework. At week's end his teacher told Neil that his arithmetic error was in omitting a comma in a six digit answer.

When Neil's mother spoke to the principal, he commented that Neil would need to put commas in answers if he was to graduate from secondary school (eight years hence), and further, he had been watching Neil since he was transferred to his school from the aphasic class. He stated that the first time there was any problem with Neil he intended to place him in the class for the educable mentally retarded. Subsequent to that, Neil's parents did not mention any mishandling to the principal, no matter how flagrant. They were so anxious about exclusion that they pressured Neil into appearing to be the model child. A fight with schoolmates who had been picking on him was sufficient to occasion parental terror that Neil would be removed from the normal stream.

Alienation from Professionals

In many instances, parent's and child's feelings of fear, alienation and isolation have been unwittingly increased by professionals. Before a family discovers the volunteer association and can be steered to professionals who are committed to specific principles, the family probably already has been in contact with a number of professionals—school psychologists, the family physician, the psychiatrist or neurologist to whom he referred the child, and so on. They may have experienced several instances in which some of the diagnostic information was withheld from them, or explained to them in terms they could not comprehend. They may have been treated in a manner that they interpreted as implying that they were unintelligent or neurotic. There may have been an implication, if only by the questions the professional asked in taking the case history, that the disability was caused by the parents. Of course, parental guilt causes them to look at each question almost as an accusation. However, this does not excuse professionals from generalizing that a less functional child is equated with less functional parents. A few years ago all behavior disorders were thought to be learned from the family. Vestiges of this oversimplified theory still cling to many professionals, which makes the parents of the l.d. suspect. Why else are parents of the hearing handicapped and trainable mentally retarded provided with a home training program when their children are preschool age, yet parents of the l.d. are told that they will harm their children if they work with them?

Professionals may share information on the child with the school or other agencies without parental approval, and parents may feel that the professional judgment was faulty and the information prejudicial to the child. (In some instances the sharing of such information has had tragic consequences.) In a similar fashion to educators, other professionals tend to exclude parents from the team. I recently asked a social worker whether parents were included in her agency's case conferences when posttreatment placement was decided. "Oh no," she responded, "We have a structure to our case conferences, which parents would mess up. But we do meet them afterwards to tell them our decision!" Shortly afterwards this woman complained to me that physicians do not know how to handle confidential information and some even share the entire treatment center report with the parents, including facts such as marital problems!

Fortunately there is a slow movement towards parent inclusion, and more professionals are questioning the practice of blaming child-rearing practices as the etiology of all developmental problems. Nonetheless, if parents do not protect themselves from indiscriminate professional exposure, the likelihood is great that they will encounter the above mentioned attitudes.

In some instances, professional avoidance may be related to unfamiliarity with learning disabilities. Many of today's practitioners did not study this disability in the university, nor is it mentioned in any but the most recently published textbooks. Its manifestations, to the unversed practitioner, are elusive and deceptive. His attitude may parallel that of the lay person who perceives that the l.d. child is a normal child who merely needs more limits. Rarely is the child in his office long enough for many of the l.d. difficulties to become apparent. He, however, is irritated by the hyperactive child who grabs his stethoscope and clears his desk of papers. His primary urge is to be rid of this irritant as speedily as possible.

Professional avoidance may represent an unwillingness to become involved in an extended course of treatment in which facilities are scarce and treatment practices controversial. In addition, demands are made on his time for which there is less than customary reimbursement, and results are slow and laborious. Professionals tend to see their cases as having specific problems which they are to work through, with successful termination of the professional-patient relationship when the problems are solved. This may not be the case with the l.d. child whose life more typically is a series of crises for many years. The professional may resent, or feel angry at the patient who exhibits slow progress, whereas dealing with other children may bear much more tangible and immediate rewards. Then, feeling guilty because of his anger, he avoids patient and family.

Diagnosticians are much more prevalent than treatment personnel. The C.E.L.D.I.C. report (Leonard Crainford) states:

Our field visits revealed a much greater availability of assessment
or diagnosis than of treatment. There is no doubt that it is easier

to diagnose than to treat emotionally disturbed children but there also may be a tendency on the part of clinicians to be satisfied with the intellectual excitement of grasping the dynamics of the case and to avoid the exacting task of becoming involved in a therapeutic process which may be long and arduous. This shortage of treatment, and the isolation, selectivity, and scarcity of clinical services for children with emotional and learning disorders, mean that a heavy burden rests on the families and school personnel who are responsible for the day to day care of these children. This has led to some particular problems between community health services and the schools which have further fragmented the delivery of care and hindered the development of comprehensive services for children.[4]

Professionals who do concentrate on treatment generally deal with specific aspects and not with the child's global program. There is no one to direct his overall program, no one to say that if the child is receiving itinerant remediation in school he may need no additional tutoring but should receive language therapy or motor therapy. No one examines the specifics of a child's program to point out gaps or overlap, and virtually no one tells the parents what they should or should not do at home. In other words, there is no catalyst. Parents, in an effort to help their child and improve an untenable and deteriorating situation, visit a succession of professionals. Because they do not know where to turn for help and because of the preponderance of diagnosticians, parents often turn to a succession of diagnosticians. When they persist in telephoning these professionals to seek direction, the diagnosticians often are unprepared to devote follow-up time to the family. They feel that, after all, they are diagnosticians, so they may be curtly limiting.

What does all this mean to parents? Withholding diagnostic information from them reinforces their feelings that the disability is shameful and that they are unworthy. They are caught in an untenable dilemma: they have to depend upon professional expertise and judgment and cannot alienate the professional because he controls the intake for services and school placement; he might perceive their points of disagreement as neurotic behavior, yet the parents feel that professionals largely have abdicated their role as helpers.

Desertion by Authority Figures

Our society is profoundly complex. Its healthy continuation requires a vast array of experts plying their specialties efficiently. When any of them default in judgment, the repercussions tend to be considerable. We expect the politicians to protect our country's interests and maintain peace and prosperity, our police to maintain law and order, physicians to diagnose and treat our ills, dentists to prevent and relieve toothaches, mechanics to repair our automobiles, accountants to steer us in financial matters, and on and on ad infinitum. As expert as we may be in one or two areas, we are dependent in all else. The structure must continue to work for us if we are to function effectively. When it breaks down in critical areas, we respond with fear, aggression, or paranoia.

Parents generally do not seek professional advice about their children's difficulties unless the problems are consequential, because the seeking of a professional opinion means that the parents have faced the real possibility of the existence of an extensive problem. Therefore, when professionals do not meet the expectations of pinpointing the difficulty and providing alleviating procedures, the family finds that it has a child on whom society has placed specific demands, with serious consequences for minimal deviation, yet society has withheld its support. This perceived desertion by professionals significantly contributes to the family's feelings of isolation and alienation. They are frustrated and helpless. What, indeed, will happen to them and their child if he is not provided with a crash course in conformity?

Summarily, the family feels that an integral part of their existence is neither shared nor understood by the outside world. Furthermore, society demands that their child conform to social, behavioral, and academic expectations, such conformity to be achieved regardless of cost, or extent to which the child's outward behavior is related to inner comprehension. In other words. complete the assignment correctly, regardless of whether you understand the principle behind it. Behave quietly and politely, even if such behavior is achieved by force or bribery and the reasons for it not comprehended. Understandably then, the family feels that the rest of the world cannot be bothered to learn what a learning disability is, pretending that lesser status differences in children are nonexistent and, if the disability can be denied, our experiences related to the disability also can be denied. (We feel more comfortable with superior functioning, which is a high status difference; hence we reward it rather than punish or ignore it.) The corollary of ignoring a disability is not providing for it, which is one of the important reasons behind our difficulty in obtaining services.

The following interview with Rick, a highly intelligent twenty year old, illustrates the alienation the l.d. feel and the defensive attitude they adopt in reaction to their feelings of not belonging. (If the world won't accept me, I'll beat them to the punch and declare that I don't want any part of society anyhow; in that way I'll protect myself from some of the pain.)

"I feel different than other people. In some ways I'm not as good as other people but think I am more sensitive. I have rejected society in my own mind and ultimately will have to live alone. I always felt that there was something missing in my interpersonal relationships. Therefore, I feel that I'll have to live alone.

"I'm undecided about the future; this isn't typical of the learning disabled but is typical of all young adults. I think I have good potential but my learning disability gets in the way of my potential. If I can't go to university and do what I want to do, I may opt out entirely and go in the mountains and meditate.

"Kids my own age don't have much to do with me. They sense that I'm different. Sometimes I turn them off because I talk too much and too loudly. I think that I am missing certain social skills. When I went on my first date, Dad had to tell me to compliment the girl. I noticed that she looked nice but I just wouldn't have thought to mention it. I don't feel that I can accurately measure what I have to offer and choose friends who are prepared to buy what I have to offer. Sometimes if a girl is giving me a hint, I don't pick it up although I sometimes understand subtle humor or sarcasm. Voice tones are tricky. At times I could tell when a teacher said something but meant something else, but not always. Sometimes my honesty got in my way like when Mrs. B. asked whether I liked her earrings and I said that they looked cheap. I think it is related to my impulsivity and misperception. I think it is a temporal problem because I can perceive most requisites of situations, but not in time. Sometimes I'm unsure of how to show my feelings so tend to hide how I feel and disappoint people.

"I think that learning disabled kids fall into two categories, more or less normal and more or less abnormal. There are lots of kids who manage to pass with no help. Then there are the type who seem normal but have trouble functioning, and this confuses people. Finally there is the type who have real trouble and people tend to think of them as having another exceptionality. People used to ask me why I was two grades behind and I just told them it was a long story because I thought they wouldn't understand what a learning disability was and think I was retarded.

"I resented the narrow demands of school. I felt that I and others were much more intellectual than our schoolmates, yet had tremendous trouble. I resented spending large blocks of time on some subjects yet doing so poorly. Teachers don't punish the disability; they punish its manifestations. I dreaded French tests and computer science classes. I resent the fact that in our society people are just a cog in the machine like in China. I have felt sorry for myself, bewildered and helpless that I couldn't fit in. I don't know why society is so inflexible and why I am not allowed to progress in things I do well without being forced to do things I can't do.

"My mother overreacted to some of my behaviors such as my always losing things and getting depressed about girls. Life was a lot harder for mother because she had to do much more for me. She also always had to look for new academic routes. Dad felt helpless in the face of my learning disability. He couldn't relate to me and found it hard to face my problems because he was too close to them. I find it easier to discuss problems with an older male friend than with Dad. My younger sister (also l.d.) definitely feels ashamed of me. She doesn't like me because I'm not cool. Even though I'm more intelligent than she, she feels superior because she won't admit she's learning disabled. I have a normal relationship with my younger brother.

"I don't compare myself to the average Joe but to superior guys. I don't envy the guy who is moderately popular, just guys who are very popular. I have never been depressed that I'm learning disabled, but from some of its limitations. I dream a lot of a secure place for me somewhere in the world where everything will be all right for me, my wife and kids tomorrow."

Reducing Isolation

As learning disabilities become increasingly understood, accepted, and provided for, the child's and parent's feelings of isolation and alienation will be less acute, and this has proven to be the case with some families in the past decade. The process of educating as many people as possible with whom the child comes in contact is bound to effect greater understanding and reduce fear, although it is not a panacea and should not be viewed as such because feelings about defects are not entirely reversed by knowledge. This education program can be sparked by the volunteer associations and can utilize the public media. Volunteers also can impress university authorities on the importance of including courses in learning disabilities in all the relevant faculties. Finally, the parents themselves can educate family, friends, neighbors, physicians, teachers, club leaders, Sunday school teachers, ministers, and others. In order to assist the parents in this task, I have included sections in this book on communicating with these parties. The information in these sections should be augmented by specific details about the child in question.

The Role of the Volunteer Association

Membership in the volunteer association is a good vehicle for reducing feelings of isolation. Suddenly the parent discovers that he or she is not alone with his problem, learning that others have lived through the same experiences or worse, have suffered the same rejection and punishment, and felt the same alienation. Coping techniques are shared.

The volunteer associations have proven to be remarkably effective vehicles for dealing with the emotions of fear and anger. Parents have been taught the steps whereby they can pressure for services for their own child and collectively participate in frequently successful legislative thrusts for all l.d. children. In this way they find channels for their aggression and hostility, learning to control it and use it constructively. (When pressuring parents drive professionals crazy, they should remember how therapeutic the channelled aggression is for parents!) One of the most important therapeutic gains is that the debilitating feelings of impotence are reversed. Instead of feeling hopelessly alone, one of millions of citizens of a complex society whose government is much removed from the individual, the parent becomes centrally involved in the process of effecting change. Feelings of guilt are atoned for in redeeming one's errors by working to improve services for the learning disabled. Thus the parents sense that they have regained control over their environment. Their judgment and experiences need no longer be considered faulty or not to have existed, nor their child-rearing abilities suspect. They have a strong sense of identification and purpose. This support and power has enabled many parents to handle the succession of stages with relative ease and to be confident, supportive, accepting parents and spouses.

Becoming Part of the School Team

It is possible to have parents and educators feel that they are working together toward a common goal. Parents need to realize the limitations with which the teacher is working, the number of children in the classroom, the amount of outside assistance and available consultants, and the limitation in training the teacher received. Any requests which parents make for individualization must take these factors into account. Some suggested ground rules for parents might be:

- When you are angry at the school board for the shortage of services, do not blame the teacher.

- Regardless of how many poor teachers your child has had in the past, or how ineffective you feel the current teacher to be, do not approach her accusingly. If you do, she will raise her defenses and nothing will be accomplished. However, if you initiate the interview on a positive note, telling the teacher how much you appreciate something she has done, she then will be more receptive to hearing your concerns.

- Tell her your expectations for the school year. If she realizes that you do not expect Johnny to bring home perfectly spelled, neat assignments, but have realistic goals and do not seek miracles, she will be relieved.

However, although we cannot expect that the classroom teacher will cure our child's learning disability, we have a right to expect that she will not violate our child's sense of dignity, that she will respect his individual needs and meet them whenever possible. I will deal with this in more detail in Chapter 14. We also can expect that the teacher will not give up on our child just because she has more difficulty reaching him academically, but will anticipate teaching him a significant number of things in the course of the school year.

Educators can involve parents more comfortably if they recognize the following:

1. Parents hope that when their child starts school that his problems will disappear. Therefore, a summons to the first parent-teacher interview threatens to shatter this hope, and usually does. Parents dread the thought of successive interviews because they are terrified that their children will be removed from the normal stream, or be excluded altogether from the education system. Parents of the l.d. become so negatively conditioned to such interviews that they even are in a state of terror preceding interviews about their nonhandicapped children. This means that the teacher has to exert extra effort at the beginning of the interview to assure the parents that the child is not about to repeat his year or be removed from the class or the school system. The interview should begin with a description of the child's assets and contributions to the class. When you do mention the child's difficulties, do not imply that the parents were the cause of the problem or are expected to do anything to alter the child's classroom behavior. (After all, what can we do immediately about a child who will not sit still, writes sloppily, calls out in class, cannot read or catch a ball, except feel impotent? If it is possible, replace some parent-teacher interviews with relaxed meetings involving a few sets of parents in the teacher's lounge, school library, or a parent's home. Such meetings could involve a mutual sharing of progress and concerns as both parents and teachers see them.

2. Include the parents in your planning. If they feel that you are dealwith them honestly and not withholding information from them, they are much likelier to accept the limitations of present services. They likely will be prepared to work with you on efforts to obtain better services.

3. Listen to the parents. Some will be unrealistic, but many will know their child well, and their judgment of the school stream into which he would be most suitably placed may be very realistic. Do not set yourself up as an authority. Many parents of the l.d. are more knowledgeable than most professionals.

4. Do not erect fences. The minute you do, there will be a party at either side with an impossible barrier in the middle. School systems that perceive the parents as important allies discover that they have many cooperative friends among the parents. Alternatively, educators who assume that there is a conflict of interests find that the parent-educator polarization is very real—the battle lines clearly drawn.

Altering Professional Attitudes

Today's parents of the l.d. are unique in that they have become expertly versed in all aspects of the disability. While this super, if somewhat narrowly educated cadre of parents has served to alienate a few professionals, it has earned the respect of an even greater number. The professionals observe these objective and constructive efforts toward effecting change, which far exceed the few hysterical efforts, and they cannot help but note the healthy methods whereby the cadre copes with stress. It becomes more difficult for them to rationalize withholding information on the basis of parental ignorance, lack of intelligence, or neurosis. Robert Russell, a psychologist and past president of the U.S.A. Association for Children with Learning Disabilities commented:

> Parents have been outspoken in their criticism of professionals. Much of this criticism was justified, as the professionals now seem ready to admit: the preoccupation with labels and definitions, the lack of remedial programs, the unwillingness to make the parent privy to critical information. The professionals have countered, and with considerable justification, with their own criticism of the parents: shopping for a palatable diagnosis, anxiety if not downright neuroses, unrealistic goals, unwarranted optimism, unwarranted pessimism. Now, however, these two groups would seem to be moving closer together. This may be attributed in part to the large population of parents who have joined the ranks as paraprofessionals. It may be attributed in large measure to the parents who have never stopped searching for new information, reaching out for broader knowledge, pressing for innovative legislation. It is our feeling that, more often than not, it is the parent who has grown and developed and become."[5]

Nonetheless, the parent-professional dichotomy is still very real. It cannot be explained away solely by the different values of outsiders and insiders, or different expectations by professionals and parents of the professional role, though these are critical issues. I feel that there must be some basic changes in professional training, changes which will affect knowledge, attitudes, and practice. Suggested models of professional training easily merit the writing of another book. Failing that, I would like to settle for second best, which is a few suggestions:

1. Some universities have initiated the method of cross-professional training and internships. This should be much more generally adopted so that physicians in training routinely intern with school boards, teacher-trainees work with language therapists, and so on. The multiprofessional team must include two more persons: the parents, and, if sufficiently old, the child himself. Parent inclusion should be practiced so routinely that professionals will think of the parents as part of the team.

2. The necessity of the successful professional becoming involved with client and family is being more widely recognized. This concept requires greater application and stress in professional training.

3. Perceptive parents should have a role in professional training. They have much to teach the fledgling practitioner by sharing their expectations, feelings, and experiences.

4. Generalists (general practitioners, teachers, social workers, etc.) should be well versed in remedial principles. Once they recognize the parent's need to hope, to be provided with something to do in order to atone for their guilt, the generalist can provide the parents with techniques of management and therapeutic child-rearing practices as well as direct them to sources of remediation. This type of constructive action can function to deter parents from seeking questionable improvement, yet assist the parents in finding procedures which might prove helpful.

5. Professionals require periodic reminders of the crudeness of their diagnostic tools and the possibility of professional error. Long-term observation, even by subjective persons, should be given consideration in arriving at a diagnosis and treatment plan.

6. There should be an examination of the kinds of information that is appropriate to share with persons working with the child, be they lay or professional, and such information should be shared promptly so that confidentiality does not work against the child's chances of receiving services. Suggested information that is appropriate to share

might be: the child's areas of strength and weakness, and known methods by which he responds and learns. The entire concept of withholding information from family and child should be examined. Parents should not have to demand to see reports that are about them and their child. The number of parents who will abuse information that is shared with them is more than offset by the many who will use it constructively. There always are professionals who will misuse confidential information, yet it is not withheld from them.

7. More emphasis should be placed on teaching counselling procedures to diagnosticians, treatment personnel, and educators.

8. Professionals should become more involved in the social action efforts of the parents. This will alter the assumption that professionals should be above the rough political games which must be played before change is effected in our system. More important still, this involvement will provide professionals with a comprehension of the desperation of thousands of families whose children are neither being recognized or helped, the deterioration of these children and the frustration of unfruitful efforts to effect change.

My son's pediatrician said to me, "You know more about your son's problem than I do. You do whatever has to be done in the way of assessment and treatment, just keep me informed." We operated that way throughout my son's childhood. I consulted our pediatrician on referrals to otologists and other medically related needs, and he and I together read the reports that I had forwarded to him. He commented that he had learned much from me and my son about how to treat other l.d. children, and he kept the reports for reference when my son "graduated" in adolescence to a general practitioner. This was a professional who treated me, a parent, as a person of worth and knowledge. Our relationship was warm and positive.

Chapter 3:

Why Did It Have
To Happen To Me?

AS THE CHILD'S DIFFICULTIES INCREASE, rationalizations for denial cease to suffice. As more is demanded of him, and as outsiders become less tolerant and more impatient with the denial game, all but the most persistent families progress to the next stage, which includes anger, envy, and resentment.

While the manifestations of denial are clearly recognized and restricted in focus to child and family, anger tends to be diffuse, as Elisabeth Kubler-Ross phrases it, ". . . displaced in all directions and projected onto the environment, at times almost at random."[1] Thus, when a parent is angry at rejecting neighbors, an insensitive teacher, or a nonsharing psychologist, he may redirect this anger at family members where the consequences can be predicted with some accuracy and are relatively safe. Conversely, anger toward the child is displaced onto other professionals, particularly educators.

One of the most intense forms of anger is that which is directed at the spouse. He or she is accused of being genetically defective. "He takes after your family. Your uncle Charlie never could spell." Or, "Aha, you failed Spanish in school; now I know why our children have learning disabilities." At an open meeting a parent asked me, "Why don't you say more about the genetic basis of l.d.? Don't you think that rejecting fathers are l.d. children grown up?"

When the anger is directed at the child, the cause may be that the parent was embarrassed by her own behavior in public, or ashamed at her behavior in dealing with a professional, or frustrated by a teacher's account of her child's nonconformity. The parent is angry at the child for causing her to lose face, for making her appear ineffective, and for placing her in positions where more demands are made of her maturity than are made of other parents. Not meeting the challenge of all the demands, she is ashamed of her behavior. She really is angry at herself and the world, but lashes out at her offspring, the instigator of this chain of feeling. Then she feels guilty that she punished him when he was not at fault, yet she is irrationally angry at him for not being "normal," not being a source of greater satisfaction.

Some of the anger directed at professionals obviously is unwarranted, such as imagining that the obstetrician was negligent. Some of the anger is partly justified, such as blaming the pediatrician or diagnostician who examined the child in his early years and failed to provide the family with a program which ostensibly could have prevented some of the many errors the parents made. Parents are not content to learn that knowledge of l.d. was not general a few years ago and that medicine and psychology are not exact sciences. They feel that if the knowledge was somewhere to be found and not utilized in helping their child, their anger is justified.

Many parents have unrealistic expectations of teachers. It is easy to displace anger onto teachers, blaming the child's learning problems on poor teaching. At times poor teaching is the culprit, but often it is not. There is much justifiable anger directed at educators who too often are insufficiently committed to individualization and stubbornly unprepared to accept l.d. as a genuine disability for which allowances must be made.

If the parents' anger is greater than their fear, they are likely to be hostile or aggressive. If the fear surpasses anger, the parent is likely to be passive. The latter parents will be unable to mobilize their aggression to make even the most justifiable and elementary demands on behalf of their progeny.

The Outsider's Anger

When an outsider meets the l.d. child, he develops assumptions about the child based on his knowledge of the child's family, subculture, and extrinsic cues, such as clothing, household furnishings, and conversation. He expects the child to live up to his assumptions. Initially, upon observing the l.d. youngster who appears alert and whole, the adult assumes that the child will fulfill his mental image of the child. If the child fails in this, the outsider tends to be "put out." If the child handles himself differently than expected, even if the expectation merely was that he would be able to read a street sign or menu, and the parents have not prepared the adult with an explanation, he may feel that the parents have "put one over on him."

This creates a problem for parents. A child's learning disability is complex, and if the parents explain it to everyone with whom the child comes in contact, the disability might be misunderstood as mental retardation or emotional disturbance. Because of the usual fears and prejudices that are associated with these exceptionalities, the outsider might be inordinately uncomfortable in the child's presence, and he might underestimate the child's abilities.

Conversely, if the parents do not alert outsiders, and the child does stand out as different, resentment is engendered. Since we parents often do not know what demands each new situation will make of our child, the decision of whether to "tell" or "not to tell" is a difficult one. Either way it is a calculated risk. The parent, too, harbors some feelings that if he withholds information, he is, in some way, involved in a kind of deception.

The parent and child both live with the constant dilemma that, even though they may have come to terms with the disability and no longer feel that it is a source of shame, many outsiders may not be at that point. The quandry of whether to tell or not to tell occurs with each new neighbor, girl or boy friend the l.d. youth dates, club leader, or prospective employer.

The Child's Anger

The child's anger is understandable, but most of the time we react to him as if it were not. He is angry at a fate which has denied him his birthright, at people who expect him to accomplish everything that his peers accomplish, and this within the same period of time and with the same degree of efficiency. He is angry that tutors and remediation rob him of his playtime. He is angry at parents and professionals who act as if something is wrong with him, yet pretend that there is not, and refuse to share their concerns with him. He is infuriated that we have led him to expect that he is "normal" and "thrown him to the lions" with no protection. He is angry that his parents cannot face his problems. He is resentful that we do not allow him to succeed in his strong areas without having the constant burden of improving all his weaknesses.

It is true that all children experience some degree of hostility towards their parents, but the anger of the l.d. child includes unique factors; for example, he resents his parents because, somehow, they have not insured that he was born a whole child. He may be afraid to display his anger because of his fear of the supreme rejection, the abandonment of being sent away. As he reaches adolescence, this fear is replaced by the fear of being thrust into independent living before he feels capable of handling it. Parents, in their desperation with untenable situations at home and school, may even threaten to send the child away. Because l.d. children cannot organize themselves or their world efficiently, they are more dependent on their parents than are their peers. The more dependent a child is, the more he resents those on whom he is dependent, and the more fearful he is of displaying his resentment because of fear of abandonment, particularly if he does not feel worthy.

Leonard is a handsome, athletic, intelligent nine-year-old boy with learning problems. He becomes completely unmanageable when faced with any sitting down task, even arts and crafts. His behavior tends towards belligerance and constant testing. When Leonard was at a camp for l.d. children, the staff confronted him with his unspoken concerns about being retarded and his fears that he would be institutionalized (as was his sister). Our most important task with Leonard that summer was to teach him what learning disability was and assure him that he was not retarded. Leonard is now at home, and continuation of this reassurance plus placement in a specific l.d. class has resulted in excellent progress.

If the child's anger is greater than his fear, he is likely to be rebellious. We should consider that an aggressive stand is likely far healthier than turning the anger inwards to self-destructive behavior, such as taking drugs. If his fear is dominant, he is likely to be compliant. Consequently, we must deal with more than the surface rebelliousness and not necessarily consider compliancy as a blessing.

JUST AS THE CHILD'S hostility toward his parents may not be expressed openly because of the various forms of supression mentioned above, the parents also experience the frustration of unresolved hostile feelings. Every one of our children is a disappointment to us in a number of ways. Perhaps our child is born with our mother-in-law's forehead, our brother-in-law's nose, and our husband's temper. Perhaps he is loud and pushy when we treasure submissive behavior, is materialistic when we tend toward the spiritual, or is artistic when we prefer practicality. When any of our children fail to meet our expectations of the ideal child we are disappointed, but our pride in our l.d. offspring may be vastly reduced a number of times. We cannot boast about his school achievements or athletic prowess, and perhaps we cannot even be proud of his behavior. He thwarts our goals, rewards our efforts with little change and minimal improvement.

Therefore, the anger of parents, child, and outsiders tends to be random, irrational, and displaced. Even persons who should know better react to this anger with hasty conclusions about its cause, and they rarely consider that it might be a justified hostility. Thus we encounter conclusions which sound like this: "No wonder he's a difficult child, just look at the angry parents," or, "No wonder he has so much trouble in school, just look at his attitude!"

Regardless of how justified they may be, neither parents nor child can show their reactions to the cumulative extrinsic and intrinsic experiences of their lives without inviting rejection and termination of services. If, after having encountered a succession of professionals who have behaved in a superior, accusative manner, not sharing information and not being helpful, the parents are defensive or hostile when they approach a new professional, their attitude might work against the child. The child's problem is likely to be diagnosed as "neurotic parent." Self-protective parents and parent's organizations learn that they must treat all professionals in a cool, objective, and relaxed manner.

Similarly, no matter how many unrealistic and punitive teachers a child has encountered in the past, he nonetheless must be a well-behaved, cooperative student or suffer the consequences. The mother of a fifteen-year-old boy told me that her son behaves as though every teacher is guilty unless proven innocent. Needless to say, that young man's school career is doomed unless he learns to "play the game."

Teachers, parents, and camp counselors will sometimes set the stage so that the child has to react negatively. Then they use this as proof that the child is the cause of his own difficulties. Mr. S., the secondary school biology teacher, was gruff toward all his students, but he was especially punitive to his l.d. students—sometimes overtly, sometimes subtly. He refused to review or reexplain the work to them when they requested assistance, called them "stupid, clumsy idiots," would not allow them into the classroom if another teacher detained them for a minute overtime, and he would not provide them with a way of making up the work they missed during that period. He insisted that his students work in pairs, and when no one chose the l.d. student as a partner, he berated the l.d. adolescent for his uncooperative attitude. While his "normal" students were able to dismiss his punitive approach as being "just him," and find ways of working around his pronouncements so that, indeed, he did let them enter the classroom late, or did explain missed work to them, the l.d. students were less fortunate. They tended to take everything he said literally and did not possess the subtle social skills to work around his rules, thereby mellowing him into acquiescence. Furthermore, his l.d. students already had been exposed to at least eleven or more years of this type of punishment, and instead of rendering them expert at the game, it left them defeated and particularly vulnerable to his ploys. The most remarkable aspect of Mr. S.'s approach was that he created the problems, caused the l.d. students to react, then accused them directly and on their report cards of disinterest and lack of cooperation—even the l.d. students who always had been positive, contributing youngsters in school.

Scapegoating

G. W. Alport, in *ABC's of Scapegoating*, states:

When people are frustrated they tend to become aggressive and when they cannot aggress against the actual cause of their frustration because it is unknown, inviolate or other reason, they tend to look for someone or something else to blame for the frustration and to aggress against.

The ideal scapegoat is as similar as possible to the real cause of the frustration, is easily identifiable, is different from the frustrated person and cannot retaliate.[2]

The l.d. child, by reason of his lack of power and low status, lends himself well to the scapegoating tactics of some families and outsiders. The family is beset by the frustrations of too few services and too little understanding. The l.d. child creates severe strain on family integration, makes vastly increased demands above the perceived duties of parenthood, and bestows less than the expected gratification. Consequently, an understandable reaction is to blame the child for the family problems. All members of families that choose this model of behavior learn to play the game in order to preserve family integration, which bases its intactness upon continuation of the scapegoating. Some parents whose child-rearing practices are poor lay all the blame for family difficulties and for the l.d. child's problems on the learning disability, on the child himself, and on the failings of the school system, thereby avoiding being accountable for their parenting techniques.

Parents who do not blame the child still tend to blame much of the less acceptable behavior and a variety of problems on the l.d. itself, and they teach the child the same form of escape. This has important implications because one of the goals of child-rearing is to teach our children to assume responsibility for their behavior. With this kind of scapegoating, we not only convey to our l.d. child that he does not need to develop inner controls but that control must be imposed from without.

Norman W. Bell and Ezra F. Vogel, in *A Modern Introduction to the Family*, comment on scapegoating:

While some of the families did, at times, have strong feelings of antagonism toward various members of the community in which they lived, they could rarely express this antagonism directly. Even if at times they were able to manifest their antagonism directly, this usually led to many additional complications, and the family preferred to scapegoat its own child.[3]

Bell and Vogel further point out that channeling hostility through the relatively powerless child was safer than risking the anger of the spouse against whom the hostility really was directed. They discuss the phenomenon whereby the scapegoat in some families was the child who resembled a parent. The family focused on the child's undesirable traits even though the parent had the same traits. The parent, whom the child resembled, may have been somewhat unhappy with the scapegoating, yet joined his spouse in this behavior to keep the burden of problems away from himself.

Scapegoating is employed by some teachers who find expedience in blaming the child's inability to learn, attend, and be interested, on a defect within him. Such a teacher blames the classroom problems on the presence of the l.d. student in the class, rather than examine his effectiveness as a teacher. An easy out, as well, is for the teacher to blame the parents' child-rearing practices for his current problems with the child.

In a similar fashion, the less adept, weak child is a ready scapegoat for peers and adults in some social situations. It seems that a common reaction to growing and living under the pressures of our complex culture is to vent our frustration and anger on the nearest lower status or weak person who is unlikely to retaliate.

I think that it is valid to assume that the l.d. child more frequently is the recipient of hostility and aggression from parents, siblings, educators, and outsiders than are his nondisabled peers. Perhaps some children's hyperactivity is an attempt to be a target that shifts too frequently for careful aim.

Envy

Both parents and child feel that fate has dealt them a "dirty hand" and they agonize, "Why did it have to happen to me?" One mother commented to me, "My neighbors are not very bright, yet their children take ballet and music lessons and maintain their interest in these arts. They also read a great deal," she continued. "My children don't maintain interest in any lessons, and never pick up a book, yet my husband and I are so intelligent!"

You will recall what Rick, the twenty year old, said in the interview: "I don't compare myself to the average Joe, but to superior guys. I don't envy the guy who is moderately popular but guys who are very popular." Some parents are so envious of their friends' and neighbors' children, the effortless manner in which they excel scholastically and athletically and their parents' pride in such attainment, that, at some stages, they cannot bear to be in contact with those families. North Americans cherish the myth that everyone is owed the right to a perfect life, to be fulfilled and enjoy oneself much of the time. To find oneself with less is to feel cheated, thereby to resent everyone who is better endowed.

Managing Anger

Anger can be more appropriately channeled by providing parents and child with acceptable or constructive outlets for their aggression. With parents, perhaps it is teaching them to fight for services, and with children, perhaps it is providing them with a punching bag, clay to pound, or teaching them to run around the block. Because the disability may be perceived as punishment for excessive hostility felt toward one's parents, siblings, or child, the feeling or expression of anger can be guilt producing. Our culture discourages the expression of murderously angry feelings at one's parents or one's child, particularly a disabled child, and certainly does not condone rejection. As a consequence, the child and parents may not feel that they can air their anger with anyone, even a spouse. They need to be provided with such opportunities (but not at the expense of someone else's rights, obviously), perhaps in groups of children, parents, siblings, families, or in individual counseling. They should be helped to realize that anger felt towards a child, parents, teachers, or others is not sinful but quite normal. I remember how surprised I was to hear a friend of mine remark, "I could kill my kid!" I learned that other parents occasionally felt murderous impulses.

Many families require coaching in communication skills so that they can learn ways to direct their anger to the anger-evoking situation or person, and channel it appropriately, without being destructive or feeling guilty. Dr. Chiam Ginott's books and articles deal with constructive methods of expressing anger and are worth perusing.

Chapter 4:

Guilt, Bargaining and Magic, Depression and Mourning

IT IS A COMMON DISTORTION of the principle of cause and effect in our society to say that the parents are somehow the cause of the child's learning disability. Parents of l.d. children are highly susceptible to the guilt related to this notion, and the mother is particularly affected. She may spend a lifetime ruminating over every bad deed or thought which would have occasioned her punishment for bearing a learning-disabled offspring. She rehashes every moment of the pregnancy, delivery, infancy, and early childhood, flogging herself for actions which she thinks caused the disability. Every cigarette smoked, alcoholic beverage consumed, and energetic activity in the prenatal period is suspect. Every diaper unchanged or cry unheeded comes under scrutiny as negligence likely to have damaged the infant. The mother's guilty imaginings are reinforced by literature or lecturers who provide pat etiologies for learning disabilities, such as insufficient movement experiences or insufficient stimulation in the preschool years. Because we are unsure of the etiology of most children's learning disabilities, the parents can rarely lay the blame on a specific causative agent, so that their guilt wanders rampantly.

As I have mentioned, every parent feels angry at times toward his children, and when the l.d. is discovered, it seems to the parent to be a fulfillment of his hostile impulses. Learning-disabled children typically have exhibited some degree of maladjustment from early childhood onward. They may begin with colic or food allergies and progress to such other difficulties as undue distress with changes in routine, slow development, poor language or coordination, hyperactivity, repetitive behavior, tantrums, and frequent frustration. Consequently, the instances whereby the parents feel angry at the l.d. child are likely to be far more frequent than the number of times those feelings are evoked by the nondisabled. Therefore, when the child is diagnosed as disabled, the disability is perceived as punishment for excessive hostility.

The extent and duration of these guilty feelings depend on the parent's general confidence and whether he feels that "to err is human." His reactions are related to his own upbringing and the degree to which he was made to feel guilty for his behavior. Not only have adults in our culture integrated the concept that parents are supposed to be perfect, but we teach this expectation to our children. They then are primed to stoke our guilt when we fail—in little and big ways—to fulfill their image of the perfect parent.

When the parents are consumed with guilt, they are most vulnerable to the promises of each new therapeutic fad. After all, they feel, if they do not offer the promising treatment to their child, they will be unable to make peace with his deficits, knowing that the new treatment might have cured him. This guilt is reinforced when they meet other parents of the l.d. at gross-motor groups or lectures. The other parents talk about devoting unbelievably long hours to remediation, and the listening parent feels that she is failing her child. In actuality, the other parents may not be spending as much time as they claim to be and need to declare their steadfast devotion to their child's cause to quiet their own pangs of guilt. Or they may be working long hours with their child, subjecting him to pressure and conveying their constant disappointment in him. Or they may need to encourage other parents to adopt their current treatment program, thinking that its validity will increase as more people undertake it. However, the listening parent rarely comprehends this. He feels inadequate as a parent, with a low score in the competition of "who can do the most for his child."

After years of remediation, when parents and child have come to terms with the disability and prefer to devote their energies to the global processes of living rather than continue remedial efforts, this decision causes anxiety in other parents who still need involvement in a remedial program. They try to seek confirmation of their own efforts by pressuring the nonconforming parents into a resumption of therapy.

Feelings of guilt and rejection toward the child may result in overindulgence, inconsistency in maintaining limits, and the combination of over- and underprotection. The parent feels compelled to "make up" to the child for having caused the disability. The child's inability to function competently in a few areas are generalized to his total functioning. He then is protected from exposure because the parents cannot handle the anxiety occasioned by such exposure. When parents feel comfortable in their love for a child, they can impose limits, see that they are carried out, help the child achieve increasing independence, and know that he is still secure in their love. However, it is the parent who feels that somehow he has caused the child's problems and harbors a fair amount of hostility who is afraid to be firm with the child lest he view the firmness as rejection. Such parents are afraid to have him leave home, perhaps to travel in the city, or attend camp, because they feel that he might view this as being sent away, the ultimate rejection. In other words, if you sometimes feel unloving towards your child, the tendency will be to guard against him sensing this by not providing any situation that he could construe as rejecting. It is somewhat analogous to being overly polite to someone you detest.

Parents suffering from severe forms of guilt sometimes resort to a variety of neuroses, such as obsessive behavior patterns and hypochondria. Pervasive or extended guilt requires counseling, since attempting only to alter its manifestations (such as overprotection) often meets with failure.

Siblings also feel guilty that their hostile and competitive feelings may have caused the disability. They are jealous of their l.d. sibling for having usurped their position in the family, and feel that their parents are not as aware of their needs as they are of the needs of their brother or sister. They then feel guilty for harboring feelings of envy.

The l.d. child feels the guilt and shame of having fallen short of family and social-class expectations. Teachers, neighbors, and family constantly reinforce his unacceptability, wrongness, and naughtiness, and he feels guilty for being bad so much of the time.

Virtually every North American community has a shortage of services for the l.d. Parents who are too fearful or insecure to fight for services for their child must live with the guilt that their own failings may have denied their children the opportunity to achieve normalcy. Parents who persist and succeed in having their child enrolled in a service then live with the guilt that their aggression served to displace equally needy youngsters.

Bargaining and Magic

I am always intrigued at the facility whereby children and adults revert to the primitive rituals of bargaining and magic when confronted with a crisis. Not only people whose religion suggests such cause and effect relationships as, "Do a good deed or perform a virtuous act and your prayer will be answered," but agnostics, also, revert to this type of bargaining. This method of reasoning dates back to childhood, when we frequently indulged in magical behavior. We were firmly convinced that if we stepped on a crack, we would break our mother's back, and when we sat down to write an examination, our magical aura would ensure that we would pass. Our cultural orientation is that reward is a consequent of good behavior. Therefore, a natural reaction to an unwelcomed situation is to enter into a pact with God, or less well-defined powers, promising that if improvement is effected, we will perform some daily ritual in payment, or conversely, if we perform some ritual, we will be rewarded with a cure. Perhaps we keep our house especially clean or engage in some other virtuous act to entice the fates into reversing themselves. If this pact is perceived to be answered, we do not maintain our original promise of asking for nothing more, but enter into another pact. The child, too, employs bargaining and magic in an attempt to compromise with his fate. It would be worth exploring the extent to which magical behavior in the l.d. can be locked into his need for extensive structure and whether this progresses into obsessive rituals.

Some treatment programs and personnel contribute to ritualistic behavior. These programs involve routine procedures that appear to family members to have only a vague relationship to the areas of dysfunction, and they demand daily practice if improvement is to be effected. Thus the program is seen by child and family not primarily as a therapeutic technique with a rationale based upon a sequence of development, but as a series of magical steps which offer expectations of cure upon completion. Consequently, when the parent neglects the therapeutic ritual for a day or more, he may feel very guilty. Treatment personnel should examine their procedures for signs that they may only be contributing to ritualistic bargaining. The elements of structure in a therapeutic regime should not require daily rituals that foster unrealistic hopes of the recipients as to the end result.

Both child and parents practice a magical game of imagining that the next important juncture in the child's life will be the one in which he will function normally. We encounter unspoken expectations, such as, "He'll be fine in the next grade," or, "He'll be fine at camp." It is for this reason, as well as fear of exclusion and devalued treatment, that causes parents to withhold information from teachers, camp directors, and others. Because they harbor this hope, they are bitterly disappointed each time the hope is shattered. Educators and other therapeutic personnel also have been known to resort to magical behavior, developing profound expectations for improvement based upon the use of one therapeutic technique or principle.

Depression and Mourning

When the discrepancies between demand and achievement no longer can be ignored, and the bargaining has failed, then the involved persons have been stripped of delaying devices and suffer feelings of deep loss. The parents can no longer pretend that the child is likely to achieve greatness and perfection. The child has lost his earlier expectations of being a "normal" person with all the concomitant privileges afforded normalcy. He must settle for the permanent state of being a devalued person. His intelligence, mental health, and general worthiness as an individual are suspect, and he acts the part, rarely to excel or be rewarded. He will suffer from the prejudice of teachers, peers, and employers. He will have to work longer and harder to achieve what others come by effortlessly, and his opportunities and time for fun and social contact are likely to be restricted.

In the mourning stage he and his parents think of the l.d. as all-encompassing, a tragedy of major proportions. The child neither views himself, nor is he viewed so by his parents, as an essentially normal child suffering only from specific dysfunctions which need not exert global limitations. L. F. Kurlander and Dorothy Colodny describe it in this way:

> He may be slowed and depressed. But there need be no loss of loved one, no loss of love nor even hostility turned inward. Instead, we see a genuine loss of self-esteem based on a consciousness of helplessness and inability to survive emotionally—a peculiar sadness as the child gives up his many losing battles.[1]

The parents may feel depressed because they imagine that they failed the child by bestowing him with a defective inheritance, or failed him when they erred in early child rearing.

The devastation may be so profound that some parents and children will react with permanent personality changes. In *The Child Who Never Grew*, Pearl Buck recounts how life's joy had been lost when she discovered her daughter was mentally retarded. She no longer was able to enjoy human relationships, landscapes, flowers, and music.[2] Some parents have told me how they no longer could pursue a previously satisfying hobby, or how their *joie de vivre* or abandonment seemed to have been lost. When in the mourning stage, parents tend to overidentify with the disabled child. As long as they see the child as an extension of themselves, they will develop anxiety around his poor performance, when the anxiety more rightly belongs to the child. The child will take his cue from his parents' level of anxiety. If they are very anxious, he then will assume that his disability is of profound consequence; if they are relaxed, he will be relatively unconcerned.

Prolonged mourning requires intervention. However, transient mourning has important psychological value. Beatrice Wright refers to it as a healing period. Both the parents' and child's need for this stage should be recognized and allowed. Even after the acute mourning stage is passed, intermittent mourning will occur with lessened frequently, as more positive solutions are substituted.

Humans are incapable of existing in a state of acute crisis for extended periods of time. If we are forced to live in continuing crisis, protective mechanisms seem to take over and, subverting the crisis, we go about the process of living. This phenomenon has been demonstrated by the populations of countries that are in a constant state of war or anticipating war. Thus, the all-consuming tragedy of having a learning disability retreats to a more realistic position within the total process of living as child and family recommence their tasks and pleasures.

Families should be supported and encouraged in this process of relegating the l.d. to its position as just one facet of the life experience. Their readiness to lead a well-rounded life without sacrificing duties or pleasures should be rewarded so that they will have the strength to resist succumbing to the "therapy driven" syndrome. Parents who return to a state of wholeness and who appreciate the value of global life experiences for the child should not be confused with parents who are still in the denial stage, doing little for their child therapeutically.

Mourning diminishes as both child and family gain the realization that the youngster possesses many strengths and abilities and, with luck, can lead essentially a normal life. A realignment of values takes place in the healthy family, and attributes other than academic achievement attain positions of importance. In order to have the child progress to more productive stages of functioning, he must experience success. He must feel that he is a valued person to family members, adults, and peers. He needs to acquire mastery of some things, such as hobbies, being a successful member of a club, scouts, or swimming, and he must be rewarded for some aspects of his school life.

For some parents, the compulsive need to talk about the disability may have to run its course. As well as being a bid for sympathy, it alerts others to modify their impressions of parenting abilities, telling them not to relate the child's behavior to his upbringing. However, the sympathy elicited often has too few elements of understanding of either the parents' feelings or the child's condition or prognosis. Sharing experiences with other parents of the l.d. can be more productive, and it prompts sympathy which is more realistic, but self-pity—in parent or child—should be discouraged. One can agree with the child that indeed his lot is a hard one, but he should be cheerfully reminded, "That's life, so let's get to work." Rather than contribute to the child's self-pity, we should provide him with an atmosphere in which he feels free to share his feelings, disappointments, and concerns, without meeting denial.

Chapter 5:

Apathy, Group Identification, Myths, Secondary Gain, Professional Mixed Messages

They tried to make us into
nonpeople and we were afraid.
Then a few men told us
we had value and worth,
and we took courage.

UNTIL THE 1960s, "apathy" was an apt word to describe most parents of the learning disabled. Guilt, and fear of massive retaliation, kept us sub-missive. Before this point in history, the professional's attitude toward parents tended to contribute to their feelings of guilt and shame. The Freudian approach to exceptionalities pointed an accusing finger at parents, blaming their sex life or toilet training techniques. Many parents seemed only too ready to accept this approach. Perhaps it served to feed their guilt and their need for simple answers.

Then the breezes of change began wafting through a few diagnostic centers. A handful of professionals began to understand that parents were not the certain cause of the disorder. The occasional diagnostician even ventured so far as to furnish the parents with a written report and remedial program. Thus, from the mass of immobilized parents, a small group emerged who had been led to believe that they were competent and worthy. They knew that if they initiated the fight for the rights of the l.d., there would be a few professionals who would not think that they were crazy or misdirected. This afforded them the strength they needed for the difficult task that was ahead.

No one can say for certain what it was that suddenly afforded us the courage to seek one another and press for change, but it is certain that the newly emerged activism of parents of the l.d. is not isolated from the general pattern of change which has become manifest in the American culture. This pattern seems to be related to a growing need for personal fulfillment that has its roots in earlier periods of American history. Pioneer life in America consisted mainly of labor that had one purpose—survival. As long as individual energy was thus directed, the American had little time to seek other means of fulfillment.

The early pioneer days were followed by the opening of new territories, the building of cities, industries and communication systems, and finally, engrossment in wars and a depression. Man in America was too busy ensuring survival and growth to be concerned with self-actualization. Those who were, found that a society involved in swift expansion, with a small population and not-yet-stratified requisites for position holding, offered them limitless opportunities for advancement. Then came technology, affluence, and population expansion. This trilogy terminated the era of man being directly responsible for his own and his family's survival, decreased the number of available jobs, and drew clear lines of requisite for position-holding.

Once man became freed of the necessity to work for survival, he developed the concept that work should be personally fulfilling. Following this philosophy further, Americans expect, as their human right, to be fulfilled in school, in love, and in recreational pursuits. The current rebellion against the irrelevance of education and the increasing divorce rate seem to indicate that the expectation of fulfillment has reached its apex in our time. We are not deterred, in the least, by the reality that few of us do, indeed, find fulfillment in all of these spheres, but continue relentlessly to pursue it on our own behalf and that of our children.

Our education system always has been essentially undifferentiated. Some young people always emerged largely uneducated from our academic programs, and we expected this attrition. However, in this "age of fulfillment" we demand every student's equal right to learn, rather than the longer standing expectation of equal right to be taught. We demand that our children receive the prescribed education for entry into vocational and professional training. It is these expectations which spawned the volunteer associations. In *The True Believer* Eric Hoffer postulates that activist movements arise in times of promise, when people have reason to hope for improvement, and this has held true for the l.d. movement.[1] The American's collective commitment to equality seemed to gather strength in the post-World-War-II era, and we gathered strength from this commitment.

In the early 1960s, the mere initiation of a social action group, with its outspoken positions on diagnosis, treatment, and education, forced the professional community into pro and con camps. The first efforts toward change were met by subtle forms of suppression. Professionals informed the parents that their goals were askew, that there was no such entity as l.d. or that it was a rare phenomenon, that remedial techniques had not been researched, were highly suspect, and the prognosis guarded. A few professionals lent open support to the fledgling volunteer associations, a few others offered behind-the-scene support but did not risk exposure, many adopted "wait and see" attitudes, and some engaged in powerful opposition.

The parents, shaken by the opposition, were less certain of the rightness of their position. Nonetheless, they continued their dogged struggle. Contrary to popular belief, many were not fighting for services for their own children, but for the next generation of l.d., so that their paths might be strewn with less ignorance and pain. This group *proved* that their activist efforts did not harm their own children. Suppressive techniques eroded their confidence, but, to my knowledge, no retaliation against their children ever occurred.

Regardless of this assurance gleaned from the pioneer's experience, parents universally still harbor the fear that social action will result in a backlash against their children, and professionals exploit this fear. Billy is a nine-year-old l.d. youngster with a normal intelligence. He has been in a school for the trainable retarded for two years. Billy believes that he is as retarded as his schoolmates and is not progressing socially or academically. When his mother suggested to the clinic psychologist that she remove Billy from school until a more appropriate placement could be found, the psychologist threatened that if she did this, Billy would be made a state ward. Consequently, Billy's parents have been rendered impotent.

Apathy of the parents of the l.d. is on the increase. Many parents are prepared to settle for transient or inadequate services, or live with the service provided today, without looking toward tomorrow, rather than risk any discomfort by "rocking the boat."

There seems to be an attitude on the part of many parents in the 1970s that their children are someone else's responsibility, that if their children have problems, the school should solve them. Parents also seem less willing to work for services for l.d. children other than their own. Once their own children have been adequately provided for, they lose interest in the volunteer association.

Because parents have no court of appeal or ombudsman, they do not initiate the process whereby their children will be assessed by school personnel and, depending upon the assessor's verdict of the child's dysfunction, assigned to special class placement or remedial assistance or denied such help. As long as parents delay the process of labelling and placement, they can maintain the hope that their children eventually will receive appropriate assistance. However, once they initiate the process, the school authorities carry it through to completion. Parents then must gamble with the real possibility of a misdiagnosis, which tends to follow children for years, or placement in an inappropriate education track, which can effect the child's entire future. This absence of a court of appeal contributes significantly to parent's feelings of impotence, anger, and apathy.

The twentieth century has been characterized by the apparent toleration of barbarism, the massive tragedies wrought on our fellow men, and the assaults on people's right and dignity. Many of us have acknowledged these conditions as being grieviously wrong, yet too many of us have done nothing to ameliorate them, nor have we even protested. We rationalize our inaction by thinking, "What can one person accomplish?" In reality, we are afraid of endangering our current position. Regardless of how unsatisfactory that position might be, we always fear that activism could make it worse. We parents of the l.d. now have a vehicle through which to channel our efforts, and the assurance that they are unlikely to result in retaliation, yet many are still apathetic. It is important that we now separate the impotence of parents who felt inadequate, who felt shameful that they had caused their child's disability, from the impotence that is the apathy of the self-protective.

Group Identification: Our Place in the Pecking Order

Notwithstanding the current reluctance to become involved in social action, both child and parents evolve to the point where they recognize themselves as having manifestations and experiences in common with other l.d. and their families. However, to ensure that outsiders perceive the child in as functional a light as possible, they may identify only with some segments of the group, so that one readily encounters distinctions such as, "My child is dyslexic, not l.d.," or, "My child is l.d., not brain injured," or, "My child isn't l.d., he's just a hyperactive, poor reader."

Many of us shun identification with more severe or lesser status handicaps, lest people identify us with one another. Some of our groups and services also resist such identification. Mark's mother wouldn't reenroll him in the camp for the l.d. because one of his cabinmates had been epileptic. Some parents resist more global identification with the l.d. because of the publicity emanating from the volunteer association. It is, of necessity simplistic. Its descriptions of the behaviorisms and the consequences of lack of services tend toward the extreme, and they are composite descriptions, rarely describing one child. Much of the publicity is geared toward public sympathy and support, so it accentuates the differences rather than the coping abilities. Thus we parents eventually carve ourselves a place in the pecking order, and we guard our high-status position on the exceptionality scale from the encroachment of, and the identification with, the more devalued. Having parented exceptional children ourselves, we do not necessarily empathize as insiders with families in which there is a member with a handicap other than l.d. We are too busy assuring ourselves and others that they are not like us.

Our own group identification primarily is acknowledged only when parents of the l.d. are together, with outsiders excluded, with the exception of the spokesmen and leaders. Thousands of parents have telephoned me about their children, yet when I see them at social affairs or on the street, they never mention our previous contact. They are silent in their shame and fear that outsiders will misunderstand.

After parents have put forth a number of years of effort for the volunteer association, many find that the increased confidence they have acquired in this work replaces their need for the support and camaraderie of the group. They depend on the association less, confidently coping with outside friendships. A few others will discover that the group has provided their lives with meaning and devote the major portion of their time and interests to the volunteer association, becoming expert "professional" speakers, writers, or lobbyists.

The Implications of Group Identification for the Child

While many parents tend to accrue considerable benefit from affiliation with other parents of the l.d., there is less gain for the child who restricts his socialization to other l.d. children, the only obvious benefits being protection and companionship. He might ostensibly enjoy many of the same benefits his parents do, if we were to structure the segregated groups in a fashion whereby he could share experiences and feelings which arise from his l.d., but we rarely do. Since he values normal attributes, the other l.d. children serve as a reminder of attributes with which he prefers not to be connected. It further serves to remind outsiders that he and the other l.d. children are alike. We learn social appropriateness by modeling the behavior of others. Other l.d. children, with their own often inappropriate behavior, tend to be poor models. Being less aware of acceptable behavior, not attentive to relevant interaction, and egocentric, they do not provide sufficient feedback to positively reinforce appropriate behavior or to discourage that which is inappropriate.

In some lesser status groups, such as juvenile offenders, the deviant behavior, although not valued by society, is considered prestigious by the other offenders. However, this is not the case with the l.d., and segregated social togetherness contrived by others may suggest to the child that he is neither allowed to, or capable even of playing with "normals." Because learning disabilities are, in no way, related to interests, the l.d. individual may have more in common with non-learning-disabled persons than with a group who have similar handicaps. Our criteria for delegating l.d. children to segregated or integrated social situations have been crude to non-existent. In the chapter on recreation I shall propose a few ground rules.

In *Stigma*, Goffman states, "The nature of an individual, as he himself self and we impute it to him, is generated by the nature of his group affiliations."[2] Group identification with the l.d. threatens to change the way people see a child. Instead of being primarily an individual with his own constellation of interests, attributes, abilities, and goals, with an incidental l.d., he becomes a learning-disabled child, with the disability paramount. His self-identity may be further subverted by the readiness of parents and outsiders to stereotype.

If the l.d. person breaks the law, outsiders are prepared to generalize that all l.d. turn to a life of crime. Parents lean to optimistic generalizations. Thus, if the l.d. person graduates from college, we do not consider the extent of his motivation, intelligence, degree and type of dysfunction, and the multitude of favorable factors prefacing his success. We insist on displaying him as an example for all the l.d. to aspire to, along with other such atypical models as Churchill, Einstein, and Edison.

Even children who, disability notwithstanding, are not college material, now that they have a l.d., can aspire to a college degree. After all, do not the literature and lecturers reinforce the concept that the l.d. can be retrained and graduate from college? It is reminiscent of the anecdote of the boy who broke his arm and asked the doctor if, when his arm healed, he would be able to play the violin. When the doctor responded affirmatively the boy replied, "That's great, because I didn't know how to play the violin before!"

The Implications of Group Identification for the Adolescent

The adolescent is at the period of his life when he places the greatest importance upon being a member of the high-status group. He is in the process of breaking away from the family life style and seeking his own identity. He looks for peers on whom he can try a variety of interactions in order to find his own style. He wants to share ideas, feelings, and emotions with peers, not parents, and wants to be desired both by males and females. If he is identified with other l.d. youth, his opportunities to be part of the "in" group, to be accepted socially by the high-status adolescents, are greatly reduced. If he is seeking his own identity, he does not want to be stereotyped with the l.d.

Ironically, the same pressures which impel him to seek high-status friendships are the ones that will increase the likelihood of the other adolescents rejecting him. The latter generally are unprepared to compromise their attained status by befriending the young person who is "low on the totem pole." The l.d. adolescents who do "make it" socially often will indulge in any behavior which they think will secure their position in the prestige group and fervently avoid anything that will identify them with learning disabilities.

Identification with the Family

The child's first group is his family. He shares the same subculture and physical attributes with other family members, yet may feel less affinity with his family than perhaps is felt by his siblings. Whereas all the members of a family share similar traits, such as being Jewish, Black, Catholic, wealthy, impoverished, or middle class, they do not share his l.d. Therefore, just as parents of the l.d. feel that outsiders do not comprehend their experience, the child also will feel alone in his experience.

The child's loneliness will be accentuated if the parent's denial prevents him from sharing his reactions and concerns. Before he learns that there are other l.d. persons, he may imagine that he is the only person in the world with his problem. He may indeed stand out as being different from his family. His clumsiness or language processing difficulties may result in mannerisms that are not shared by other family members. A quiet, slow-moving family may find itself with a dynamo in its midst. A family that carefully weighs and considers each decision and action may find itself with an impulsive offspring clashing with its modus operandi. His poor skill in choosing appropriate clothing, or his lack of coordination to dress neatly, may contrast with the stylish family. With his clumsy table manners, spilling the food, he may be a source of irritation to the fastidious. Athletes may sire an uncoordinated offspring and professors beget a poor academic achiever. The child who often says and does the wrong thing appears noticeably out of place in the politician's family. Furthermore, the child realizes that he may be unable to realize the expectations of family and subculture, so, indeed, he is "odd man out."

Robert Coles points out that Negro families, from a child's early years, teach him who he is, where he may not go and what he most probably will be and cannot be.[3] However, because the l.d. usually is not an experience shared by other family members, they neither can prepare the child for what will happen to him or shield him from pitfalls.

Myths

We parents of the l.d. have created some of our own myths, and they serve us less effectively than the truth. They are:

1. *Learning-disabled children are born only to special families.* (The implications are that we possess special abilities to meet the challenge and that to have the l.d. child is some type of blessing.) Some of us do rise to the challenge commendably, but it is not related to special endowment, and whereas the l.d. need not be a tragedy, it assuredly is not a blessing. Many children and adults do experience additional growth because of the adversity, but they pay a heavy price for such growth.

2. *Learning-disabled children are handsomer, more sensitive, etc.* They look like everyone else, and not being as perceptive, some may be less sensitive.

Our culture cherishes many myths, which all of us tend to believe. The l.d. and their families also may believe the following myths, only to have them destroyed, one-by-one. They are:

1. *This is a just society.* As long as we continue to believe this we will agonize over the multitude of injustices that are the lot of the l.d. However, if we function from the premise that life in our culture is not always just, we then can mobilize our resources to work for increased justice.

2. *Hard work is rewarded.* The child often works and tries very hard, yet is penalized. Temara Dembo, G. L. Leviton, and Beatrice A. Wright state:

In our society, people are frequently compared with each other on the basis of their achievements. Schools, for example, are predominately influenced by the achievement or product ideology. High grades are not given to the one who worked hardest but to the one who performed best. Under certain circumstances, of two persons who reached the same performance level, the one who did so with greater ease is considered the better. He is seen as potentially a better producer than the one who had to work harder. Thus effort is not only considered a positive value, but paradoxically, sometimes a liability.[4]

3. *All that is expected of you is that you do your best.* What we really mean is, "All that is expected of you is that you do as well as everyone else."

4. *Everyone is treated equally in our schools. Everyone is afforded equal opportunity in our society.*

5. *Good people will be rewarded.*

Secondary Gain or How to Succeed at Being L.D. Without Even Trying

We have to assume that children would not elect to become l.d. and that families would not elect to beget the l.d. child. Nonetheless, when faced with the reality that the disability is likely to persist for some time, child and family react in certain ways and sometimes realize that other's responses to their behaviors carry a degree of satisfaction. Many of the attributes emerging from the presence of the l.d. family member can be exceedingly positive, such as the possibility of greater maturity, depth, sensitivity, empathy, and sense of purpose. Some parents who would have led unremarkable lives if they, had been untouched by this accident of fate, effect impressive changes in their direct or indirect efforts for the l.d. Some families achieve greater closeness among family members. Because our children's dignity so often is affronted and respect not forthcoming for their individual abilities, parents tend to direct much thought to human dignity, kindness, and other vital, basic attributes. This realignment of values has resulted, in many instances, in the emergence of some l.d. persons and their siblings who are caring, hard working, and goal-directed.

However, secondary gain can also be less lofty. Thus we find the parent who plays the "Authority" game. He establishes himself as an authority, speaking on television, lecturing to audiences and directing his own gross-motor group. He personifies the simple answer that all parents seek. Some authority types are ruthless in their condemnation of parents with different answers than theirs, or parents who carry out less remediation with their children than the authority feels they should. Some merely seek the glory of publicity and adulation. Even the humble authority who professes not to be the perfect parent, or have all the answers, sets himself up as a competent, mature parent merely by that humble admission.

The "Messiah" game is played by the parent who claims to have wrought the miracle of creating a functional child from a very disabled one. In reality the child's improvement may be as attributable to intrinsic development as to superb parenting. The "Messiah" makes little attempt to correct the patronizing oversimplification of outsiders who gushingly commend him for converting a "vegetable" into a human being. He is a ready lure for the magic seekers.

The "Successful Me" game is played by the parent whose child has "made it." He has managed to survive the school system, though the price of survival may have been high. The child then is touted as the model of success for other l.d. to emulate. It never occurs to "Successful Me" that she or he might have been a greater success if the child had settled on a career that did not require such high academic achievement, in which he could have functioned more comfortably.

The "Martyr" game is played by the parent who is sacrificing her life for her l.d. offspring, and enjoying every moment. If her spouse resists involvement with the child's l.d., her enjoyment is enhanced because she then is the only person saddled with all the responsibilities, worries and chores.

The "Poor Me" game is played by parents and children who bask in self-pity and thrive on other's sympathy. They find more reward in this behavior than the efforts to effect change.

"Dumb Me" is the "cop out" for the parent who prefers to be too inept to do anything for her child, and for the child who finds this game safer than trying and failing.

The child may use the disability to avoid the push towards independence, and the parents may use it to avoid the anxiety of decreased dependence. Some families, too, develop a life style which takes the disability into account, and the child may feel compelled to continue acting learning disabled to merit the approach the parents use. Coleen, at age nine, had been used to living a highly structured life, which she probably needed in earlier years. When she first came to camp we found that she kept asking what was going to happen next and where she had placed items. With encouragement she was able to figure these things out for herself and organize her own activities. When we told Coleen's parents of her growth, they were somewhat anxious about reducing the structure, and Coleen attempted to revert to disorganized, dependent behavior when she returned home. Many parents would be prepared to alter their expectations and approach as the child improves, but, due to the limited availability of long-term follow up personnel, there generally is no one to suggest a modified approach. Thus the cycle of overcompensation continues, while the child plays the game of being more disabled to merit the parents' "assistance."

Some children use the disability to demand attention, interrupt, disrupt, or punish the parents. When Rick is moody because of his limited success with female socialization, he will refuse to talk to his family or he will take a walk in the middle of the night, worrying and punishing his family.

There is no conscious payoff for the behaviorisms associated with the disability (and by behaviorisms I mean learning behaviors, as well) because both the learning disabled and the non-learning-disabled value normal behavior. There is great pressure on the child to produce normal behavior even if it is a facade, such as when the parents do the child's homework. Consequently, the maladaptive behaviorisms are not consciously rewarded. However, if the child discovers that they can evoke parental concern, or exclude him from chores and decision making, there may be considerable gain in preserving the manifestations of disability. It may be his only claim to fame: if one does not think that one can attain a unique position by excelling, one may elect for the uniqueness one presently has, of being different. Defensively, if peers and others will not accept you, you may elevate your differences to a type of superiority. "I'm different. I don't want to be part of their stupid goings on."

Perhaps the l.d. is the parent's only "claim to fame." If the child allows himself to improve sufficiently to "pass" in society, where will the parent get his "kicks"? The parent may have become so involved in the l.d. that denying him this may plunge him into his former state of purposelessness. The parent who has to continually demonstrate how much he is doing for his child may have a child who will oblige him by always needing something done for him.

All l.d. children and parents find some secondary gain, but in many instances the gains may be healthy, such as satisfaction in working for the volunteer association. However, those who perpetuate the disability because it seems the safer, more comfortable or rewarding route, need to be taught new styles of functioning. They need to discover that the payoff for being normal is sufficiently worthwhile to risk relinquishing old patterns of behavior.

Professional Mixed Messages

When the family has made peace with the disability, the father, mother, and the child often decide to conclude the search for new cures and the years of remedial effort. They are prepared to live with residual deficits, while being fully aware that further remediation might occasion continued improvement. They may have concluded that there now are more vital priorities for their time and their child's. Perhaps they feel that the hundreds of hours that they and their child have devoted to remedial efforts are all that they should direct toward that goal. The child's current ability to cope is one of the factors in this decision, but is tempered by other considerations, since one child may have received massive doses of remediation yet copes marginally, whereas another received much less help yet manages with relative ease.

The point at which the family decides that "enough is enough" will vary from family to family but, most typically, occurs when the child is in adolescence. The decision is related to the adolescent's more global interests, the demands, stresses, and pressures on him, which surpass those of the non-learning-disabled adolescent, and the fact that the parents are becoming older and wearier. The resolution to live with the disability and stop running is accompanied by a great sense of relief. No longer does each new article read or speaker heard compel the parents to pursue the new cure. They can view each new promise philosophically, knowing that they have seen the simple answers achieve popularity, occasion a flurry of activity, much expenditure of money, and, oftener than not, result in deep disappointment. They have tried many treatments themselves and learned their limitations the difficult way.

The professional community should respect the family's decision to forego further remediation unless that decision has been arrived at too early in childhood. Only the family appreciates how much it has been through and done, how much it and the child can handle, and what has to be sacrificed for remediation. Often their decision to concentrate on a well-rounded life is a sign of real health which must be respected and supported, as indeed it often is. However, there are many pressures working against such a decision. Relatives and friends still in the earlier stages of adjustment perceive cessation of remediation as abandonment of the child.

There are also professionals who, even after the family has stopped seeking them, find the child and readily offer their thoughts on what is the matter with him and what should be done about it. All they see is where he is now, not what has gone into bringing him to this point. Many fail to take into account the fact that the family has lived through years of differing diagnoses, facing the implications of each. Continuing to ply the family with diagnoses and recommendations undermines their adjustment to the disability and undermines the adolescent's confidence in his parents' judgment. They have told him what his disability was and decided with him to terminate remediation. When teachers, principals, guidance counsellors, education consultants, vocational counsellors, physicians, et al., ply the family with confusing and contradictory messages, they place the family in the position of not knowing which message represents reality.

The Children's Hospital, Washington, D.C. study, "Brain Damage in Adolescence," discovered that the l.d. adolescents in their study did not show the expected discrepancy between their verbal and performance intelligence test scores, nor were they low on the subtests, such as block design, in which one expects a low score in l.d. children.[5] If this is indicative of the test picture that l.d. adolescents show, it is not widely known by psychologists who consequently tell some adolescents and their parents that they no longer are disabled. If the child is still l.d., yet the parents accept the diagnosis of normalcy and impose normal expectations on the child, the results can be devastating. Conversely, if they doubt the accuracy of the diagnosis of normalcy and continue to perpetuate the idea of a disability, the child is likely to meet parental expectations by functioning as disabled. No healthy parent wants this to occur. If the child is told that he is not disabled, he likely will resent his parents for having stigmatized him by perpetuating a supposedly nonexistent disability, and furthermore, he returns to the community to find that he still cannot compete with "normal" peers. Who and what is he to believe?

At age eighteen, in grade eleven, Neil began to experience serious problems in school. He had a past history of moderate deficits in coordination, language processing, visual organization, and memory, and previous diagnoses of cerebral palsy, mental retardation, and dysphasia. He had been in "normal" classrooms since grade three and had "held his own" without utilization of ancillary school system resources. However, when Neil became overwhelmed in grade eleven, his parents contacted the school guidance department, school psychologist, head psychologist, school social worker, and consultant in special education in futile attempts to obtain intervention. The special education consultant declared that she could not approach the school unless a request for her services came from the principal, which he was unprepared to make. The head psychologist declared that there were so many l.d. secondary students in crisis in the school system that there were no resources to assist them. The school psychologist suggested that Neil drop one subject at the end of the first semester, and he assured him that he would receive credit for it. He arranged with the principal to have Neil pick up another subject the next semester. Although Neil dropped the suggested subject, he did not receive the promised credit, and when he attempted to register for the agreed upon new subject, he was told by the assistant principal that the class was filled.

The school psychologist told Neil's parents that Neil should receive remediation in reading comprehension and recommended a clinic that specialized in crawling and developing unilaterality. The parents knew that whatever Neil did need, he did not have a problem with reading comprehension. After years of motor, optometric, and academic therapy, they were most reluctant to once again initiate a therapeutic regime or to subject a young man to crawling. Their dilemma was that the psychologist seemed to be the only available resource for intervention, and if they ignored his recommendations they might burn their only bridge. Not one of the above mentioned professionals had interpreted Neil's problem to his teachers, or attempted to discern the demands of each subject and individual teacher's expectations to determine whether Neil could meet them or how they could be modified.

Neil's parents convinced him of the validity of entering a nondiploma course in a community college in lieu of grade twelve. They arranged a vocational assessment in order to determine the course he would enjoy and could handle. The psychologist at the vocational counseling agency told Neil that he had no disability, that his only problem was his parents who had led him to believe he was incapable, and that he could handle any subject, including spelling, foreign languages, and geometry. She suggested that Neil should become a psychologist, lawyer, or social worker and wanted to inform his school that he was not l.d.

Following her suggestions, Neil enrolled in grade twelve and fell flat on his face! At this juncture his parents insisted that the school invite the special education consultant to speak to their son's teachers. After her conference with the staff, she informed the parents that Neil's learning and language handicap was hindering his ability to handle academic demands so extensively that it would be impossible for him to pass grade twelve in a "regular classroom." "It really is a miracle that he got this far," she remarked. She felt that Neil needed his family, should not go away to school, and suggested that she try to place him in the resource classroom. After a month of uneasy waiting, she was unable to place him and complained to the frustrated parents, "If only you had contacted me earlier!"

Neil enrolled in a residential school for l.d. youth where he progressed well. He required his first semester's credits from his secondary school in order to have sufficient credits to pass grade twelve. However, the school would not supply the credits, stating that one credit per subject is not earned after one semester although two credits are awarded at year's end.

The Desire for Simple Answers

I have described the tendency of outsiders to stereotype, to see l.d. in absolutes, either obviously handicapped or nonhandicapped. Parents also tend to seek simple or total answers. They may be disappointed in a professional because he is not forthcoming with a solution for all of their problems. They look for treatment programs that will be the total answer to their child's disability, and they find professionals who claim that their remedial approach is the one answer. I have participated in workshops with the "one answer" people, and I bleed for those persons in the audience who latch on to this new-found approach as the solution for their children. Once again most of these parents and their children will be dashed onto the rocks of disappointment. The irony is that these approaches, oftener than not, are the therapy of choice for some types of l.d., but fall short of being everyone's cure. The simple-answer people speak at workshops sponsored by reputable professionals and institutions, often are articulate and charismatic, and appeal to the hopes that parents hold.

Parents need to be apprised that effecting improvement in a l.d. child is an ongoing process which involves the use of many different approaches at home and at school. Some of the most knowledgeable practitioners attempt a variety of remedial methods with a child before one technique or a combination seem to reach the child. Therefore, even to suggest that matching disability to remedial approach is the answer, is simplistic. Parents should reassure themselves that if there were one simple answer or cure for l.d., it speedily would be adopted by our education systems and treatment centers. Similarly, there often are not simple answers to problems at home.

When I spoke to parent's groups around the continent I used to feel compelled to furnish a wise answer to all their problems. My difficulties in being a sage were alleviated somewhat by discovering the ploy of throwing the question back to the audience from which someone frequently would come forth with a far better suggestion than I ever could dream up. However, the best solution, by far, arrived one day with the realization that there simply is not an answer for everything. My mistake as a speaker (and hence parent figure) was that I felt that I always had to provide an answer. The parents' mistake was that they, too, felt that they must provide solutions for their child.

For example, let's look at the youngster who is miserable because in school he is two grades behind his twin. He really does not feel any better when we tell him that at age forty it will not make any difference whether he was ten or twelve years old in grade four. The relevant factor is that he is twelve years old now, in grade four, and feeling very much out of place. We would be far more empathic parents if we faced up to this reality. Chances are that he would feel better if we acknowledge his feelings about being academically retarded. That does not mean that both he and his parents need spend a great deal of energy on self-pity. It does mean, though, that he has a right to feel badly.

Also, let's drop the "con job" that emerges sounding like this, "You may be behind in school but you're a wonderful athlete," or, "You may be behind in school but you're a delightful, obedient son." Any child worth his salt will react to these irrelevancies with a resounding, "baloney!" The reasons are these: (1) If we really enjoy some aspects of his achievement, we do not need to verbalize it, he will know it; (2) There is no relationship between school failure and proficiency as an athlete or being an obedient son; (3) When he is upset about grade attainment, his concern at that time is his prestige in the eyes of other children, and we are mixing this up with our values.

Chapter 6:

Developing a Realistic Self-Concept

IN ELISABETH KUBLER-ROSS' delineation of the stages whereby one comes to terms with a terminal illness, acceptance immediately follows the stage of depression. However, with the l.d., acceptance cannot be achieved until the child appreciates who he is, his attributes and weaknesses, the contribution he can make to others, and they to him, and his present and eventual role in society.

The fact that many l.d. children function with a self-concept that is somewhat askew has been noted frequently in the literature. The blame usually has been placed on poor body image and school performance. Body image has a role in the development of self-concept, but in the case of the the l.d., it would seem to be a lesser role than the incredibly complex galaxy of factors working against the development of a clear identity.

Familial Factors

A learning disability is considered by society to be a defect. This is clearly implied in the words and terms associated with l.d.: "disability" in the term *learning disability*, "dysfunction" in *minimal brain dysfunction*, "handicap" in *perceptual* or *neurological handicap*, and "injury" or "damage" in the terms *brain injury* or *brain damage*. Thus it is considered to represent a cluster of defective and undesirable traits, and the overwhelming emphasis of remediation is directed toward normalcy. The possibility of continued disability, however mild, is untenable to families for many years because it implies reduced functioning and reduced opportunity for upward mobility.

Each family's unspoken pact with society is that it will prepare its children to carry on the cultural components and contribute to the social, technological, and humane development of our civilization. Society strongly imposes this expectation on the family, and it is powerfully internalized. The l.d. child appears unlikely to meet one or more of these expectations, and this failure to meet the commitment is unacceptable both to child and family. Therefore, they shop for cures and society contributes to the concept of cure by gearing its programs to such a goal, while fully cognizant that complete cure is rare. This means that if the child accepts his disabilities, which are an integral part of himself at any given time, he is failing his family and society. (The extent of the disability may change with time and demands, but at a given point in time they are part of what is him.) Indeed, we teach him that he must *not* accept his disabilities but must work hard to overcome them.

Even when we encounter an adolescent whose disabilities have resulted in an academic deficit so severe that our educational structure cannot provide allowances for the extensive recouping he requires, we still tend to ply him with remediation. This says to him, in effect, that he still must not accept his areas of dysfunction, but must continue to fight them.

The child has difficulty figuring out who he is because the games people play prevent him from receiving honest feedback. In some families one parent conveys to the child that he is disabled and the other maintains that he is the all-American boy. Within these polarities are the mixed messages of hope and disappointment. Then there is the tendency of parents, teachers and other adults to praise the child for poor production and "destroy" him when he has exerted genuine effort. The parents allow him to behave one way at home and punish him with embarrassment when he behaves the same way in public. People are so concerned with their own feelings about disability that they distort the feedback they give the child. The youngster's confusing pattern of abilities and disabilities makes it difficult for him to figure out who he really is. Mark's father commented to me, "Mark doesn't know how he fits into the scheme of things."

The confusion surrounding prognosis makes early adjustment almost impossible. There are many types and degree of disability falling into the l.d. basket, and many variations of intellectual capacity even within the limitations of the description, "normal to above normal intelligence." There are numerous known and unknown factors affecting prognosis. Consequently the prognosis of any l.d. individual remains in an unclarified limbo. We do know that mentally retarded persons tend to remain that way, that autism rarely is completely reversed, and that cerebral palsy remains a handicap throughout life. However, we find that some very involved l.d. make remarkable gains, whereas some who appear promising show little progress. The literature tends to be unspecific, but where prognosis is mentioned, it generally suggests that remediation leads to recovery. However, when one traces most of the literature mentioning prognosis to the parent's associations, one has to temper the statements by taking into consideration the parent's need to hope and the possibility that the literature is oversimplified.

The first generation of the diagnosed l.d. are in young adulthood, so only now do we have an opportunity to relate supposed prognosis to actuality, yet few of their attainments have been recorded. As a consequence of this, parents really do not know what will become of their children. This makes goal setting and adjustment difficult indeed.

As long as the parents are actively seeking remediation and are unaware of how the child will respond to it, they really do not know how much the child will progress. Normally, from their early age, we tend to point our offspring in the direction of their aptitude. When ten-year-old Adam, who has accelerated in school and excels in mathematics, announces that he is going to be a professional hockey player when he grows up, his mother responds with, "You think you're going to be a hockey player now, but I imagine that you'll probably be an accountant." However, with our l.d. children, we are not sure what they will be able to do. In the development of self-concept, there needs to be an emerging mental image of one's adulthood, and we cannot direct the l.d. in this process. Rollo May, in *Man's Search for Himself* states:

> . . . man's consciousness of himself is the source of his highest qualities. It underlies his ability to distinguish between "I" and the world. It gives him the capacity to keep time, which is simply the ability to stand outside the present and to imagine oneself back in yesterday or ahead in the day after tomorrow. Thus human beings can learn from the past and plan for the future.[1]

Many l.d., being unable to conceptualize a temporal future, have no image of themselves as adults, and are bound to the immediate present. Unlike others, they can enter into no dialogue with their destiny.

The Capacity for Consciousness of Self

May elaborates:

The capacity for consciousness of self also underlies man's ability to use symbols, which is a way of disengaging something from what it is, such as the two sounds which make up the word "table," and agreeing that these sounds will stand for a whole class of things. Thus man can think in abstractions like "beauty," "reason," and "goodness."[2]

Since the l.d. is a disturbance of the symbolic processes, this difficulty with some forms of abstract thought is bound to affect the awareness of self. May continues:

> This capacity for consciousness of ourselves gives us the ability to see ourselves as others see us and to have empathy with others. It underlies our remarkable capacity to transport ourselves into someone else's parlor where we will be in reality next week, and then in imagination to think and plan how we will act. And it enables us to imagine ourselves in someone else's place, and to ask how we would feel and what we would do if we were this other person.[3]

The l.d., being bound to the concrete present, experience considerable difficulty imagining themselves in someone else's shoes, or manipulating time, place, and circumstance in their minds in order to imagine themselves in a situation occurring anywhere other than the present. Sol Gordon describes l.d. as a deficit in the ability to discern the impact of one's behavior on others. Similarly, the l.d. experiences difficulty perceiving the other person's feelings. Without this perception being well defined, one cannot feel much empathy towards others.

Because the l.d. has trouble imagining events that will occur in the future, he cannot always weigh the consequences of his behavior. These frequent errors in judgment and demonstrations of poor self-control cause parents to impose their judgment and control on the child more often and for a longer period of time than they do with the nondisabled. This gives the child the impression that his judgment, decisions, and control system are defective, and it diminishes his self-confidence and his desire to trust himself to make future decisions. Consequently, he has fewer opportunities than his peers to express his individuality as distinct from the stand his parents take.

Parental concern about the child's ability to exert reasonable judgment, and their feelings of rejection and anger toward their child convey to him the message that he is unlikely to receive consistent parental support in his attempts at independence. He has had so many failures with exaggerated parental response to those failures that he realizes that he is not allowed the privileges of the nondisabled child, which is to make some incorrect decisions and to fail some of the time.

Our swiftly changing, multistress culture offers a meager sense of structure and constancy to any parent. Parents of the l.d. find that society has been less supportive of them than of families in which there is no l.d. member. They harbor many reality-based anxieties around the child's performance, opportunities, and future. The child takes his cues from his parents concerning the gravity of his disability, and the more anxious they are about him, the more anxious he will be about himself. Furthermore, their anxieties will lead him to believe that the outside world is a dangerous place in which to attempt to become oneself.

As I discussed in the section on secondary gain, if the parents are unable to derive as much pleasure as they seek from the child's achievements, they may begin to exploit the disability as a source of gratification. The child then realizes that he cannot develop his ability to be a responsible, functioning self without losing parental support. He rightly could ask, "will they love me only if I am disabled and dependent on them?"

The child whose daily diet consists of an overdose of failure cannot be expected to like himself or others. Should he resort to self-pity, he may feel temporarily comforted, but even further demeaned.

In order to strive toward an independent adulthood we seem to need to fuel ourselves with a modicum of anxiety about our future achievement. The l.d. creates a crippling anxiety about current situations, and it generates considerable nonspecific anxiety in the family and others, but probably not enough productive anxiety based upon a knowledge of future role requirements. If we want to alter the "Walter Mitty" behavior of some of our l.d., in which they accept few challenges while dreaming grandiose dreams, we may have to reduce situationally-determined and generalized anxieties and create some anxiety which is geared to competition with oneself and achieve-related to future goals.

May states that the self is the organizing function within the individual. The l.d. person demonstrates difficulty in organizing his sensory impressions, his body in space, his perceptions, concepts, and attention. It is reasonable, therefore, to assume that he has difficulty organizing the various roles he assumes, the relationships and feedback which, when considered in totality, provide him with an image of himself.

The Etiology of Aspiration

When outsiders, particularly professionals, encounter the l.d. adolescent who has unrealistic aspirations, they frequently blame his parents for not accepting the disability. But this often is not the case. The child internalizes the family's attainment as his desired goal. If both parents are college graduates and voracious readers, the child is not likely to be impressed by his ability to read at a grade two level when he is ten years of age, or by the prospect of a vocation such as plumber or electrician, regardless of the worth of these vocations, and his parent's realistic attitudes. The child also conforms his goals to the aspirations of his subculture. If his greater family and their friends value scholastic achievement, he will as well. If they value wealth or prestige, he is likely to internalize these values. Neil's parents were realistic in their goal setting for him, discouraging a college career despite his high IQ. However, when a relative asked him what he wanted to do for a living and Neil stated that he was considering joining the merchant marine, the cousin cautioned, "Don't do that; you'll meet undesirable types!"

Many of the child's values are integrated before he and his parents even know he is l.d. This will have a definite bearing on the importance he places on his deficits and his coming to terms with them. We also should not minimize the significance of peer-group values in the development of his aspirations. Whereas the peer group often responds negatively to outstanding academic achievement, they also think poorly of the child who cannot maintain the academic pace. As long as the child's ability level falls far below the attainment goals of his immediate family, greater family, peer group, subculture, and society, even if his parent's expectations are realistic, his may not be. It is well and good for the parents to reward his honesty, creativity, or what-have-you, but if he still is "odd man out" at school day after day and year after year, he will want to be like the others rather than be himself. The child's adjustment also will be related to the parent's ability to be relaxed and honest about his disability as contrasted with parents who discuss it in a tight voice, or not at all, or who may encourage the child to hide the fact that he is l.d.

In *Human Dilemmas of Leadership*, Abraham Zaleznik describes the phenomenon of consistency in expectation and reality.[4] If a person's job and life style is consistent with his own expectations and the expectations of his family and subculture, he will be content. Conversely, if he feels that he should be accomplishing more, and his family and friends feel that he is "cut out for better things," he will be status inconsistent, or unhappy with his lot. Status inconsistency is an apt term to describe many of the l.d. Typically, their levels of accomplishment fall below the expectation for persons with their intelligence, and below the expectations which they and others develop based upon their intact areas of functioning. They are on a perpetual teeter-totter, not knowing whether each situation will be one in which they are respected for their competencies, devalued for their deficits, related to as able, or considered handicapped. They frequently cannot identify with either the nondisabled or the handicapped. Thus they are denied the opportunity to develop an image of themselves which says to them, "I am on this level, which is similar to the level of my fellow students and friends."

Ironically, many parents of the l.d. also have become status inconsistent. In order to help their child and others like him, many parents have become more knowledgeable about exceptionalities in children, diagnoses, and remediation than some professionals. Because of their acquired knowledge and professional attitude, some professionals treat them as equals, whereas others are patronizing. They may be asked to lecture at a University, yet be denied enrollment in the same institution. Each time they come in contact with a professional, they do not know whether they will be related to as a fellow professional or as a "stupid parent."

The Phenomenon of Spread

The process of developing a realistic self-concept involves taking stock of all that makes up a person, and appraising it without distortion. This means that the disability must take its place in this appraisal, without exaggeration. However, for a number of years this is a difficult expectation to make of the child because outsiders, in their simplified thinking, will either insist that he is normal or that the disability is pervasive, effecting all areas of his ability to function. Have you noticed how people may shout at a mentally retarded person or non-English-speaking person, generalizing the fact that if he is retarded or foreign born, he also must be deaf. (This phenomenon of spread is operant when educators and other professionals generalize that parents of the l.d. must have undesirable traits such as poor parenting abilities or neuroses.) The parents also experience an extended period in which the disability is uppermost in their minds. At that time every move, every behaviorism is viewed as it relates to the disability so that the child also learns to generalize and think of himself as totally inept. By viewing all behavior in terms of the disability, we narrow our concept of the child and his concept of himself into that of a one-dimensional person; thus we reduce our ability and his to perceive himself as a multifaceted being.

This creates the most cogent argument for parents and child to be knowledgeable about the disability. In the l.d. field, ignorance is not bliss. When both parents and offspring are afforded the respect of having assessment information shared with them, they will understand the areas of deficit and also the many intact faculties with which he can relate to the world as completely as others, thus conveying to others the fact of his adequacies. Parents can discourage the askewed stereotyped thinking of their friends if they correct distortions. If parents allow outsiders to persist in the game of "great you, you brought him to this point from a vegetable," they will reinforce the distortions because even though they supposedly brought the child a long distance, a former "vegetable" is indeed a very different being.

Profoundly handicapped persons tend to spend much of their lives in sheltered situations where there is not only a special physical environment but expectations and feedback are special also. They so obviously cannot cope that we modify their world to ensure success. The l.d., being relatively functional, spend most or all of their time in the world of the nonhandicapped. However, we do not modify the world so that they can cope, succeed, and thus learn what they can do. There always is the discrepancy between what we expect of the child, what he expects of himself as a member of normal society, and what he can achieve. How often are his environment and external expectations altered in the classroom, in the physical education program, and on the street? The more intelligent the l.d. child is, the greater the difficulty he will have in coming to terms with his achievement.

Some self-concept tests, modified especially for the l.d., are designed in such a way that the child with the most realistic self-concept will test out as having the lowest self-concept. A negative answer counts against one's score, and some of the questions are of this type: "The teacher likes me," or, "Other children like me." Surely a good self-concept must be realistic, yet the l.d. child who scores highest on such a test may be most unrealistic. I wonder whether a test exists that can measure the attributes a family and subculture award, the extent to which they award these attributes, and how good a child feels if he possesses some of the awarded attributes.

The World Is Our Mirror

One of the ways we develop an image of ourselves is through the process of action and reaction. Nature probably made young animals and humans particularly appealing so that a chain of positive action and reaction would be initiated. This furnishes the young child with sufficient feelings of being appreciated and wanted, and he then is able to cope with the inevitable negative reactions that also are part of the humanizing process.

Thus, the infant smiles, coos, or involuntarily lays his floppy head on our shoulder, and we respond with appreciation. He is quick to learn that such behaviors elicit pleasurable responses. Before long, he attempts variations and monitors our response to these. If the response is positive, the variation is varied further or added to another positively reinforced behavior such as smiling and reaching out simultaneously. If we react negatively, he is less likely to repeat the negatively reinforced behavior, preferring to respond to that which evokes pleasure.

By this means of negative and positive reinforcement, humans modify their behavior throughout their lives. Thus, when someone says, "I enjoy you; you're very witty," we try to be wittier oftener. Conversely, if someone queries, "Why do you act like that?" we try to act less offensively from that point on. More typically, the cues we receive are less overt—a slight turning away of the head, or a grimace.

In order for a person to maximize the action and reaction process whereby we learn to develop into vastly complex social beings, a number of factors must be operant.

Output

In order to react to a behavior, there must be a behavior to which to react. If the infant proffers reduced output in critical socializing areas, there will be no reinforcement and there is likely to be negative reaction, a reduced interest in the baby. If he does not smile, we do not smile back, and he is not much fun. We are content, even delighted with crude, sometimes accidental social gestures performed by the infant: rewarding gas smiles, accidental vocalizing, a chance reaching of the hand towards us. However, as the child matures, our expectations of social behavior become increasingly complex. We allow the human a short time in which to amass a vast array of complex social skills, some consciously taught, many merely assumed and assimilated through the process of accurately assessing and relating subtle cues. In order for the person to benefit from this learning process, he must provide the expected social output to which people can respond at each stage of development.

Literature on deafness describes the impoverished environment of many deaf children. Their handicap in communication results in reduced output to which the family can respond, so that they are often ignored and excluded from interaction. This reduced ability and opportunity to interact impoverishes the entire experiential cycle, which results in immaturity. The child has failed his parents' expectation of how a child should communicate, so disappointment and possibly rejection further contribute to the exclusion. Finally, our frenetically paced culture dictates that communication be speedy and effortless. People lose patience with the person who fails to hear, to comprehend, to respond appropriately or not at all, or who requires more laborious or slowed down communication. This is particularly noticeable when we communicate with stutterers. It is easier to exclude than include.

When output is absent or faulty, the quality and depth of relationships tends to be reduced. For instance, from the ages of six or seven onward, an assumed expectation of the child is that he will reward family members and friends every so often. We expect him to comment, "I enjoyed the dinner," or "That was a cool thing you said in school." However, some l.d. children never have internalized the concept that mentioning positive attributes is an important aspect of interaction. In the past, when other persons in his environment rewarded people, he may have been attending to unimportant stimuli, and not noticed, or he may not have recognized rewarding behavior as important and stored it as a communication tool, or his inept system of organizing, storing, and recalling past experiences for current use may be working against him. Regardless, his conversations and actions are then likely to be immature and self-concerned. Because he is deficient in this and other requisites of interaction, the relationship is less rewarding to the other person, and is not actively sought. The consequent reduction in quantity and depth of interactions affords the child reduced opportunities for behavioral feedback. He almost never is told the real reason why people are less interested in him, primarily because the interactors may not be conscious of the reasons, often blaming surface manifestations such as manner of dress, for the friendlessness.

We all have occasion to wonder why we were rejected by someone. The l.d. child rarely knows whether the rejection occurs because of the person's discomfort with the idea of a disability, whether he just is not compatible with the person, whether he has said or done the wrong thing, or whether he has failed to perceive the other person's expectations of the interaction.

Deficits or exaggerations of output could be catalogued endlessly. The hyperactive child who never is still long enough to hug or converse with his parents does not produce positive social behavior to which a positive response can be directed. The perseverative talker will bore people so that they will become impatient, but possibly suppress showing their impatience because they pity the child, or alternatively they may avoid him. Either way his output has resulted in unsatisfactory or reduced interaction, and the feedback does not clarify the reason. The tendency toward impulsivity may render some output as spontaneous reactions to impulse rather than cognition, which may make the behavior unrelated to past social learning of the current situation.

Output should be viewed not only as vocalization, but conceptualized within the total context of a person's expressive system. It is not only what we say, but how we say it—voice tone and volume, facial expressions, use of the body, clothing, perfume, hairdo, manipulation of time and space—that expresses the ideas we wish to convey. For instance, the clumsy body of some l.d., its plasticity (the infant-like total body response to emotions), may be misperceived by others. Stefanie Greene, in "Life Styles in Adolescents with Brain Dysfunction," comments:

> The first thing I would like to do is to try to describe this group
> of adolescents, because often their physical appearance tends, in
> subtle ways, to set them apart from normal youngsters—so much
> so that other members of our clinic staff would inform us after a

glance that one of our subjects had arrived at the waiting room. About 40 percent of the subjects were physically unremarkable in appearance, but the rest could be distinguished by obvious immaturity, high activity level, neurologic handicap, obesity, wooden, expressionless faces, or an overall sloppy, gawky, or awkward appearance. We photographed these youngsters, and they seem to have a peculiar asymmetry—often because their heads are cocked and their bodies slumped over to one side. Several were dressed in dark, somber suits that would have looked more appropriate on their fathers. The three girls in the study were immature, awkward and rather unfeminine in appearance. Their clothes were appropriate but they looked as if someone else had dressed them and hadn't done too good a job of it.

More striking was the social awkwardness and inappropriateness of the subjects. They were less able than controls to make "small talk" before or after the interview, and more awkward with such things as opening doors for the female interviewer (most of them didn't attempt to). Eight could not refrain from asking inappropriate personal questions, telling bathroom jokes, or trying to be seductively flattering. Perhaps also indicative of the problems with inhibition or modulation of activity, the experimentals tended to be more uninhibited in speech and to laugh and giggle more often. Seven showed moderate or marked press of speech, and in twelve the interviews were full of trivial details and digressions. They tended, as a group, to be more concrete and to have more difficulty with an unstructured interview, forcing the interviewer to ask more focused questions.[5]

In summary then, output bears a distinct relationship to the development of a self-image. Faulty or missing output results in no reaction, negative reaction, reduced interaction, and interaction with less depth. In other words, if you persist in not giving something to a relationship, you will receive less in return. The child learns that the things he says or does may not always be well received, yet the reasons for this poor reception are not always clarified for him. This is because the reactors are unsure of why they reacted negatively, which quality or combination "turned them off." Additionally, our cultural pattern is one of avoiding the less rewarding person without explaining the reasons for this avoidance. If the child is inept in perceiving or assessing the subtle cues in response to his output, he may never learn the reasons for his reduced acceptability. At least faulty output evokes a response, whereas missing output cannot be responded to, which reduces the likelihood that the person will acquire the desired behavior. Consequently, the l.d. person may find himself with few in-depth relationships, which further reduces the opportunities to plumb reactions to his mode of expressing himself. The existential concept is that a person's actions portray the true him; in other words, "I am what I do." However, if the child cannot determine the effects of what he does, how will he be able to develop a concept of who he is?

Henry V. Cobb, in "The Attitude of a Retarded Person Toward Himself," describes the differentiation of one's self from the environment as that which gradually emerges from the experiences of thwarting and gratification.[6] However, he points out that if frustration is too great, the infant is helpless to obtain gratification and the coping self cannot emerge. If we assume that some l.d. proffer fewer positive social behaviors to which persons in the environment could respond, we then can deduct that those persons will give less to the child. He thus will be gratified less frequently and thwarted oftener. The propensity of the l.d. infant's system having difficulty adjusting to the physical world has been noted. Colic, food allergies, and other upsets further impede the acquisition of comfort and consequent gratification.

Then, of course, we must take his own deficiencies into account and recognize the likelihood that they will frustrate him from an early age. The clumsy child, unable to differentiate shapes, sizes, and his spatial world will likely prove unable to feed himself accurately, crawl and walk adeptly, make contact with objects for which he reaches, steer them to his desired destination, or manipulate and master many of his toys. The child with language memory problems will experience early difficulty processing the expression of others and expressing himself. Jean Piaget and Barbel Inhelder state, "When symbolic functioning appears, language representation and communication with others expand this field (development of self-awareness), to unheard-of proportions and a new type of structure is required."[7] The language of others tells us about ourselves, and our own language molds our thoughts. We shape what we are and our destiny through language, and when it is limited, then we are limited in how we can structure ourselves. Even the seemingly most verbal of the l.d., on close scrutiny are found to be deficient in their ability to process and manipulate spoken and written language, which we must take into account in considering the development of self.

The l.d. become frustrated from minimal provocation. This propensity to ready frustration may be primary behavior, or secondary behavior resulting from accumulated failures, or a combination of both. Regardless, we then can assume that the child will feel frequently frustrated and cease trying to succeed in difficult tasks. He then will experience failure, and with failure there can be no gratification or developing awareness of what he can accomplish.

We tend not to allow the l.d. child as much leeway to be himself as we do his nondisabled peers. Much of his behavior tends to be attributed to his disability, which we feel will show his "mark of Cain" to the world, so it must be discouraged. A nondisabled child can have his times of frustration, irritability, impulsivity, clumsiness, and other inappropriate behaviors, yet elicit only the expected negative reaction to such behavior. The pattern of the l.d. is one of exaggerated behavior evoking exaggerated response from which we expect normal learning to ensue. Our cultural bias is to discourage expression of feelings, and the l.d. child is particularly discouraged from expressing his feelings because they are too painful or too overt for others to handle, couched in language that distorts their meaning or serves to embarrass, expressed at inappropriate times or to the wrong people.

Input

In *The Communication of Emotional Meaning* J. R. Davitz describes his research which found that sensitivity to voice tones, facial expressions and the emotions they convey are directly related to verbal intelligence, abstract symbolic ability, knowledge of vocal characteristics of emotional expression, ability to discriminate pitch, loudness, time and timbre of auditory stimuli, and ability to distinguish figure from ground in a visual perception task.[8] He views the ability to communicate feelings as a symbolic process. Davitz found significant positive intercorrelations between a person's ability to express his feelings vocally to others, self-perception, or ability to identify one's own vocal expressions of feeling, and ability to identify feelings expressed vocally by others. In the same text, John B. Turner states: "It seems reasonable to expect some correlation between accurate auditory perception of emotions and adequate interpersonal adjustment, whether adjustment affects perception, perception affects adjustment, or both.[9]

This research seems to bear great relevance to the interpersonal behavior of the l.d. The above-mentioned attributes, which are directly related to one's ability to monitor his own and other's expressions of feeling, are the same attributes which are associated singly or in the total cluster, with the l.d. Certainly, the l.d. is a deficit in symbolic ability, often accompanied by temporal confusion. It seems reasonable to conclude, therefore, that an undetermined but likely significant percentage of the l.d. experience difficulty accurately monitoring their own and other people's output. If they are less skilled in perceiving their own expressions with accuracy, inevitably they will be handicapped in matching expression to response. In other words, you may have thought you were conveying interest, yet the perceiver may have interpreted your expression as boredom. Consequently, he will react to your supposed boredom and you will assume that his reaction is to your expression of interest. Even if you interpret his reaction accurately, you will store it as a response to interest. As a consequence, when you encounter the reaction in the future you will think it's a response to interest, thus having learned nothing from the input. Furthermore, you did not monitor your expression as boredom so you will have no way of realizing that you need to alter your output to convey interest. Similarly, if you are inept in processing the expression of others, you cannot respond appropriately or store their reactions to use in modifying your future behavior. The apparent egocentricity and lack of sensitivity observed in some of the l.d. may well be attributed to their difficulty in using emotions to "feel" others out and adjust their behavior to the response.

Summarily then, others are our mirror. We shape our concept of ourselves from the messages we receive from others. Communication is a circular process with the onus on the child to initiate the cycle. We can modify our behavior and sophisticate our social skills only if we can assess our output and input with relative accuracy. If our output is unfulfilling to others, they will not give us the message that our friendship is valued or rewarding. Since we are social beings who need to feel important to others in order to feel important ourselves, the implications are enormous. If our input is inaccurate, our image of ourselves becomes distorted.

Development of Identity

How does the human organism develop to become an individual within our culture and world? He attempts to organize and comprehend the world, then design his role in it. He needs to determine the meaning of life as he perceives it, and decide how he intends to relate to that meaning or to confront it. In order to develop true individuality he cannot totally adopt other's meaning for life as his own, or completely submerge his identity in the infinite, or whatever his belief, but must establish an ongoing relationship between the meaning behind "being" and himself. He needs to determine the ways he can relate honestly to that meaning.

We have taken the first step in assisting him in his identity search by actively assisting him to organize and comprehend the world. However, if man is to become comfortable with self, he must have respect for himself. It is impossible to respect yourself if others tell you that you have no control over yourself or your destiny, that control must be imposed externally and that you have difficulty making choices so that you will be excluded from decision making about yourself. How can you develop your unique philosophy about the meaning of life if much of the environment revolves around you and feeds into you rather than you giving to it? How can you develop a philosophy towards which you can behave with integrity if much of what you do is discounted?

Perhaps the most important remedial thrust might be that of developing a sense of time in the organism. As long as he continues to live only for the present, he can develop no ongoing plan, no blueprint for implementing through living experience the meaning he attributes to his existence. He must learn to weave past actions and experiences into a base for present and future behavior. A life predicated upon momentary fulfillment largely is meaningless. The next step is acquisition of independence skills. Only when you have achieved mastery over yourself and your environment can you function as an individual.

Acceptance of Disability and Self

Acceptance implies coming to terms with that which a person *will* be able to do as well as that which he is unlikely to accomplish. Self-image is not static in any of us; but we undergo constant changes related to our experiences of success and failure. Self-image relates not only to what you can do now, but what you should expect of yourself, given your innate capacities and likely opportunities. The vast majority of the l.d. possess the potential to function in the nonhandicapped world of employment and socialization. This means that the child and family should adopt goals for themselves leading to integrated adult functioning. A suggested list might be:

1. Expects to be able to exert control over his own behavior and assumes an increasing responsibility for controling himself. Does not blame behavior on the disability.

2. Strives toward adaptive methods of handling his difficulties, rather than maladaptive. For example, frustration can be overcome by kicking a soccer ball rather than screaming; overstimulation can be handled by removing oneself rather than displaying a tantrum.

3. Accepts consequences of his behavior.

4. Does not allow himself to be caught up in a situation in which he cannot cope but explains his difficulties so that demands can be modified. By this means he gains some mastery over his environment.

5. Is confident in his strengths and feels that he has something to offer other people and society. Neither distorts his strengths or weakness.

6. Has a number of interests where the disability retreats to a minor place in his life. However, he does not pretend that the disability does not exist or feel that he has to compensate. Rather, he is content to do those things that he does adequately.

7. Does not overreact or underreact to stimuli.

8. Expects others to accept him. Is not defensive and does not magnify rejections out of proportion. Takes a reasonable amount of initiative in interaction.

9. Is interested in other people and the well-being of society and the world.

10. Expects to be able to cope with independent adult life.

These goals might take a lifetime to achieve, but they are predicated upon attitudes which can be inculcated in childhood and worked on as the child grows. "Acceptance" means feeling good about yourself and then being able to relate comfortably to others.

Hope

The last stage that Elisabeth Kubler-Ross delineates is one of hope, and for the l.d. and their families, that stage is realistic. Many l.d. can hope for a life of normal fulfillment and accomplishment. The mere fact of maturation seems to work in favor of many of the l.d. who, like some fine wines, seem to improve with age. Then, because adults do not have to meet most of the expectations that children have to meet in school and on the playground, they can choose a life style that maximizes their coping skills. No longer need they be faced with baseball, algebra, geometry, or Spanish. Their mobility allows them to seek a spouse and friends from a wide selection of adults, so they can select persons whose interests and skills are compatible with theirs.

Although the disability probably will not have disappeared, the adult who learns to ask for added structure, clarification, or the organization he needs, is likely to function quite adequately. Perhaps it is a matter of stating, "I'm sorry, I didn't understand what you said. Could you please explain it more simply?"; or having one's spouse read to one, or asking someone for directions to a street, or having a secretary handle the spelling, or listening to lectures on tape. The l.d. person should be able to "make it" in adult life if he possesses adequate social skills, is flexible, has learned to organize himself, and can read sufficiently to cope with signs, menus, and simple written instructions.

Part One / Notes

Chapter 1:

1. Robert Coles, *Children of Crisis: A Study of Courage and Fear, Part One* (Boston, Mass: Little, Brown & Co., 1968), p. 328.

2. L. F. Kurlander and Dorothy Colodny, "Pseudoneurosis in the Neurologically Handicapped Child," *American Journal of Orthopsychiatry*, Vol. 35, No. 4 (July 1965), p. 733.

3. Beatrice A. Wright, *Physical Disability— A Psychological Approach* (New York: Harper & Row, 1960); Erving Goffman, *Stigma: Notes on the Management of Spoiled Identity* (Englewood Cliffs, N.J.: Prentice-Hall, Inc., 1965); Elisabeth Kubler-Ross, *On Death and Dying* (New York: The Macmillan Co., 1969); Bernard Schoenberg et al., *Loss and Grief: Psychological Management in Medical Practice* (New York: Columbia University Press, 1970); Coles, *Children of Crisis*; Edward T. Hall, *The Silent Language* (New York: Doubleday and Co., Inc., 1959); Joel R. Davitz et al., *The Communication of Emotional Meaning* (New York: Mcgraw-Hill Book Company, 1964); Kurlander and Colodny, "Pseudoneurosis in the Neurologically Handicapped Child."

4. Kubler-Ross, *On Death and Dying*, p. 42.

5. National Institute of Neurological Diseases and Stroke, *Early Recognition of Learning Disabilities* (film produced by Churchill Films, 1969).

6. Temara Dembo, "Sensitivity of One Person to Another," *Rehabilitation Literature*, Vol. 25, No. 8 (August 1964), pp. 232-233.

7. Ibid., p. 233

8. Kubler-Ross, *On Death and Dying*, pp. 31-32.

9. Schoenberg et al., *Loss and Grief*, p. 56.

10. Ibid., p. 58.

11. Wright, *Physical Disability*, p. 257.

12. Kubler-Ross, *On Death and Dying*, p. 32.

13. Wright, *Physical Disability*, p. 92.

14. Schoenberg et al., *Loss and Grief*, p. 96

15. Doreen Kronick, *They Too Can Succeed* (San Rafael, Calif.: Academic Therapy Publications, 1969).

Chapter 2:

1. Gerd Jansen and Otto Esser, "Hostility to the Handicapped," *Time Magazine* (December 20, 1971), p. 67.

2. Alice Thompson, letter to the author.

3. Leon Eisenberg, *The Disabled Reader, Education of the Dyslexic Child*, ed. John Money (Baltimore, Md.: Johns Hopkins Press, 1966), p. 12.

4. Leonard Crainford, *One Million Children*, (Toronto: The Commission on Emotional and Learning Disorders, 1970), p. 158.

5. Robert Russell as quoted by Betty Lou Kratoville in "Promises to Keep," *Academic Therapy*, Vol. 8, No. 3 (Spring 1973), p. 346.

Chapter 3:

1. Kubler-Ross, *On Death and Dying*, p. 50.

2. G. W. Alport, *ABC's of Scapegoating* (Chicago, Ill.: Central YMCA College, 1944).

3. Ezra F. Vogel and Norman W. Bell, *A Modern Introduction to the Family* (New York: The Free Press, 1960), p. 427.

Chapter 4:

1. L. F. Kurlander and Dorothy Colodny, "Pseudoneurosis in the Neurologically Handicapped Child."

2. Pearl S. Buck, *The Child Who Never Grew* (New York: The John Day Co., Inc., 1950), pp. 29-30.

Chapter 5:

1. Eric Hoffer, *The True Believer* (New York: Harper and Row, 1951).

2. Erving Goffman, *Stigma: Notes on the Management of Spoiled Identity* (Englewood Cliffs, N.J.: Prentice-Hall, Inc., 1965), p. 113.

3. Robert Coles, *Children of Crisis*.

4. Temara Dembo, G. L. Leviton, Beatrice A. Wright, "Adjustment to Misfortune—A Problem of Social Psychological Rehabilitation," *Artificial Limbs*, No. 2, 4-62 (1956).

5. Elsa S. Greenberg, "Brain Damage in Adolescence." A ten-year followup study of the children in the Montgomery County Project, Children's Hospital, D.C. Paper presented at the Orthopsychiatric Conference, California, 1970.

Chapter 6:

1. Rollo May, *Man's Search for Himself* (New York: W. W. Norton & Co., Inc., 1953), pp. 85-91.

2. Ibid.

3. Ibid.

4. Abraham Zaleznik, *Human Dilemmas of Leadership* (New York: Harper and Row, 1966), Chapter 6, "Discontinuities in Status and Self-Esteem."

5. Stephanie Greene, "Life Styles in Adolescents with Brain Dysfunction." Paper presented at the Orthopsychiatric Conference, California, 1970.

6. Henry V. Cobb, "The Attitude of the Retarded Person Toward Himself," in *Social Work and Mental Retardation*, ed. Meyer Schribner (New York: The John Day Co., 1970), p. 127.

7. Barbel Inhelder and Jean Piaget, *The Growth of Logical Thinking from Childhood to Adolescence* (New York: Basic Books, Inc. 1958), p. 343.

8. Joel R. Davitz et al., *The Communication of Emotional Meaning* (New York: McGraw-Hill Book Company, 1964).

9. Ibid., p. 129.

Part Two

The Socialization Process

Chapter 7:
The Communication Components of Time, Space, and Relatedness

OUR CULTURE has explicit and implicit rules that provide order to time and space. Without communication, time and space have no meaning, and conversely, without having integrated the feeling of time and space, and the communicated meanings conveyed by our use of time and space, we are hampered in our ability to relate to others. When we deposit our pet at a kennel, we cannot explain to him that this space is a kennel and that we will fetch him in a week. He likely feels abandoned forever in a strange location. Thus, without communication, there is no time and space.

THE COMMUNICATION COMPONENT OF TIME

We are well aware of the difficulty with which the l.d. child develops a feeling of time and the problems he encounters in learning to handle the measurements of time. He experiences as much trouble learning to "read" the clock as he does to read a book. For him, days of the week, months of the year, the number of this year, seasons, holidays, weekends, time of day, and calendars may require infinite patience to sort out. This is the child who calls lunch "breakfast" and asks repeated questions about when something will occur. He seems completely lost when trying to comprehend our casual expressions of time, such as, "I'll be a few minutes," "In a little while," "Pretty soon," or, "It seemed an eternity before the phone rang."

We further confuse the child by our tendency to minimize or exaggerate time with such expressions as, "I'll just be a second," or "This is taking forever to do." Concepts such as *past* and *future* tend to be so amorphous that they may be impossible for some l.d. children to grasp. Assuming that the concept of self develops with the process of gaining control over oneself and the environment, and contrasting this with infantile dependence upon the environment and the consequent inability to separate one's identity from its surroundings, we can see that the temporal world must be mastered in order to achieve mastery over one's present and future. As long as the child is lost in time his vulnerability and inability to control his destiny are profound.

Developing a "feeling" of time is implicit in achieving competent social behavior. When someone tells us to return in five minutes or an hour, we must know how much time we are allowed before returning, how far we can travel in that time, and, even without a watch, must know when to check the time to ensure a prompt return. We need to determine how long it will take us to travel to an appointment, whether walking, driving, or by bus, and leave for that appointment neither too soon nor too late. When the student casually chats with a schoolmate he must "feel" when the time has arrived to return to school so that he will not be penalized for tardiness. He must judge how much homework he has, how much time it will take, how much time it merits, and set aside that amount of time. In addition, he must subdivide the homework time so as to apportion temporal blocks for assignments based upon their length, importance, and difficulty.

The young person who is unable to organize homework time may find that bedtime has arrived before he has even begun. The student who is assigned a project that is to be completed in a month needs to determine when to begin and how much time to allow. If the child has no feeling of one month's time, he may not complete his project or even begin it. The student who hands in an assignment and must wait two or more weeks for the teacher's reactions may feel that it is forever. Subsequently, he may neglect his assignments unless the teacher adopts the practice of instantaneous feedback. Children who are lost in time may return home from school at recess instead of lunchtime or after school, and may fail to appear at mealtime.

In his book, *The Silent Language*, Edward T. Hall describes the informal patterning of time in our culture.[1] Informal patterns rarely are explicit so that generally we learn them from observation and modeling. If we are two or three minutes tardy for an appointment, we tend not to apologize, but we are more likely to do so if ten minutes late. To be later than this is considered bad manners and calls for an extensive apology. If invited for a social visit at 9:00 P.M., we do not arrive early; it is customary to arrive as late as 9:30 P.M., but no later. I once appeared at a formal reception at the stated time and had to live with the embarrassment of being the only guest present for one-half an hour! To be late for a dinner party is considered rudeness, yet to be late for a cocktail party is accepted behavior. We might keep a good friend waiting for a period of time before appearing for a preset date, but it would be unwise to keep our boss or a prospective employer waiting. Since our American and Canadian cultures are obsessed with the productive use of time, adherence to formal and informal temporal customs assumes considerable importance. We cannot assume that the informal customs are perceived by the l.d., and while we do not consciously teach them to our nondisabled children, we may need to carefully teach them to the disabled.

As any comedian can testify, timing is a critical component of communication. Often, *when* you say something is more important than *what* you say. We have copious informal cues associated with the proper and improper times for certain types of communication, and these rules rarely are consciously taught. For instance, dirty jokes, sex, and the process of elimination are considered inappropriate table conversation. However, dirty jokes and sex may be considered very appropriate for an all-male or all-female social event, and elimination is an appropriate topic of discussion with one's physician if it is a professional visit rather than a social occasion, We do not joke at a funeral, or with people who just have received shattering news. We do not awaken people to impart trivial information.

Temporal awareness helps us determine the length of time to discuss a topic, when to interrupt, when to pause, and when to listen patiently. We need to learn that pauses and silences can denote sadness, quietude, anger, and punishment. ("I'm punishing you with my silence.") We should learn that slow movement might signify illness, reluctance, or enjoyment, and fast movement might cue us to urgency, lateness, or anxiety. We need to interpret the drawl of the hesitant and the rapid speech of the agitated. Our responses must be accurately timed.

Temporal awareness is required for prediction, and prediction is central to social interaction. What will he do or say next? What will he expect of me? What happened before I arrived and what will happen in the future? Time and trust are related. If I tell you that I will return in an hour or so, and you have no inner awareness of time, you may feel deserted after one-half an hour. The temporally lost child who is sent to camp for four weeks may feel that he has been permanently deserted.

Impulsivity is behavior produced without allowing oneself the time to think of the consequences. In order for a person to appreciate the consequences, he must be able to relate action to a later reaction, that is, to predict the future. Impulsivity also may be the replacement behavior for a defective ability to control one's environment through language and other means.

Mastering Time

The most important beginning for ordering time is to teach the child to tell the time and to learn time sets, such as, periods of the day (morning, noon, etc.), days of the week, months, seasons, and the names of customs in which we participate at those times (supper, dinner, Thanksgiving, Christmas, etc.). There are a number of suggestions in my book, *They Too Can Succeed*, for teaching these concepts.[2] Payoff is most important as a motivating force. If, by reading seven o'clock on the clock, the child will know when his favorite television program will start, there is a high probability that he will succeed. If a treat is promised when the child reads seven-thirty, he will have a stake in the correct answer. If he can read the hour or half-hour before the cuckoo calls, the call itself can be the payoff.

Give thought to the temporal language you use. Perhaps you have wondered why your child does not respond to your admonition, "Don't wake me up so early," not realizing that he has no concept of the meaning of *early*. Attempt to use the more defined measures of time rather than the loose ones until the child grasps the former with ease. In other words, rather than stating, "I'm going shopping and will be back in a little while," tell the child who cannot tell the time when you will be back in terms of an event. "I'll be back before we eat supper," "I'll return home at the same time as your television program begins," or "You'll return home from camp before we go to Grandma's cottage," (assuming that you go to Grandma's cottage annually so that he has a feeling of when that event occurs).

If the child is beginning to learn to tell the time, set the hands of a cardboard clock and tell him that you will be home when the real clock says the same time. When he becomes proficient with clearly defined time you can tackle the more amorphous delineations of time. Structure for him what our loose temporal expressions really mean, for example, *a few* typically signifies four or five. Before you attempt to teach *earlier* or *later*, be certain that he has a feeling for temporal sequences. Practice a great deal with *before*, *after*, and *next*. Ask him what he did before he ate breakfast, what he ate after his cereal, what he will eat next. Play such games as, "Before we take a bath, what do we have to do?" "After children eat breakfast, what do they usually do?" or "Who came in the house before Dad, was it Tom or Susan?" Then try to teach the concepts such as *early* or *late* by commenting, "It is early in the morning," which defines *early* a bit better than, "Why did you awaken me so early?" or "It is late in the morning," or "We are all ready to eat supper and Dad is late returning from work," or "Gina left the house earlier than Tom," or "We'll have to wait because we arrived too early."

The parent or an older student will need to teach the l.d. youth to organize studying temporally. He needs to be taught how to assess the amount of daily homework he has, how important each assignment is, its time requirement, and how he can maximize his use of time by learning what is important to study. Similarly, long-term projects will require the same approach, and the child should read sample tests to practice subdividing the total time allotment according to the importance and length of each question. Some children should be taught to start a class assignment or oral test immediately and not to fall behind by checking previous answers. This is often helped by practicing such things as dictation of spelling words and paragraphs at home. The first number of times you may have to state, "One, two, three, go!"

Play games with the timing of speech and with inflections. Many l.d. children seem to have difficulty perceiving pauses in speech and the raising or lowering of the voice. To avoid his guessing of mood from the words alone, use neutral language, such as, "The postman has brought the mail." Say it slowly, quickly, hesitantly, in an agitated fashion, sadly, as a question, and in disgust, having the child guess your mood in each instance. This game is sufficiently interesting to involve more than one child, and the additional person(s) can act as a safeguard that you are not distorting what you are trying to say.

The child whose speech is jerky, too slow, or too fast, probably could benefit from some general rhythm games and experiences. Several are described in *They Too Can Succeed*.[3] Exercises such as singing, clapping, and tapping to music are good. Then you might try tapping with your hand on his arm, hand, or knee while he is speaking to establish a rhythm to his speech.

THE COMMUNICATION COMPONENT OF SPACE

It frequently is noted that the l.d. have difficulty organizing their bodies in space, and we are readily aware of their problems in comprehending our measurement tools of space. Inches, feet, ounces, pounds, cups, pints, quarts, and miles may be understood by the children as measurements and representations of space, yet they often prove helplessly mired when attempting to translate these symbolic representations to the spatial world. Space and time are connected so that control over one must go hand-in-hand with the mastery of the other. Each minute covers a "space" of sixty seconds. It takes a minute to drive a mile when traveling at sixty miles per hour.

It is interesting to note that l.d. children who are not obviously language handicapped still exhibit remarkable deficits in their ability to name objects in space, from parts of their bodies to coffee tables, basins, faucets, closets, attics, trap doors, water tanks, and so on. A "naming walk" is a good tool to determine whether these deficits exist, and also to learn the names of objects in space and then reinforce the learning.

In my experience, l.d. children are even more strikingly deficient in delineating the parts of space, such as a stove element or switch, window ledge, sill, or pane, stair rise, rung of chair, arm of sofa, head or foot of bed, light switch or cord, neck of lamp, tines of a fork, and toilet tank. They may be unable to appreciate the fact that although objects in space may remain constant, the space can change, or that space can remain constant but the objects in it can change. After nine-year-old Noah left for school in the taxi, we moved to a different house. The taxi returned him to his new home that afternoon. Two weeks later Noah was still querying me when the family was going to move to the new house. Finally, in exasperation I curtly replied that we had moved. "Oh," Noah responded with real surprise, "the furniture is the same!" Whenever we changed our clothing, Hersh used to ask us who we were and commence to feel our hair and face to establish our identity. It took several years for him to learn that people could remain constant though their clothing might change.

While some spatially disordered people can learn to handle some aspects of space well (perhaps developing accurate judgment of an inch, foot, or yard), they still may be unable to develop a stable pattern of their spatial world. Such a pattern would enable them to remember the door they entered and corridors along which they walked to get into the building, so that they would be able to leave independently. It would orient them to the north, south, east, or west parts of the city, and which street is north or south of which, so that they could travel without becoming lost. They would be able to remember where they hung their coat without accusing people of theft when they are unable to find it. When their back is turned away from the shower faucets, they would be able to translate the space behind them sufficiently well to increase the flow of cold water without turning on the hot and scalding themselves. In school they would be able to make sense out of geometry, the perspective lesson in art, sewing patterns, and industrial arts blueprints. They would be able to sit down on a chair without having to place their hand behind them to feel the seat and avoid the risk of falling on the floor.

Persons who have difficulty stabilizing space might compensate for this insecurity by rigidly carving out small spaces for themselves which they structure into constant and known quantities and demand that they remain untouched. Such a child might demand to sit at the same place at the table, using the same dishes each mealtime. He may prefer not to share his bedroom and insist that every object in the room remain in the same place. This extreme behavior is an attempt to organize one's space and use it as a refuge in a spatially disordered world. If this purpose is achieved, the child should be able to tolerate gradual expansion of his spatial world. He can be helped to structure space through his more intact perceptual systems.

Space can be verbalized when you teach the child to tell himself, "We turned left when we got off the elevator." Space can be felt when you trace geometry configurations with your finger. Space can be visualized and manipulated if you make a small model of the city, stressing the main arteries, and have the child run a toy car up and down Washington Street, and east and west on State Street, or help him to "walk" it with his fingers. He can be taught to stabilize space by learning to notice landmarks and relate them to a specific position in space.

Parents should recognize the child's need to structure his space and not feel that they must introduce him immediately to frequent changes of seating at the table, or moving of furniture, in order to teach him flexibility. We can be flexible only after we have stabilized our base, and premature pressures for change only force the child to cling rigidly to whatever constants he has established. However, if the child's excess structuring of his living space results in ongoing resistance to change or to outward movement, then the structuring has been a tool for withdrawal rather than organization.

The Use of Space in Interaction

The use of space is a critical factor in interaction. You sit on a child's bed and cuddle or stroke him when you want to express affection. You advance toward someone to whom you wish to communicate aggression, yet maintain a distance of a foot or more in casual or formal interaction. However, if you stand any farther away, the person may imagine that you find him offensive. The child who has missed perceiving these spatial cues may advance too close or pull away too far, thus distorting his message. The child who cannot determine the distance between himself and others may shout too loudly and antagonize, or whisper too softly to be heard. The child who cannot comprehend *bigger than, smaller than, thinner than*, and so on, cannot respond to many directions or understand some language. The child who cannot determine where a person began his movement, his path and probable destination, is locked in the spatial present without the ability to predict.

We position people in space to denote status, task, and worth. The teacher sits at the desk in front of the classroom, whereas her pupils sit at smaller desks facing her. The boss has impressive furniture in his own private office, whereas his employees have smaller desks and chairs in a communal office. Law students learn that it is psychologically sound to post bail for one's client before the trial so that he will sit beside his lawyer rather than in the prisoner's box, and they also learn to ensure that he is wearing a suit, tie, and polished shoes. His position and accouterments in space cause the jury to make assumptions about his guilt or innocence. A seat at the head of a table implies status, as does a seat on a stage, position behind a dais, judge's bench, or throne, though the elevated status may be situational and related to the status of the current company. Regardless, these positions in space command specific behavior which we learn by modeling and which the l.d. child may not learn without conscious teaching.

Where we place ourselves in space has other unspoken social meaning. If we enter a room at the same time that an aged person or crippled person enters, we should not usurp the only chair. If we stand in front of a person, thereby blocking his path, or view, he likely will perceive our action as belligerence or rudeness. If we stand in front of a group of seated people, it generally means that we have a message to impart.

The use of the body in space is a communication tool of some importance. Dr. Albert E. Sheflen, of the Albert Einstein School of Medicine, stated that nonverbal communication patterns are learned about the same time as language is learned, and they are taught in approximately the same manner.[4] We do not overtly teach our child the language of the body or other nonverbal behaviors, such as clearing the throat, and facial expressions; rather, we expect him to pick these up from observation. If he perceives and organizes his spatial world inefficiently, and is distractible, he may not discern or remember some forms of nonverbal expression. Thus, he may not realize that scratching one's head signifies confusion if performed in one manner, and an itchy scalp if performed in another context. He may not have learned that a stiffened back probably signifies anger, or that one would be wise to avoid the teacher when she places her hand upon her waist. When our dog wagged her tail, Hersh did not recognize this as a gesture of friendship. There are body gestures that are universal to our entire culture, and others that are idiosyncratic to our subcultures. Ideally, the child should learn both if he wishes to comprehend and communicate effectively. He should learn that social acceptability is predicated on responding to spatially related commands, so that, for example, when he is told to wipe his nose he does not wipe the bridge of his nose.

He needs to learn that in casual communication, in our culture, we do not generally touch people, though it is acceptable for boys to throw their arms around a buddy's back, or pound him in sheer comaraderie, but that neither gesture is antagonistic. I always am saddened when I observe the l.d. child's peer or counselor move to place an arm around him—and the child flinches at the upraised arm. He also needs to learn that persons of the same sex never hold hands, unless one of them is a young child, that men never kiss in public and rarely in private; it is done only after lengthy absence and with someone with whom we have deep affection. Women rarely kiss women in public, and oftener than do men in private, but this also is exclusive to women who are close. We might hold a girl's hand on the first date, but not when we first walk her home from school, and so on.

Our cultural patterns for use of the body in space have deep importance to us. This was graphically illustrated to me when thirty Mexican children enrolled in our camp. We began to notice that our campers from U.S.A. and and Canada increasingly avoided the Mexicans. When queried, they complained, "They always are touching us, kissing us, and standing too closely." The situation was clarified by a counselor who had lived in Mexico, and who explained to us and the campers the uses of the body and space in Latin American interaction. Once armed with this new understanding, the children were more tolerant, but remained quite uncomfortable with the unfamiliar customs. We can assume, then, that the l.d. person who violates our unstated use of time and space in interaction may create discomfort in others, and that they may avoid interaction.

How can we teach these cultural patterns to the l.d. child? In addition to giving him careful verbal instructions in the rules of temporal and spatial interaction that are not normally spelled out, we can involve him in "play acting" the formal and informal interactions. He can learn such things as how far away one should stand to convey a specific impression, when to shake hands, not to sit before the boss does, and a variety of body messages as well as what to say in situations. These help the child and adolescent feel more adept in communication. The adolescent can playact applying for a job, talking to a policeman who has given him a speeding ticket, conversing with the school principal, and taking a girl on a date. If he cannot process spatial, temporal, vocal, and body messages, either his own or others, simultaneously, playact using only one or two of these communication components, and when he becomes adept, add one more at a time. Rick's first two dates were times of agony for him. He sidled up to his date while waiting in line for a movie, and ended up pushing her. When attempting to place his arm around her shoulders in the theatre, he poked her in the head with his elbow.

Because the l.d. child may lack a finite sense of timing, the ability to judge space and move through space with speed, he frequently ends up being the "fall guy." The children may have teased him for weeks and initiated a fight, yet he is the one who is caught and punished. Joey was asked to keep a beer bottle in his school locker by a classmate who claimed that his lock was broken. The l.d. child is ready to comply with requests such as this because he is so anxious to have friends. Predictably, Joey's poor spatial judgment meant that he placed the bottle on the edge of the shelf; he opened his locker and the bottle smashed onto the floor, just as the principal walked by. "But, sir, it isn't mine!" struck the principal as being a lame excuse.

Not only is there a time to say certain things, there are correct and incorrect places. We do not tell an off-color story loudly in a streetcar, classroom, or church. We do not involve the supermarket clerk in a deep political discussion as we check out our groceries. We do not tell our mother that our trousers are torn the minute she returns to her hospital bed from surgery. We do not go into the room where our parents are hosting a formal dinner party, to tell them that there are mice in the house, or that we have worms again. We do not announce to visitors in our neighbor's living room that our unmarried sister is pregnant.

The way space is used provides vital cues to elicit certain behavioral responses from us. If our car breaks down in a hamlet consisting of unpainted cabins backed by crooked outhouses, we will make a number of assumptions about the villagers and base our initial interactions on these assumptions, creating speedy modifications if the villagers we meet prove some of our assumptions invalid. A spotlessly clean formal parlor implies one type of behavior; a casual, random assortment of well-used furniture will provide another message. Think for a moment how rapidly we make assumptions from such objects in space as pews and a coffin, a disordered kitchen, a tablecloth with fine china, wine glasses, and lit candles, a cake with candles on it and a platter of sandwiches on the dining room table, a decorated evergreen tree with presents beneath it, the cat on the table beside a spilled pot of jam, muddy boots, a black lunch bucket and man's work jacket hanging up, an extensive collection of classical books, a living room with paintings by the Great Masters, an ambulance with the back doors open, and on and on.

Colors offer important cues. Light pink or blue often are associated with a baby, and although girls may wear blue, boys rarely wear pink unless they have hand-me-downs. A pink powder room is likely to be a very feminine woman's domain. Purple or lavender often are associated with femininity, old women, or royalty. Bright colors convey flamboyance, fun or flaunting; subdued colors convey rest and refinement; black or grey convey dirt, sadness, oppression, subdued taste, or the unknown; dark green bespeaks of institutions; and white tells us of sterility, starkness, or an institutional environment. Mixtures of color in decor or clothing tell us about a person's taste. Patterns convey taste, personality, and mood. We automatically assume that the person wearing a red-striped shirt with green diamond-patterned trousers and purple socks is flamboyant or unrefined. The l.d. child often needs practice in learning the languages of the objects in space, colors, patterns, and the messages we receive from odors so that he can use those nonverbal means to express himself and accurately monitor the cues in space to become a sophisticated interactor.

He also must learn the ways we make assumptions about the care of the body, the way we clothe it, and the extensions of the body. Consider the cues we derive from: a man in an undershirt, holding a bottle of beer and needing a shave; a person dressed all in black; a woman in a hostess gown; a woman in a T shirt and jeans; a dirty baby with soiled diaper; a man in a conservative suit, vest, with handkerchief in pocket; a man in a smoking jacket with pipe in mouth; a man in jeans and riding boots with a crop in his hand; a girl with a frilly dress and a hairbow, carrying a box wrapped with tissue. Each set of cues implies a set of assumptions as to what preceded what we now see, what is likely to occur, and what is expected of us.

Up to the latter half of the twentieth century our customs were relatively stable. We had clearly defined (but not always stated) rules for the appropriate clothing to wear for occasions, the expected behavior of males, females, adults, and children. We had distinct customs for dress and grooming which denoted masculinity and feminity, and well-defined concepts of the appropriate behavior of males and females for each exigency. Although the customs were complex, they were stable; thus, it was possible to teach them to one's children.

Now they are fluid and ever-changing. This allows most of us a much appreciated leeway in functioning. We can use pottery and paper napkins at a fancy dinner party; women can wear slacks to a formal affair; men can wear frills to accompany their pony tails; and the child who stands up when elders enter a room, or who is seen and not heard, may be considered an anachronism. Nonetheless, this creates a difficult task for parents who attempt to structure social exigencies for their l.d. children. We find that there still are numerous unspoken expectations for behavior, which, if violated, will single the person out as being inappropriate. Our problem is that by the time we have figured out what those expectations are, they have changed. There are modes of dress for young people which are considered "cool," but they shift so rapidly that it is hard to keep apace. Regardless, we have no choice but to do the best we can. A couple of ground rules are: teach the child manners and politeness, even if we err toward the old fashioned, because the mannerly child will evoke positive responses; and teach him to be clean and try to have him emulate the hair style and clothing of his peer group.

The l.d. child, if he is to respond appropriately and feel that he has mastery of a situation, needs to learn the communication possibilities of spatial cues, metaphors, generalizations, exaggeration, sarcasm, the rules of casual conversation versus serious conversation, how to perceive mood through voice tones, facial expressions, body stance, and body use. Many of these communication tools can be learned through "play acting."

Have the child close his eyes and guess the emotion you are conveying as you say some neutral statement such as, "I'm going shopping now." (This same device was mentioned in the section on mastering time. After the child achieves facility with the temporal meaning, the emphasis can be shifted to mood.) Some of the emotions you might attempt to depict are: anger, fear, sadness, distrust, surprise, happiness, weariness, love, and hate. Another time the game might be that of guessing a person's feelings using only facial expressions, or body stances or gestures.

Turn on the television but without sound, and, after a glance, turn it off and have the child guess the mood, the situation, what has happened previously and what is about to occur, making his assumptions from the nonverbal cues on the screen. Do the same with magazine pictures. Initially he may be able to deal with one aspect only, such as mood.

Have him express moods using timing, voice tones and quality, face, and body, both singly and collectively. Have him express body gestures by drawing stick figures, or using pliable plastic or wire-structured toy people. (You can bend stovepipe wire into the shape of a person, cover it with a nylon stocking, and tie it at the neck, joints, etc.) Pinch your nose with your fingers, put thumbs down and have him guess that and other forms of body language.

Place doll-house figures in the rooms to portray specific emotions. For instance, if the child doll is talking to his mother and she does not turn around to face him, what does that mean? Is she angry, upset, or too busy? How can you use other cues and knowledge of what preceded the current situation to decide which of the emotions she is portraying? Set up the doll-house furniture and other props you make to augment the situation (such as paper tablecloths, plasticine cakes), and guess what has happened in that room, what is about to happen, and what would be expected of him in that situation. Then have him set up the room and you guess the messages and implications.

An hour or more after a meal, have him describe the items that were on the table. Subsequently have him describe the items he would expect to see on the table at breakfast time, lunch time, etc. Have him tell what he would expect to see on the table if he went to a fine restaurant for dinner and what he would expect to see on the counter of a "greasy spoon."

Have him describe how a room would look if someone were having a birthday party, Halloween party, or Christmas celebration. Walk with him into different rooms in your house and have him pretend that he has not seen the room before. Ask him what generalizations he can make about the use of the room, the age, sex, habits, and personality of the people who use it, ensuring that he is explicit as to which cues give him which messages. With practice, he may become so adept that a glance at the bathroom alone will enable him to make a number of generalizations about the family. Nylon stockings hanging to dry tell of a woman's presence; a plastic duck implies that a baby lives in the house; the size and number of toothbrushes allow him to guess the number of family members and their ages; and the degree of disorder and cleanliness should enable him to make some generalizations about family habits.

Have him guess the cues that odors give him at home, in other people's homes, in food markets, on the street, and at the library. Sometimes closing his eyes will facilitate his ability to concentrate on the odors. Tell him the occasions for which you use perfume and why or when his father uses shaving lotion. Subsequently have him guess why members of the family smell the way they do.

Part of being close with family members or friends is developing the ability to guess what people are thinking or feeling from their expressions or from assumptions about what has happened or currently is happening. The l.d. child may need to verbalize what he thinks people are feeling and why he came to those conclusions until he becomes adept at perceiving cues. Therefore, he should be frequently asked, "What do you suppose John is feeling now?" or "How do you suppose John felt when . . . ?" This also will serve to make him more conscious of the fact that other people also have emotions. Games such as the above teach the child selective attention, and this is a skill which needs to be learned by many of the l.d. who may learn to perceive accurately, but are distractible. Therefore, as part of each game, the child should point out which cues in the environment offer no relevant information and should be ignored.

Mastering the Language of Space

Determine whether the child knows the concepts, *higher than, lower than, deep, deeper, shallow, more than, less than, fatter, thinner, heavier, lighter, under, above, below, behind, beside, taller, shorter, broader, narrower,* and all the other terms we use to denote position and size in space. If he is unsure about some of these concepts, you might try teaching position in space by having him assume those positions with his body. For example, he could stand beside, behind, or in front of someone, climb under and over the chair, and stand behind it. Then he can place an object in each of the positions, and finally, draw pictures where an object is under, over, or beside something. Then graduate to teaching him where he is in the world. "We live on State street," and when that is well learned, teach the city, then the state, country, continent, and then other countries in the world, making the latter alive with stories about the people and customs. Use a globe to show him where his city, state, and country are positioned in space, and have him draw a map of his street, showing the houses and other relevant distinguishing features. Then have him draw a map, in less detail, of the way he walks to school or to a friend's house. Have him draw a ground plan of each floor of your house, and have him describe the position of furniture, drapes, windows, closets, and pictures in each room of the house when he is not in that room. Have him look at strange rooms, close his eyes, and tell what objects he remembered in the room, and their position.

Teach him the size of objects in space by commenting, "He is taller than I am," while holding your hand up to demonstrate the principle. Do this several times before you ask him, "Who is taller, Dad or I?" Then have him draw pictures in which someone is taller, shorter, fatter, thinner. Teach only one concept at a time, making certain that it is thoroughly integrated before progressing to the next concept. Then return to the old concepts regularly to ensure that they are retained. The next step is to have the child arrange objects according to size and weight, such as glasses filled with different amounts of water, different size jars, and a random assortment of objects that weigh different amounts. Teach the words *circle, oval, square, rectangle, triangle,* and *hexagon* one by one, and have him guess the shape of objects inside the home and outside.

Position a person at the opposite end of the room and have the child tell you the path the person will have to take, and the objects he will have to sidestep, in the order that the person will walk them, so that he can reach a given point. Then expand the game to include two rooms in the house, and finally, have him describe the person's path from outside to inside the house.

Teaching Conservation of Space

Place a set number of buttons in a short, fat glass, and then pour them into a tall, fat glass. Ask the child if there are more, less, or the same number of buttons. Do the same with a set amount of water. Have the child cut an apple in half and ask him if there is more apple then, or the same amount.

If he feels that there is more, place the two halves together again to demonstrate the principle. Then cut the apple in quarters and repeat. Break a chocolate bar into pieces and ask him whether there now is more chocolate. If he feels that there is, place the pieces together and compare its size to an identical bar. Change a piece of plasticine into a different shape and ask him whether there is the same amount of plasticine as before. If he feels that there is not, remold the plasticine into its original shape, then back to the new shape again.

The Concept of Object Permanence

The child needs to learn that no matter where an object moves, it remains essentially the same, and does not disappear. Play games where you hide an object in different parts of the room and the child has to find it. Play "button, button, who's got the button?" Show him where you store the winter skates and clothing, pointing out that those items will be returned to the drawers and closets next winter. Purchase several sets of doll-house furniture and have him rearrange the furniture regularily, placing the unused furniture in a specific place.

Reversibility in Space

The child needs to learn that operations are reversible. Have him walk to a given point, then reverse it by walking back to the point of departure. Then have him climb over obstacles to reach the same destination and reverse his path by climbing back. Then have him climb in one direction and walk in the return direction. Finally, have him proceed from one point to another, using one form of locomotion, and return by using another. (Hopping, skipping, crawling, wriggling on belly, walking backwards, for example.) Have him combine four individual objects to make a whole four, then break the whole into all its possible components, $3 + 1$, $2 + 2$, $1 + 1 + 1 + 1$. At a later stage you can progress to the various ways we can multiply, subtract, or divide objects to achieve four.

Problem Solving in Space

Make a variety of obstacle courses and have the child work his body through them. Then make obstacle courses and have him tell you the steps his body would have to take, in proper sequence, in order to navigate the course. Then have him judge whether his body would fit into a space or what he would have to do with his body to fit the space. Have him guess whether the bodies of other family members would fit the space. Ask him whether specific objects would fit into specific spaces. Have him figure out how high he would have to lift his arm to reach something, whether he could reach an object, and if not, how high a stool or reaching pole he would need. Have him demonstrate how high he would have to lift his leg to reach a step, then try it out to determine whether his estimate was correct.

In *They Too Can Succeed* there are several suggestions for games to improve a child's ability to problem solve in space.[5]

As the size, shape, and position of signs give us messages, so do the size, type, spacing, and execution of print. We can generalize from signs and advertising symbols the type of product being advertised, the population it is geared to, whether it is attempting to appeal to our esthetic or baser instincts, and its approximate price range. We can generalize from signs and and advertising symbols whether a store will be expensive, concerned with the creative arts, or likely to handle antiques. We can make accurate assumptions about whether a restaurant specializes in seafood, short-order cooking, or fine food. Take walks with your child and have him guess the messages implied in billboards and the many signs and symbols he sees. Have him do the same with television advertising.

When printed or written invitations come to the house, we often can predict several things from the quality and color of the stock, print, and decorations. Have the child guess the quality of the affair to which you are invited by the cues the invitation affords, and have him suggest the clothing you should wear. When the mail arrives at the house, have him guess the nature of the contents of each envelope by its size, shape, whether it has a window, whether the address is printed, typed, or written, whether the stamp is metered, color of the ink, and handwriting. When parcels arrive at the house, they can be felt, jiggled, and guesses can be made about their contents based upon their size, shape, weight, wrappings, and mode of delivery. You can play a game of deciding what items would go into household containers according to their size and shape.

Games such as these teach the child to be observant and to make relationships and assumptions. They also teach him that spoken and printed words are only one aspect of communication, that we learn a considerable amount from symbols in space. As he becomes more adept at this, his ability to predict from spatial cues will make him more comfortable with the new and the unknown.

Practice is the key to proficiency, which means that exposure to real situations is essential. If the child's out-of-home behavior is at all acceptable, he should have exposure to every conceivable real situation, from chatting with house guests to visits to other homes and public institutions, in order to try out the skills he has learned. Before he leaves the house, he may need to practice the way a child his age is expected to conduct himself in the upcoming situation. When he is exposed to an unplanned event, he and a parent may need to step aside for a couple of minutes to discuss the behavioral requisites determined from the cues thus far perceived. The parent should let the child do the talking, with the parent merely filling in. Sometimes we are so eager to have our children learn quickly and so impatient with their groping that we supply the answers and they learn little. Have the child exposed to the situation only as long as he can tolerate it comfortably. As soon as possible afterwards, have him tell you the behavioral cues he picked up, how he behaved and how appropriate he thinks it was for the occasion. If you wait too long, it likely will be an intellectual exercise with no carry through. Praise him if his behavior was more appropriate than in previous similar situations, even if not ideal; if he is to feel that he is a person of worth, he must learn that he has some degree of competence. Do not intellectualize about his behavior and do not become Freudian. Suppose he and Tommy had an argument. Confine your discussion about it to the facts, such as, "What did you say?" and, "What do you think you could have said?" or, "What might you say next time a similar situation occurs?"

When he leaves a friend's home ask him what messages he received about the kitchen, living room, etc. Did they convey a message of hospitality and if so, what cues conveyed that? Did he receive the message that the host is artistic? What gave him that impression?

On outings have him guess what someone you see will do next, or where he will go next. Ask him what messages are given by the person's clothing and other extensions of his body. Extensions of the body might be such things as a pipe, cigarette, crutches, or pocketbook. Ask him what he thinks the person does for a living and why he made that assumption, and have him guess the person's salary. Sit on the park bench and pretend that you are a stranger who just met your child. Practice having a casual conversation. Watch people and guess whether they are joking or serious. Tell a story part way or do the same with a film and have the child predict what will happen next. Précis a story or film and have him tell what was important in the story or how the characters might have acted differently.

THE COMMUNICATION COMPONENT OF RELATEDNESS·

L. F. Kurlander and Dorothy Colodny state:

We constantly are struck by the greatest disability of all: an inability to learn casually the nature of relatedness among humans, a failure of social skills rather than a malignant inability to relate. We call this a "lesion of intuition" and see how it operates within the family and peer relationships. We believe it comes from the absorption of attention by basic physical skills such as managing bodily activity, speech, orientation in space, primary perceptual activities which are prerequisite to living with well people. Oddly enough, gifted children of this type often are as obtuse as some retarded ones. Yet we all have seen dull, neurotic or schizophrenic children with sharpened and astute perceptions of human motives.[6]

Parents often mention to me how their l.d. children, ages six, seven, eight, and sometimes older, exhibit obvious difficulty with the relatedness of people. They may not even realize that husbands and wives are married, and there certainly is much confusion about the labels, "Miss" and "Mrs." They tend not to realize that aunts and uncles are their parent's siblings or married to them, and that nieces and nephews are their aunt's and uncle's children. Equally baffling to them is the concept that grandparents are parents of one of their parents, and father-in-law and mother-in-law to the other parent.

In addition to the reasons Kurlander and Colodny attribute as the cause of this confusion, I would add the problems l.d. children experience in making relationships, and in organization, particularly if the organization required is complex, and their problems with body image. If we have not sorted out the differences between infants, older babies, toddlers, preschoolers, preadolescents, adolescents, young adults, the middle aged and the elderly, or between males and females, how then can we possibly be expected to make relationships? At age seven Bobby took a daily bath with his two-year-old sister. One evening, in the tub, he and she engaged in a heated argument because she contended that boys and girls had different bodies and Bob insisted that there were no differences. Shortly afterwards, when someone asked Bob who his father was, he gave his grandfather's name. When queried about this response, Bob replied that his mother and her sisters called his grandfather "Dad," so he assumed that he was his father also. Needless to say, Bob's father was hurt at this confusion.

As the child matures, his disorganization around the relatedness of people becomes apparent when he calls the Dr. "Mr.", calls his uncle "Mr. Smith" instead of "Uncle Ben," thereby insulting him, calls the minister by his first name, is too chummy with the principal, and not sufficiently deferential to the judge. Rarely do we realize that his current inappropriate behavior is a sophisticated form of the confusion with relationships he demonstrated at an earlier age. Instead, we lose patience with him or punish him, or he receives a week's detention for disrespect.

Teaching Relatedness

So frequently do l.d. children appear bright and knowledgeable in a variety of areas that we tend not to realize that there may be gaps in basic knowledge. In order to ensure that they have integrated concepts of categories, constancy, and relatedness, you might try some of the approaches that follow. Play games in which you ask questions such as: "Are bass, pike, pickerel, salmon, perch, all fish? If a lake had no bass, could it still have fish? Are terriers, collies, boxers all dogs? What category of living things are dogs? If a dog is a puppy, is it still a dog? What about when it becomes old or dies? If a dog is sleeping, eating, running, is it still a dog?"

Teach numerous other categories and then progress to the questions such as: "Are weeds and flowers both plants? If I bring flowers into the house, are they still flowers? If I knit wool into socks, is it still wool? Is a kitten a cat, a kid a goat, a calf a cow, a colt a horse?" Practice with categories, subcategories, and the constancy of categories (that is, that a member of a category can be any age, in any place, involved in any activity, be incomplete, dead, or altered, and still belong to that category). A subcategory can be the only ones present, yet we still say that the category is represented. (There might be only two babies in the house, which still means that there are people there, or a lake that has only bass, still has fish.)

The child then is ready to deal with the "people" category. Through the same type of questioning and games as those above, he needs to learn that infants, babies, children, adolescents, adults, and the aged are all people. Then he needs to determine which subcategories are classed as children, youngsters, youth, and adults, as well as the concepts such as "middle aged," and "senior citizen." Ask him questions such as: "If there are only women present, are there still adults in the room? If we invite only boys to your party, will there be children here?" When he has these concepts firmly integrated, teach him what constitutes an immediate family and greater family, as well as subculture (Blacks, Jews, middle class, etc.) and the fact that we all function as members of two or three subcultures. Progress to: "Can a person be Black and Protestant? Jewish and Catholic? Ukranian and Methodist? Christian and wealthy?" Then progress to: "If we have children in the room and all the boys go home, what have we left?" (Children minus boys = girls.) "If all the young and middle-aged adults left the city, what adults would be left?" (Adults minus young adults and the middle aged = the aged.) Continue with: "If the room was full of adults and all the women left, what adults would remain behind? If we had a group of preschool children and all the toddlers departed, who would be left? Will my father still be my father when I am old? Will my sister still be my sister when she marries? Will her children be related to me?"

119

Ensure that he is aware of the expected abilities and roles of each of the ages of man: "Do children usually work for a living? Do the aged?" Notwithstanding the blurring of sex roles, you and he still can play games around the tasks men and women usually do. (Men drive trains, fix cars, etc.) Talk about the games that children of different ages usually play, and the interests and attitudes of people of different ages and sexes. Does he know the relatedness of members of his immediate family? When that is integrated, expand it one concept at a time to greater family members. There are several suggestions on this in the section, "Concept Formation" in *They Too Can Succeed.*[7] Progress to: "How do you address an aunt, minister, principal, king? Do you think that she's married? What made you guess that she might be?" Does he realize that all married women and some married men wear wedding rings? "Does her sister have the same last name as she does? Do her husband and children? Is her name the same as it was before she married? Do we now call her 'Miss' or 'Mrs.'? Do men's names ever change? Do divorced women retain their married names?" If the child cannot abstract to this extent, make cardboard figures of Mrs. Jones and her family or use doll-house figures. Carry on "pretend" discussions with grandma, peers, a baby, the postman, storekeeper, telephone operator, a teacher, and the principal. Practice how you would address them, and the type of conversation you would carry on. Discuss whether you would touch them, as well as whether you would stand or sit, and the messages one's body conveys when it is in different positions (legs crossed, slumping, leaning on the doorpost, standing awkwardly, etc.).

HOW AND WHY WE CHOOSE FRIENDS

The l.d. child may be less aware, as I have pointed out, of the way he expresses himself, and less adept at monitering other's expressions. Thus he is less capable of matching their reactions to his behavior. Unselective in attention, inefficient in integrating the cultural customs and the verbal and the nonverbal cues of interaction, and deficient in manipulating the spatial and temporal components of communication, he is handicapped in selecting and keeping friends. His previous social failures have made him cautious and unsure, and his previous rebuffs have rendered his parent's protective, both of which work against his future successful socialization.

The method whereby we approach people we would like to have as friends is to tally our assets and deficits and select a potential friend whose saleable compliment of strengths and deficits, although different than ours, weigh roughly the same. (Assets and deficits are viewed within the value system of one's own subculture; the attributes that would be rewarded by inner city children might be considered negative attributes by their more afflu-ent counterparts.) Then, when we have successfully acquired a cadre of friends who are on one level of our group's desirability scale, we may make overtures to a higher-status person. If he responds, we will proceed further upwards until we are rebuffed, at which point we begin to move downwards.

This process of measuring ourselves against the ultimate predictor of our acceptability, whether a person values us sufficiently to use precious lei-sure time socializing with us, is one of the most important mirrors whereby we continually reassess ourselves. The child who has not perceived his inter-action with accuracy, or been able to determine which facets of his interac-tion people are responding to, is likely to have an unclear idea of who he is and who is likely to "buy" what he has to offer.

We have to assume that one factor in choosing a friend is to demon-strate our own acceptability by being accepted by a high-status person. The child wants his parents and the other children to be impressed by the "great kid" who chose to become his friend. Children often will avoid a friendship which they feel will devalue them by association, or they will play alone with a low-status child but scorn him in the company of other children. We cannot change the peer group's perceptions of our child's friends, but we can point out that children sometimes are ashamed of their friends, imagining the scorn of peers that will be deflected on them, yet their fears often prove to be unfounded. We all can recall our child's resistance to inviting a child to his party because he felt that the child would be looked down upon by the other children, whereas this did not prove to be the case.

We can do much to teach our child to develop an awareness of the attri-butes of others and how to weigh them, by asking such questions as, "Is he loyal, generous, interesting, fun?" It is important that we convey to him that we value certain attributes in children, but not necessarily the ones he feels he must seek in order to please us. One day Betty remarked that her class-mate, Elizabeth, is so shy that she cries whenever the teacher asks her a ques-tion and that she has no friends. "Why don't you invite Elizabeth to our house after school tomorrow," her mother responded, thereby giving Betty the message that if she has learning and social problems, perhaps Elizabeth would be prepared to weigh those with her shyness, and add it up to friend-ship. After Elizabeth's visit, Betty's mother commented that Elizabeth seemed to be a well-mannered girl who shared many interests with Betty, and she suggested further interaction. We parents have to realign our old value system because one statement such as, "Your friend isn't very bright, is he?" instantaneously conveys the message that intelligence is an important value in seeking friends, and it says much about your feelings about your own youngster's academic problems. Bite your tongue before you comment on his friend's clothing, length of hair, clumsiness, poor social graces, and so on. Develop a basic list of your criteria of behavioral "musts" such as "no stealing," and ignore all other issues.

Even though I have catalogued only a portion of the determinants of adequate social behavior, I realize that parents may be overwhelmed. Fortunately, most l.d. children learn a great many social requisites in the same manner as they are learned by other youngsters, so that no conscious effort is required of parents in those areas of adequate functioning. I think that parents of all children should develop the habit of no longer taking the components of interaction for granted; rather, they should learn to consciously observe the means whereby customs dictate behavior and the avenues from which we receive environmental feedback. Then, by observation and game playing, they can determine the areas in which their children are deficient, and practice in those areas. Practice should be fun. Much of it can be incorporated into everyday living rather than occupy a special time. In my book, *Learning Disabilities: Its Implications to a Responsible Society*, Ernest Siegel points out that, while the learning problems seem to be the paramount concern in the young child, by adolescence the problem is one of poor self-concept, social immaturity, and communication. Dr. Siegel feels so strongly that he entitles the chapter, "The Real Problem of Minimal Brain Dysfunction."[8] We then can conclude that, although the social problems do not seem critical in the younger child, nonetheless, the requisites of social learning should be taught sequentially from an early age.

Chapter 8:

Parents' Attitudes
Are Important

A STUDY CONDUCTED BY G. Langdon and I. W. Stout found that the important factors in child adjustment are, not the type of discipline used, not the socio-economic status or religion, but:

Loving them and letting them know it.

Thinking of them as people and treating them so.

Appreciating what they do, trusting them and telling them so.

Above all, letting them know they are wanted.[1]

In order to work toward these goals you should stop thinking of your child as a walking learning disability, but rather think of him as basically intact, a unique person who has some learning problems. Encourage him in every way to develop his unique interests and abilities. Fight furiously to obtain some remedial help for him in school. Once he begins to achieve, he will feel better about himself and behave better. Then the family members will feel more relaxed and comfortable with him, and hence, more loving and appreciative of his contribution. As long as his academic situation is acutely distressing, it will create a smoke screen from which few positive attributes will emerge.

Do not measure his achievements by the achievements of other children his age, his siblings, or children in his class in school. Reward him for genuine improvement based on his own time clock. Enjoy him and reward that which is enjoyable. In order to trust him, we have to give him some responsibility. If the chore asked of him is within his ability to remember and accomplish, he likely will reward your trust by being trustworthy. The l.d. child often possess great sources of strength. If we believe in him as he really is, rather than an image of how we would like him to be, he very well may believe in himself.

In the course of one waking day all of us experience thousands of successes and several failures. After all, does success not signify that we—and others who attach importance to our act—are satisfied when we complete all or part of an act? We take most of our successes for granted, as do the persons with whom we come in contact, whereas our failures evoke intrinsic and usually extrinsic reaction. We tend to feel badly about our failures for a significant period of time, and some of our failures have the power to evoke such shame and personal dissatisfaction that they remain to haunt us long after they have faded from the memories of family and friends.

We usually think that an accomplishment is successful only when it involves a task of relative importance to us. The skillful completion of commonplace or expected tasks and interactions rarely receive our own or another person's acknowledgement of success. However, failure to perform the least significant of tasks elicits a reaction from us and others. Even if there has not been a direct response to our ineptitude, we have received a message of failure whenever someone does not understand what we have said, finishes a sentence for us, completes our task, or redoes it. Thus we have been reminded of our fallibility and our momentary inability to meet our own or other people's expectations.

Some of us may run a model household yet fail our l.d. child many times daily in the little things. He may be describing an event to us in garbled or jerky language, and in our impatience, we finish his narration, ignore him, or interrupt to converse with someone else. Perhaps we become impatient at his clumsy efforts to tie his shoes, so we tie them for him. We ask him to sweep the floor and we resweep it. He spills a bit of milk, so we take the bottle from him and pour it ourselves. He twists the wire tie in the wrong direction, so we untwist it and place the bread in the basket ourselves. He hangs his coat up with the sleeves askew, or it falls on the floor, and we rehang it. Ensuring success in the little things takes time and patience, but the little things add up to a big feeling of, "I am one who CAN!" My friend Charles Drake refers to it as "the nitty gritty of the itty bitty."

How often do our children acknowledge to themselves, or we to them, that they successfully have dressed themselves, eaten their breakfast, or left the house on time for school? These and most other activities are considered routine occurrences, unworthy of our conscious recognition. Let some part of them be performed unsatisfactorily, however, and we magnify it into a big deal! What is your usual morning reaction when your child's shirt is improperly buttoned, inside out, or hanging out of his trousers, when his shoes are unlaced, or when he handles utensils clumsily at breakfast with half of the breakfast on his shirt? I know what my reaction is, and I wouldn't care to have it recorded on a television show, "Breakfast with the Kronicks."

Many of us react more consistently and profoundly to the failures of our l.d. children than we do to the failures of our other progeny. We assume that all failure is attributable to the disability and convey that impression to our child. Since our l.d. child is likely to experience a greater number of failures in the course of the day than other children, it is easy for parents, teachers, and others to fall into the pattern of constant negative reaction to the child. His failure might be in expression, comprehension, memory, behavior, coordination, socialization, and on it goes.

What are the consequences of continued doses of negative reaction? The child is likely to assume that no matter how hard he tries, he does few things well. He likely has the impression that he is a disappointment to everyone with whom he comes in contact. Since negative reaction tells him that he rarely succeeds, he feels that there is no point in trying. Furthermore, he cannot continue to respond adequately to constant negative reinforcement, so he is likely to develop the skill of not responding, to protect his fragile ego from continued assaults. Therefore, the more we communicate his failure to him, the more likely he will be to ignore us, and the more likely we will be to nag and react even more negatively to the behavior which he appears unready to change. In addition, he may figure that if he doesn't receive attention for approved behavior, he might as well continue to resort to that which affords him recognition.

Alternatively, we may "give up," since, in spite of our chastising, he undermines our authority with his apparent inability or reluctance to change. Then we become permissive parents, allowing the child to persist in important undesirable behaviors as well as unimportant ones. Neither the permissive nor the negative response on our part elicits a preferred goal, so it seems important to reexamine our approach.

Put Yourself in Johnny's Shoes

Everything is an effort for Johnny. Sometimes he overreacts because he is trying so hard. Let's acknowledge the tremendous effort he is making. While trying to reach his goal, perhaps Johnny has found a path that is not the one you would choose, or perhaps his end result is different than the one you would have elected. Rather than chastise him because his way is different, pause a moment to assess whether his method is acceptable to you. It is discouraging to try so hard with no reward. Adopt the attitude that to make mistakes is human. Just as you should not chastise yourself for the mistakes you make as a mother and wife, the child, too, should feel that mistakes are part of the learning process. Without mistakes there would be no learning.

There is a strange phenomenon in human behavior, which is that the thing we fear is the selfsame thing that is likely to happen. Parents who do not allow their young children to explore, climb stairs and furniture, because they fear that the children will hurt themselves, have children who have not learned to judge the movement of their bodies in space. When these children finally do venture out, they *are* likely to be hurt. The person who is afraid that he cannot make friends will be so anxious in his interactions that he probably will "turn people off." Similarly, the child who becomes afraid that he will make mistakes will not approach tasks with confidence, so he is likely to fail. Dr. Rudolph Dreikurs comments that parents need the courage to be imperfect—and, I would add, the courage to have imperfect children.

A mother told me that her daughter presented her with a Mother's Day card the evening before the event because the youngster realized that her sister would execute a neater, more sophisticated, and properly spelled card the following day. Beating her sister time-wise was the only way she could compete. "How can I tell her it's nice when it's such an obvious mess with things rubbed out, mispelled and all?" the mother queried. I suggested that she tell her daughter how much she appreciated the love, thoughtfulness, and work that went into the card. We should stop for a moment to think of the really important aspect of each situation, and not become caught up in external standards.

Let's Talk About Respect

We should regularly ask ourselves whether we treat our children as respectfully as we do others. If the minister came to dinner, became absorbed in the conversation and knocked his glass of milk over, would we berate him with the same invectives that we use on our children? If your husband inadvertently brought the wrong work home from the office, would you respond nastily or be sympathetic? We neglect the housework on the days when we are not in the mood to do it, yet fail to respect our child's right not to feel like doing remediation. Parents ask me how teachers can be taught respect and my answer is that they probably cannot be. Respect is learned at one's parent's knee by being respected. If everyone respected their children, thus teaching them respect, the world might be a far better place. The l.d. encounter disrespect from many outsiders. The very least we can do is show them our regard for them.

Establish Priorities

What are the most important behaviors or skills that you would like John to acquire this season? Concentrate your efforts on a limited number of goals and establish these goals with John. Then reinforce every effort, however minimal, that he makes toward reaching these goals, and provide him with immediate feedback, without overreaction when he fails. When he loses control, do not respond by losing control yourself. (I still have a broken hairbrush which is a mute reminder of how I used to respond to my son's tantrums with such fury that I whipped them into high gear by my reaction.) If he can do the task himself, do not do it for him when he fails. Do not praise him falsely or tell him that he looks good if he is a mess. If he is neater than he was yesterday, tell him that. Let's play straight with our kids.

On Setting Goals

At camp we set two goals with nine-year-old Barry. One was that he would try to speak more quietly and the other was that he would begin and complete tasks more promptly. (Note the positive approach rather than, "Don't speak so loudly and don't be so slow.") He collaborated with us on the methods we would use to try to reach the desired goals. We provided Barry with a clock and set a time past which he was not allowed to work on a task. He was to begin as soon as we said, "One, two, three, go!" This reversed Barry's long-standing pattern of manipulating everyone around him into wild frenzies because of his tardiness in executing school work, dressing, eating, and most other routines. Beating the clock became great fun for Barry. He proudly announced, in a loud raucous voice to all who would listen, how much he had completed in the allotted time. Simultaneously, we stopped reacting to Barry when he was tardy. We told him what the consequences of tardiness would be, such as missing the part of the meal for which he was late, and we imposed the consequences without fuss. In other words, we eliminated the fun that Barry used to have by manipulating adults with his lack of speed and made it enjoyable to be speedy.

Whenever Barry's voice was too loud, we reminded him quietly, but consistently, that he was shouting. We also praised him when he modified his voice, even if it did not reach our desired degree of softness. Another method of modifying Barry's voice could have been to ignore him when he spoke loudly and award him a point or token, with a number of tokens redeemable for a prize, whenever he spoke softly.

We might reward another child for remembering to wash his face, dress neatly, clean his room, share his possessions, act thoughtfully to others, go to sleep without a fuss, and so on. It may be more effective to disregard the instances in which the child fails to reach the desired goal, since that likely has been the battleground of innumerable, emotionally charged scenes.

We should realize that every task can be completed successfully only if the person has acquired the skills requisite to handling the task. Next time you feed yourself, brush your teeth, get dressed, wash your face, etc., take apart each separate skill required for successful completion. The nondisabled seem to acquire each skill effortlessly, adding skill to previous skill, in order to successfully accomplish an activity. If the l.d. child keeps spilling his food, perhaps he has not acquired one or more of the skills requisite to eating, such as tilting the spoon just as it reaches his mouth. Slowly do each of the child's tasks yourself so that you can analyze the parts and then teach it to him step by step. We often punish him for repeated failure without realizing that he does not have the skills to succeed. Afford him your physical and moral support while he is trying to master the task.

Enjoying Your Children and Their Achievements

Allison's parents shared their concern with the camp staff that they had no basis upon which they could praise her. She did not have the athletic skills or obtain good marks in school as did her brother and sister. "We try not to show our pleasure with the other children's achievements," they commented, "because we never can praise Allison for anything." The camp staff, who had lived with Allison all summer, were taken aback! She was a warm, delightful little girl, who related easily to children and adults. Although her limbs were stiff and uncoordinated, she tried every activity and thoroughly enjoyed them all. She was pleasant, cooperative, clean, and tidy. It is true that Allison was behind in school work, but was well motivated and progressing at a steady pace. Her speech was difficult to comprehend, but she never became discouraged, persisting until someone understood. Reward her? We had spent the summer admiring her determination and enjoying her affectionate, pleasant personality. Allison's parents were so enmeshed in the standardized achievements of our society, such as "A" grades and athletic awards, that they had missed discovering a wonderful little girl and denied themselves and their other children the pleasure of achievement.

We make a large error in our culture when we award only specified success, ignoring the differing amounts of effort required of people to reach the same goal. Let's forget external goals for awhile so that we can concentrate on more attainable goals. If we can move our child from one point to the next, be it behaviorally, academically, socially, or in self-care, we will have helped him to feel that he is capable, responsible, dependable, and appreciated, rather than a failure. We should ask ourselves not only what we can give to our child, but what he can contribute to us and the family.

What About Competition?

It is essential that all our children learn that it is more important to compete with themselves than with others. Some of the competition to which we subject any of our children is horrendous, and more related to the needs of the adult coaches of the hockey, baseball, or other school teams than the children's needs. Nonetheless, we have made competition very much a value in the lives of children in our culture, so they will perceive competitive success as valuable regardless of our attitude. In your own relationships with the child, or in situations where you have control, avoid competition if the child has no chance of handling it successfully. He is subjected to competition every day in school in which it is impossible for him to succeed, so he does not need more impossible competition to develop his character. However, if he has acquired considerable proficiency in an area such as swimming or crafts, by all means allow him to compete. If he does fairly well in the competition, he will feel marvelous! Some l.d. children base much of their good feeling about themselves on knowing that they "belong" in a swim team, choir, crafts group or what-have-you, and have a genuine contribution to make. Much more patient work may have to precede their proficiency than goes into making other children skilled, but the results are worth the effort.

At What Age Should a Parent Stop Helping a Child?

We never stop trying to help any of our children. If a child, or any family member cannot handle a task, we ensure that it is replaced by a less demanding task, is broken down so that the child can learn it sequentially, or we help him with it. He may always require some assistance with his school work, such as someone reading his texts and assignments to him, or taping them, or spelling words for him. He must learn to recognize when he needs help and ask for it. We do not attempt to mould our children, spouse, other relatives, or friends into perfect beings. Rather, part of being a good relative or friend is recognizing a person's weaknesses and stepping in unobtrusively to assist, or gearing our interaction in a way that minimizes and protects his weaknesses or complements his needs. We owe no less to the l.d. This is very different from overprotection. It also does not mean that remediation should go on forever. In *Helping the Adolescent with the Hidden Handicap* and *They Too Can Succeed*, I suggest several ways to determine when remediation should be terminated.[2]

How Do You Counsel the Child to Handle Taunting?

Some taunting can be reduced if the child spends time at home with parents and siblings learning the basic sequential skills and rules of game playing. For example, if he is taunted for not learning to play baseball, he can be taught at home with a plastic bat and balloon, graduating to a beach ball, then smaller rubber ball until finally he has mastered a wooden bat and soft ball. (Of course, all children will not ever achieve a finite degree of skill in eye-hand or eye-foot tasks.) Then, if he becomes adept at the game and firmly grounded in the rules, as well as proficient in social skills, he will be better accepted by his peers.

However, he may never become that adept. The teasing may persist. It is important that he should know about his l.d. (In *They Too Can Succeed* I explain what and how to tell the child.) With time and family acceptance, he should feel sufficiently comfortable, if encouraged, to educate the other children. Since this will not entirely eliminate taunting, we must accept it as an unfortunate fact of his life, while being prepared to sympathize with his pain. When he tells you that the children picked on him on the way to school, do not react with, "Why don't you punch them in the nose?" Instead, say, "How did that make you feel?" or, "You must feel very badly when they say those things to you."

If the Child Has Returned to Special Education, Have We Failed Him?

Having to enter a special program after a period of time in a normal program should not be perceived as a failure on the part of the parent or the child. Children with l.d. are often returned to the normal stream as soon as they can "just" cope. In some instances the return may be premature, or the ongoing support too minimal. Also, as the academic demands become increasingly complex, his coping abilities may not be sufficiently generalized to meet those demands. However, before a child reenters a special stream, the parents and educators should ask themselves:

1. What are the demands that he could not meet?
2. Does he require a specialized placement, or would an alteration of the area of difficulty be worth trying?
3. Is it that he really does not comprehend, or does he feel overwhelmed?
4. Would tutoring be the answer?
5. Should he be in the normal stream part time?

Whose Needs are We Meeting Anyway?

For years I taught my son to fold his trousers on the crease. The more I taught, the more he resisted learning the skill. My constant nagging and lectures sounded something like this: "What do you think I am anyway, nothing but a laundress? Every time I look into your trouser closet I have to reiron all of them! I have better things to do with my time!" Finally I saw the light. Certainly I wanted my son to look presentable, but, if anything, I was more concerned about what sort of a housekeeper people would think I was, than about his appearance. When he becomes sufficiently concerned about his appearance, he will fold his trousers properly.

We parents want our children to look and act in meritorious ways because we want people to be impressed by our ability to produce handsome, well-dressed, well-groomed, accomplished children. Therefore, whenever there is a hassle, it is well worth asking ourselves whose needs we are meeting anyway.

The Home as Asylum—But Not for the Insane

We have a fight with our mother-in-law, the grocer cheats us, or the boss was unfair, so we retreat to our home for succor and support, just as animals retreat to their lairs for protection. We do not expect our spouse and other family members to be judgmental, to make such comments as, "Of course you fought with the neighbor, you probably started the argument." We expect sympathy.

As was mentioned in Part I of this book, the l.d. experience a multitude of slights every day from peers, teachers, and other adults. However, instead of feeling that home is a warm, beckoning refuge to which they can return and "lick their wounds" within the protective confines of the family, it may only be a place where they exchange one battleground for another. The child may return home from a day at school, where he had to face impossible demands, to a lengthy session of home remediation. Home may be the place where he has rendered his mother tense and anxious; thus, he becomes the central character of his parents' disagreements and accusations against each other. His behavior might be under constant scrutiny and rebuke. He is bombarded by his parent's hopes, and he is the central force around which their disappointments revolve. Therefore, whatever has to be omitted in the way of remediation to make home a relaxed haven for the child, should be omitted. Whatever changes in attitude need to occur, should be worked at. If the child has a warm and accepting base, he will possess the courage to face a sometimes hostile world.

Don't Cut Your Nose Off to Spite Your Face

Some parents of the l.d. are very proud. Pride comes before a fall, and theirs precedes falling flat on their faces from exhaustion. They won't ask their spouses or relatives or friends for help, or ask the teacher to institute some modifications to make their child's school life more enjoyable and comfortable. In *They Too Can Succeed*, I have mentioned several suggestions on how the father and mother can work together.[3] Having a child with l.d. in the family is an added strain which needs added support. In addition to the father's help, the parents may need to approach close relatives and friends, explain the strain under which the family is functioning, and request some relief. Such relief might be: baby sitting with the other children while the parent can work with the l.d. child, taking one of the children on an outing, or holding down the home front so the parents can escape for a while. Whenever the mother feels that she has "had it," she should make whatever arrangements are necessary to provide herself with a breather, an hour or two devoted to her own pleasure. If the parent is too proud to request concessions for the child, the youngster is the one who suffers.

Chapter 9:

Dealing with Behavior

AMONG THE PROBLEMS associated with l.d., the child's behavior is one of the areas of greatest concern. We wonder how much of his behavior can be attributed to the handicap, and how much is "Johnny just being Johnny." Will he outgrow his behaviorisms in a few years, or will they affect his adult life? Behavior is a complex phenomenon, not completely understood by the most learned of our social scientists. It often is difficult to determine why any of us behave the way we do, even when we are faced with a fairly simple decision or problem. How much more involved, then, is the understanding of the reactions of a handicapped child whose behavior reflects his basic physiology, his reaction to stress, his and his family's feelings about his handicap, the ways in which family, educators, and friends have responded to him, and indeed his totality of past experience! All I can attempt to do is to describe a few ways of coping with some behaviorisms common to some l.d. children. It is worth examining, as well, how parents unknowingly may contribute to undesirable behavior.

No single l.d. child is likely to display all the behaviorisms that are associated with the handicap. Indeed, some children will show none of the manifestations, or certainly very few. On occasion, all children, handicapped or otherwise, will be restless, overexcited, anxious, repetitive, frustrated, impulsive, inflexible, or disorganized. The differentiation, then, between the reactions of the l.d. child and all children can be determined only by the frequency of the behavior and its severity.

Even though parents influence the child's behavior, we should not feel that it is solely a reflection of our child-rearing practices. Research now has demonstrated that children are born with basic personality differences. Also, a situation that is of no consequence to one child may be traumatic to another. The popular notion is that stress is damaging, but studies conducted on children who survived World War II and black children who remained intact through the abuses of the first school integration programs in the South have indicated that stress is not necessarily damaging, and that a backlog of some stressful experiences may better equip a child to handle future pressures. Stresses which are unrelieved or without any outlet might very well be damaging, but we should not assume that pressures in the home are the cause of the learning disability. Even if all behavior were directly related to the environment, the parents are merely one facet of the child's environment. Therefore, realistically, parents cannot take total credit for either their child's misbehaviors or achievements.

DISORGANIZATION

If I had to identify one behaviorism that is likely to be common to the largest percentage of l.d. children, it would be disorganization, which means that the child has developed a less than effective system for organizing stimuli in the environment which he sees, hears, and feels. His poorly developed system of sorting and storing sensory impressions and experiences renders him less able than the nondisabled to use this information. Thus, a child may learn to calculate a mathematics problem yet be unable to translate the principle involved in doing a similar problem the following day. Or he may forget the name of an object, but remember the name when he hears it.

If You Didn't Have Your Head Screwed On

Disorganization may be apparent in the everyday functioning of some children. We all are familiar with the child who cannot remember where his toys, clothing, and schoolbooks are. Mornings in his household typically are frenetic. Everyone is searching excitedly for scarves, mittens, boots, books, pens, and assorted paraphernalia in time to fling Johnny out the door to catch the school bus. By 8:30 A.M. the members of the family feel that they have been engaged in an exhausting day's work.

Such a child tends to bring the wrong textbooks home from school for his homework, forgets to do his homework in some subjects, or forgets the method the teacher wishes the students to use in completing their assignments.

Similarly, some children do not organize their time effectively. They do not formulate a productive plan of action for their free hours, and consequently spend their leisure periods watching television, reading comic books, lounging on the sofa, or nagging mother with the age-old querie, "What'll I do now?"

I Don't Know What You're Talking About!

Disorganization in language can manifest itself in grammatical structure, such as that of ten-year-old Harold who asked, "How old you are?" It is apparent in subtle ways in the conversation of thirteen-year-old Jan who forgets many words, and confuses words that are similar. She talks about "the roof that doesn't have a big enough hangover," and her friends who sleep in "hostages" when cycling in Europe in the summertime. She calls cake icing "sauce," and calls sauces "dressing," and refers to pie as "cake." Yet her disorder is not obvious to most people.

A more noticeable defect is the garbled narration of those l.d. children who have expressive language problems. They may have adopted the easy way out, avoiding language by using standard answers such as "because," or "I don't know." Others launch into descriptions of events understandable to the child's mother, but hopelessly confused to the outsider who "tunes the child out" rather than exert the effort required to comprehend his tale. In describing a birthday party or activity at school or on the street, the child repeats some events in his narration and others are related out of sequence. It is apparent that he is thinking of the entire experience and has difficulty breaking it down in the order in which it occurred.

How Can We Create Organization?

Pioneers in the field of learning disabilities used to advocate a rigidly structured and unchanging daily schedule. They felt that the child's bedroom should be stripped of all extraneous stimuli. This meant discarding the flowered or chenille bedspread and pictures on the wall, and removing exposed toys, books, etc. It was thought, too, that the child might have to eat his meal at a table upon which there were no other distractions, such as salt and pepper shakers or a patterned tablecloth, and possibly have only one food on his plate at a time. A few professionals still advocate adherence to such a simplified existence as an initial step toward the creation of inner organization in the l.d. child. Certainly this may be necessary for a child who is severely disorganized, impulsive, distractible, and hyperactive. However, the majority of l.d. children are teaching us that they are far more capable of organizing their environment than we suspected in the past. This is particularly true if they are not being faced with demands that they perceive as difficult. Thus, a school situation may require far more structure and reduction of stimuli than a recreation or home environment.

There are many ways whereby we can build inner organization. The important first step is to take your cues from your child. Does he become very upset with a change in daily routine? If he does, that is his way of telling you that he cannot organize the change in his mind. Consequently, for the present time, you should consider as unvarying a daily routine as possible. If a change in the daily schedule is necessary, describe it to him a short while before it occurs. "John, tonight you'll have your bath before supper because we'll be visiting Grandma after supper. As soon as you have finished playing outside, I'll bathe you."

Since anxiety may occur when the child cannot structure a change in his mind, describe the change to him detail by detail. If you are taking him to someone's house, describe putting on your coats, going out the door, getting into the car, out of the car, ringing the doorbell, giving the hostess your coat, sitting in the living room, etc. As the child adjusts to changes, and handles himself with ease in new situations, you can simplify your description of the change, highlighting only the areas in which the child might not know what will occur. As he becomes adjusted to your daily routine, begin to vary it, one change at a time, describing to him the changes you will make. If this upsets him, return to the old routine and attempt changes a month or two later, at a time when he is relaxed and happy.

Visitors and Parties

Your child will give you cues as to when he is having difficulty organizing a new situation. If he has children visiting him and becomes overexcited, talks in a loud voice, is aggressive and hyperactive, he is letting you know that he is anxious and needs help. You may decide that the visitors have stayed long enough, and in the future plan short, supervised, structured (preprogramed) play periods with only one or—at most—two children. Or, if you are in the middle of a birthday party and the guests will not be fetched for another hour, perhaps you can relax Johnny by sitting him on your lap and reading a familiar story to Johnny and his guests. After the party, he may need to spend a few minutes in his bedroom to unwind. Since "an ounce of foresight is worth a pound of cure," you and your child can pre-plan an entire party so that he will know in advance the activities to expect and the food he will eat. Involving him in the planning and preparation will make him feel much more a part of the process. If groups of children over-stimulate Johnny, arrange to have him spend the day with a relative when your other children have parties.

A Time and A Place for Everything

Some children cannot find *anything*. Charlie is late for school because he has rushed around the house searching for his eyeglasses, only to dash past a mirror and discover that the glasses are on his face. He becomes upset because he claims to have left a schoolbook on the kitchen table and it has disappeared. All the members of the family search the kitchen, only to learn that his language disability created added confusion; Charlie meant the dining room table, but in reality he had left the book in the living room on a chair.

For such a child there should be a time and a place for everything. He cannot drop his books in the entrance hall upon his return from school, because that will be the cause for confusion and one upset family when it is time for homework. He must have a specific place for his schoolbooks, preferably a desk in his bedroom. His clothing should be in specific piles in specific drawers. His toys should be in specific places. Toys and games with many parts may be eliminated temporarily from his toy cupboard if misplacement of the parts is upsetting to him.

When the child is young his mother will lay out his clothing in the evening for use the following day. She will pile it in the order in which the child will dress. As he matures, he and his mother will select his clothing together, and finally he will select his own apparel. To know which days to lay out gym clothes for use in school, he will check the chart he and Dad made that is posted on his bedroom door. Similarly, as he finishes his homework, he and a parent will select the schoolbooks, pens, money, and other equipment he will require the next day, and he will put them aside in a specific place to be taken to school. Eventually, he will do this without assistance.

Mornings can be less nerve-wracking if the l.d. child is awakened with sufficient time to dress and eat breakfast without stress. He may accomplish more if he is allotted a specific period of time in which to wash, to dress, and to eat breakfast. If he daudles he may need supervision and rewards for meeting time commitments. Mother could mark these periods of time with a homemade cardboard clock with moveable hands, or with a food timer that rings at predetermined times.

Breakfast is a good opportunity in which to have John relate his schedule for the day and any special lessons or equipment he will require. This verbalization will include the time he will spend playing, eating, and doing homework. This encourages him to organize his activities in his mind, in the sequence in which they will occur.

Before he leaves for school, time will be well spent in placing a fresh sheet of paper in front of his binder, so that he can make a note of his homework assignments as he receives them, and note the textbooks he will require to complete the assignments. Have him paste on the cover of his binder a timetable for the day. Thus he will be assured of not forgetting to attend each class. A checklist of the items he must take to school daily can be posted on the bulletin board in the kitchen or on the kitchen door. At the day's end, have the child relate his day's activities in the order in which they occurred.

Organizing Free Time

Some l.d. children have few friends, few skills, know few games, and are unaware of the resources the city has to offer. Hence, their free time may be poorly organized and unproductive. When they are quite young they often function best with close parental structuring of free time. This means that the parent will plan projects that can be done at home (learning a song, dancing, playing with clay, arts and crafts projects, building models, sewing doll clothes, etc.). The parents will plan, as well, many of the child's social encounters, working up from the visit of one child to the house for a short preplanned period, to longer visits of a few children, and finally to the child visiting others. As well as preplanning with the child what he will do during such a visit, it is worthwhile to explore the kinds of things about which your child might converse. Often the conversation of the l.d. tends to be self-centered, limited, and uninteresting. He needs to be coached in the things that interest children of his age. You should make him aware, as well, of the importance of showing interest in other children.

As the child matures, the structuring of free time should become his responsibility. Ask him what his plans are for the day and what time he intends to carry them out. When the prestated time arrives, be firm in seeing that he initiates the activity he has planned. Is this cruel, authoritarian, and an imposition on the child's prerogative to plan his own leisure? At the moment it may appear so, but on the other hand, it assures the development of the habit of productively using free time. The alternative is a lifetime spent lounging on the sofa.

You probably will have to familiarize your child with community facilities. Contact your local social planning council to learn which agencies have club and interest groups. Additionally, you might explore the facilities of local church, scouts, and community centers. Show your child the location of ski hills, skating rinks, museums, and planetariums. When he plans an outing with a friend, you might suggest a specific activity rather than leave the programing to chance. Generally, a child who organizes his time poorly gains a great deal from participation in an organized club or special interest group.

Father and son or mother and daughter might wish to develop a hobby or area of mutual interest together. This assures good use of some free time, and it provides an area of common interest and fun without pressure. It allows the child to develop a positive identification with the parent of the same sex. (This is particularly important in the case of sons, since some fathers may opt out of the picture.) Finally, it encourages the development of an interest or skill which successfully can be transferred to other social situations, and it motivates the child to acquire learning in order to participate in the shared interest with his parent. The important warning to the parent in this instance is: be patient. Do not become aggravated with your child's clumsiness or slowness in picking up a concept. This is a time for mutual enjoyment, not disappointment or failure. The hobby or activity can be anything of interest to parent and child, such as cooking, hiking, woodworking, sketching, model building, scrapbooks, photography, puppetry, any of the sports, or collecting butterflies, stamps, or coins.

INFLEXIBILITY

It is not uncommon for children to dislike change. That is why they order a hamburger in a restaurant rather than quiche Lorraine. Sameness represents security. They enjoy the same daily routine, the same furniture in the house, and sleeping in the same bed. Moving them into another bedroom, building a room onto a house, or taking a trip may tend to create anxiety. Some l.d. children are even less flexible than this. At some stages in their development, the most elementary alteration of their routine will be upsetting. Bob would not eat because a visitor was sitting at his customary place at the table. Cameron became upset when warmer weather required that he wear different clothing. Neil refused to visit family friends when invited. Steve made visits unpleasant occasions for everyone by talking in a loud voice, touching everything in sight, jumping on the furniture, running up and down stairs, and sometimes climbing through windows.

Inflexibility rears its head in countless ways during the course of the l.d. youngster's childhood. It is caused by his difficulty with organizing changes in his mind—before they have occurred or when he is faced with the change. He cannot picture what will happen from moment to moment; consequently, a seemingly routine change will be frighteningly strange to him. Not being able to fit the pieces of the new situation together, he therefore will not be able to select the behavior appropriate for the occasion. His uncertainty will mean that he has less energy to devote to the customary control he exerts on his behavior, often with great effort. Consequently, he responds to change with stubbornness, overexcitement, or a tantrum.

Picture yourself in an analogous situation. You are invited to a party at the home of a casual acquaintance. You are unsure of the appropriate clothing to wear. Upon arrival at the party you realize that you do not know anyone. You are ill-at-ease until you have "structured" the situation. In other words, when you have determined the interests and orientation of the guests (whether they are Republican or Democrat, feminist or antifeminist, hawk or dove) you can select people with whom you feel comfortable. You know what to say, how to behave, and your initial anxiety dissipates. You have drawn upon previous experiences at other social occasions, selecting the conversation and behavior suitable for this occasion. Since l.d. children may not have perceived previous social experiences in their entirety, nor stored them in an organized fashion in their minds, each change in schedule must be tackled as something frighteningly new.

Don't Let Yourself Get into a Corner

If your child is going to be inflexible, you will have to possess a greater ability to provide alternatives.

The family is invited to Aunt Sally's house for tea. Several relatives and friends will be there, and mother eagerly is anticipating the fuss they will make over the children. She takes extra care in having everyone dress in party clothes. Then Laura refuses to leave the house.

Inflexible solution: Insist that Laura join you. Chase her throughout the house, spank her, scream, and call her names.

Flexible solutions: 1. One parent stays home with Laura and one parent takes other children. 2. If Laura is old enough, she stays home alone. 3. You phone Aunt Sally to find out whether another guest is passing your house and can take your other children to the party. 4. If you know that this type of occasion makes Laura unhappy, you make an alternate arrangement in advance, such as having an older student "sit" with Laura.

The family is invited to Aunt Sally's house for tea and everyone has changed to party clothes except Laura who refuses.

Inflexible solution: You insist that Laura wear her party clothing and force her to change.

Flexible solutions: 1. You effect a compromise by suggesting that she change her dress, but not her shoes and stockings. 2. You let her visit in her every-day clothing since you recognize the fact that you wanted her to change so that people would think that your child is well-dressed. 3. You anticipate the problem in advance and ask Laura whether she would like to wear her red dress or her blue one.

Mother tells Ruth, who is not l.d., to set the table. Ruth protests several times. When she realizes that mother is not going to back down, Ruth states that she will set the table for lunch if her brother sets the supper table. She has acquiesced to her mother's demand and saved face by creating a proviso that she knew would be acceptable both to her and her mother. Nancy is learning disabled. When asked to set the table she refuses, and does not possess the flexibility to creat a proviso.

Inflexible solution: Nancy continues to refuse and her mother continues to insist, until the cycle of demand and refusal has escalated into a scene wherein both Nancy and mother have lost control. She is forced to set the table, and in the future, rather than face analogous scenes, mother abstains from asking Nancy to handle her share of household chores.

Flexible solution: Mother suggests that if Nancy sets the table for the meal, her brother will clear the table. (Mother provides the flexibility that Nancy lacks.)

Michael, a four year old who is not l.d., asks for a candy before dinner. Upon being refused, he cries loudly for a few minutes, until he realizes that his maneuver will not result in parental capitulation. He saves face by asking, "O.K. then, can I have a glass of water?" Billy, on the other hand, lacks Michael's flexibility. He continues to vocalize his demands for a candy. If no "out" is suggested by the parent, Billy might scream for hours, becoming increasingly overstimulated and upsetting to himself and family.

Inflexible solution: Maintain your refusal to give him a candy.

Flexible solutions: 1. Mother says, "I know you want a candy. I'll bet it would have tasted good. Too bad it's just before supper. Would you like a carrot stick or celery stick to eat?" 2. If Billy is a good eater, there is no reason to assume that one candy will spoil his appetite. Perhaps it's important to establish rules that really *are* meaningful.

Two-year-old Pam will not sit in the bathtub. Her insistence on standing occasioned several falls with nasty bumps and bruises.

Inflexible solution: Mother continues to force Pam into a sitting position. Bathtime becomes a battle of wills instead of the enjoyable time it might be.

Flexible solution: Mother takes baths with Pam, plays with bathtoys, and then bathes Pam while offering the protection Pam requires.

Fifteen-year-old Rick will not cut his hair.

Inflexible position: Parents insist because they believe in short hair.

Flexible position: Parents realize that although long hair makes them uncomfortable, they are mostly concerned about how people will react to Rick's hair being long. They concentrate on establishing the important values in Rick.

Tommy returns from school and refuses to attend physical education class in the future.

Inflexible position: Parents insist that Tom continue to attend physical education classes since that is a compulsory subject in the curriculum.

Flexible solution: Parents talk to Tom and to his P.E. teacher. Possibly intolerable demands have been made of Tom. It may be more propitious to have Tom drop P.E. from his curriculum for the present, or have Tom, parents and teacher, evolve a method whereby Tom can feel comfortable and productive in that class.

When a child is inflexible or stubborn, he is telling you that he is unhappy or uncomfortable about making a change. Perhaps he is unsure of what is involved in the change. In that instance, a description of the forthcoming activity and what will be expected of him might be all that is necessary. Possibly, too, he may be prepared to acquiesce, but not have the skills to back down with grace, so that the parent must assist the child in this. Stubbornness may represent a power play between parent and child. Thus the parent should distinguish between essential and unessential demands, being certain that the child is capable of executing the former. Then create a climate in which essential demands can willingly be executed and wherein the child has ample opportunity to exercise his independent process of decision making. Parents of the l.d. often have to rethink their concepts of how "nice" children should look and act, and ask themselves in each situation whose needs they are meeting, theirs or their child's.

Consistency is the Key

Be consistent in the demands you make, and do not make demands that you do not expect to see fulfilled. Be specific about the consequences. Idle threats are worse than no threats. All children must know where they stand, and this is particularly true of the l.d. child.

Dealing with Frustration

For a period of time try not to make any demands which the child will perceive as difficult. Engineer his environment so that he will experience success at a variety of tasks. Praise him in terms of his own progress rather than relative to the accomplishments of other children. As his confidence increases, you obviously might increase the demands upon him.

142

Make a list of situations that frustrate your child. Think of ways in which you can alter his environment to circumvent major frustration. If the tying of shoelaces has occasioned a series of upsets, and has become a cause célèbre between parent and child, purchase loafers. If multiple choices are frustrating, offer no choices, or very simple choices between two things.

SHORT INTEREST SPAN, DISTRACTIBILITY

It is common for l.d. children to experience difficulty in attending to a task for a reasonable period of time. They fidget and become distracted by sights and sounds in their environment that are irrelevant to the job at hand. Mother sends John to his room to dress, and one-half hour later John is still in his pyjamas playing with his toys. He may have meant to dress, but was distracted by his playthings, consequently forgetting to do what he was told. The teacher tells the class to complete the assignment written on the blackboard. John answers the first question, then begins to play with his pencil, listens to Susie sneeze at the back of the classroom, and then listens to the rain on the windowpane. He daydreams about his new bike, and about the fact that he is becoming hungry, so he fails to complete the given assignment. He has not been able to attend primarily to his assigned task because he has been inefficient in organizing inner and outer stimuli to exclude irrelevant sights, sounds, thoughts, and feelings.

Dealing with Distractibility

If a distractible child has a specific job to do, he should complete it in a setting where there are as few visual and auditory distractions as possible. Distractible children never should do their homework on the dining room table with the family milling around and the radio blaring. They function far better at a desk placed in a corner of their bedroom. Keep the desk top cleared of materials other than the assignment at which the child currently is working.

A distractible child needs the structure of a specific time in which to perform a task, and a specific place in which he always completes that task. He needs adult supervision to remind him of the job at hand when his attention wanders. Distractibility, like many of the behaviorisms associated with l.d., is more pronounced when the child feels that a demanding task has been asked of him. It is interesting to observe a child with a one-minute interest span spend three hours watching television.

PERSEVERATION

Perseveration is repetition. Once again we observe the inflexibility of a child who continues an action or conversation after it has become relevant to do so. Paul becomes interested in a topic and talks of little else for days. One week he is fascinated by hot water tanks and his conversation centers on that. The following week he rambles about roof tiles. Sally keeps repeating questions long after she knows the answer. Kevin uses the same few words over and over in his conversation. Joel's speech is full of repeated sounds in words. "Let's go-o to the store-ore." Donny prints and reprints the same letter. The perseverating child is like a cracked record that no one has moved on to the next phase.

Dealing with Perseveration

Perseveration may be a neurological phenomenon or it may represent the discomfort of the child in trying something new. For the child, repeating old behavior has the advantage of maintaining familiar consequences, no matter how uncomfortable the consequences may be. The adult, therefore, must move the child away from his repetitious act. When the child repeats himself in public, the parent signals to him, using cues established by child and parent. One effective cue is one finger held up for the first time a topic is repeated, two fingers held up the second time, and so on. If the child and parent are conversing alone and the child repeats a question or once again pursues a topic, a gentle, firm reminder that the question has been asked, or the topic discussed previously, is a must. Allowing the child to continue using inappropriate behavior is poor training for the future. Some l.d. children perseverate because they want to socialize and do not have a store of interesting topics on which to converse; hence, they make the same comments whenever they see a person, until the person eventually decides to avoid the child. Teach the child the types of things one says to peers, older children, and adults.

Impulsivity—Act Now Think Later

Most of us occasionally act or talk before we think. We are more likely to do so if our behavior monitors are subdued by alcohol, fatigue, or stress. Some l.d. children seem to function impulsively a great deal of the time. They are less able to measure a desire and its consequences in terms of the other factors in the environment. Johnny rushes across the road disregarding the red light. Charlie plays with matches and sets his house on fire. Sally comments on peoples' appearances regardless of the embarrassment it causes.

Danny answers all questions truthfully. As refreshing as the candor and spontaneity of the l.d. can be at times, it signifies, as well, the fact that they have not internalized all the controls of a civilized society.

Controls from Without

Adults must supply the controls that are lacking in the child. If he is unable to handle an experience safely and acceptably, he must be denied the experience until he has learned self-control; that is, a child who rushes across the road without waiting for the lights to change or traffic to stop must be protected from such a situation. The child who hits others, makes loud comments in class, laughs loudly when his classmates are working, must be controlled by adults. Remove him from the child he is hitting. Tell him that his interruption of the class is inappropriate. Let him unwind in a quiet place. It may be that an entire day spent in a classroom is more stimulation than he presently can tolerate. Teach your child the white lies that at times are preferable to a truthful response. Play games in which the family is in a variety of social situations; for example, you are coming out of church and the minister's wife asks "Do you like my hat?" What is an appropriate reply?

Accountability

Our professional leaders in the field always are talking about the need for accountability on the part of educators and administrators. Everyone who comes in contact with the l.d. child needs to be accountable, including, and perhaps especially, the child himself. Many l.d. children develop an image of themselves as total incompetents. Incompetent persons cannot be expected to be accountable for their behavior, hence, they have no stake in controlling their behavior. The child must be made to realize that even though he is hyperactive, his hyperactivity is not a license to have tantrums and that his activity level can be controlled and channeled. Neither is his l.d. a license to act impulsively, hostiley, negatively and so on. When he becomes intractible, discuss with him the fact that he is a person who can control his behavior. Then you and he work toward a goal of increased self-control.

Concrete Thinking—Literal Interpretation of Events

It is often erroneously stated that l.d. children cannot think in the abstract. To be incapable of any abstract cognition generally is a defect of a child far more handicapped than the learning disabled. Most l.d. children have the capacity for abstract cognition in a variety of areas; experiencing difficulty only in specific modalities such as mathematics.

However, one frequently notes overliteral thinking on the part of the learning disabled. Thus we see the child who becomes upset when someone says "Let's kill two birds with one stone." We note too, the child who takes jokes seriously and cannot always determine whether or not someone is teasing or "kidding." Indeterminates such as "possibly," "probably," "I imagine," "I guess," or "approximately" may be overlooked by the learning disabled. Consequently, a statement that "we may go to the museum on Saturday" could be interpreted as an ironclad oath. Or the comment that "the toys we ordered probably will arrive on Monday" might occasion repeated queries on Monday as to the whereabouts of the toys.

In addition, they may not have learned the countless colloquialisms with which we spice our language, such as "he's a dead duck," "over my dead body," or "I'm a monkey's uncle." Is it any wonder then, that l.d. children may become confused and anxious at the things they hear?

Teach the Child to Express Himself

When he stands in the corner with his head lowered, scowls or retreats to his bedroom behind closed doors, you the parent may realize what is bothering him. However, nonfamily members may not, so it is important that you teach him to express his concern, since you will not always be present when he becomes upset. You might say, "I see that you are upset but I don't know what is troubling you; would you tell me about it?" Or, to the angry child who is kicking the furniture, "You obviously are very angry; please tell me what has happened."

HYPERACTIVITY, HYPOACTIVITY

The hyperactive child is one whose activity pattern tends to be in excess of the expectation of an active child of the same age. Much of the activity seems to be purposeless; he flits from stimulus to stimulus rather than sitting down to a specific project and carrying it through to completion. The hyperactive child is particularly vulnerable to distractions, and moves his body toward the current distraction. Some hyperactive children have difficulty falling asleep and may awaken early in the morning, at which time they seem incapable of remaining quiet so that the family can sleep. Hyperactivity may be noticeable in the child's speech and language pattern in that he speaks quickly and jumps from topic to topic. The expenditure of the child's energy is considerable, yet the only persons to tire are the adults around him. Some hyperactivity may be a result of the child's anxiety concerning his ability to meet demands, and some may be a smoke screen created to divert demands and hostility.

The hypoactive child appears underactive. It takes him a long time to dress, walk to school, make his bed, and perform most activities. He is the child who occasions the reaction in adults, "If only I could light a fire under him." Nevertheless one can observe fidgity movements, short interest span, and distractibility in the hypoactive child. He may be expending as much energy as his hyperactive counterpart, because although his body remains in one place, his mind flits from thought to thought, and his attention is as easily distracted.

Handling Hyperactivity and Hypoactivity

These children may do well with structuring of their daily activities and reduction of stimuli as described for the impulsive and disorganized child. Learn the extent of their attention span and assign tasks to them in a low stimulus environment, for the extent of their ability to concentrate. Increase the length of the tasks gradually, as the shorter tasks successfully are completed. Do not expose your child to an environment in which he cannot control his activity. Give the hypoactive child specific periods of time in which to complete an activity. Supervise him to assure that he continues his task until it is completed.

Set a tone for the upcoming activity. If bedtime is approaching, avoid stimulating endeavors, exciting or frightening stories, and noisy interaction. Begin establishing a quiet tone as soon as dinner is finished. Possibly soft music, a pleasant discussion, a warm drink, and an intimate story or chat on the bed while you stroke his head will set the mood for a relaxed drifting off to sleep.

EMOTIONAL LABILITY

Many of us have experienced the child who throws a devastating tantrum in which he screams, cries, stamps his feet, kicks and throws objects. Just as quickly as the tantrum was initiated, it is dispersed and the child is laughing gaily while his parents still are shaken by his previous behavior. Emotional lability is an instability of the child's emotional reactions. His behavior tends to change abruptly, and the reaction may be grossly out of proportion to the stimulus.

Handling Emotional Lability

It should be pointed out to the child that his response is inappropriate: "Steve, the joke wasn't that funny," "Paul, I know you are amused but you are not supposed to shout in the classroom." If he cannot control his behavior he should be removed to a quiet place until he has regained control. Quench the overreaction quickly before the child has become too overstimulated.

BEHAVIOR IS A MESSAGE

There is a reason for all behavior. In some instances the reasons are indiscernible. Nevertheless, if we stop to think, we can find reasons for much of a child's behavior. Lon is a clown. He clowns in school and when he is with peers. In the latter instance the clowning may be amusing for a time, but Lon does not know when to stop. Naturally each episode of clowning in the classroom occasions instantaneous discipline. Since this has proven to be ineffective in reducing episodes of silliness, it might be profitable for the teacher to examine the demands made of Lon which initiate his bid for attention. Clowning is an effective smoke screen. People become so attentive to the antics that they forget the demands made of Lon (academic, social, etc.) in which he feels he will be a failure. There are a number of techniques used by l.d. children to avoid tasks they do not feel they can do, or to draw attention away from the assigned task. A few of these behaviorisms are daydreaming, dawdling, whining, tantrums, withdrawal, and hypochondria.

Some behavior may be a bid for attention. The child justifiably may feel that little of what he does is praiseworthy. He lives in a world of constant reprimand, punishment, and little positive feedback. He may even feel that people do not love him a great deal. Consequently he will attempt to be recognized using whatever means he has at his disposal. He may get into fights, be destructive, or demand endless amounts of adult attention. It is important for the adult not to grant attention to undesirable performance, but to recognize the child's needs and show appreciation for his *positive* contributions to family and classroom.

Manipulative Behavior

Betty has a tantrum when asked to do the most elementary task. Initially her tantrums may have been occasioned by genuine frustration and inadequacy, but now they reflect her knowledge that adults will acquiesce in order to end the uncomfortable behavior. At this point Betty "has it made." She is excused from all household chores, and the most minimal of demands. Although at age nine she easily is capable of dressing herself, her parents dress her daily. In such cases as Betty's, if the demand you have made of the child is reasonable, insist that it be executed. "Have your tantrum, but when you finish, I still want you to make your bed."

Coyness, helplessness, submissive behavior, and verbosity are other manipulations that are employed at times by the l.d. to avoid execution of demands. Any of the behaviors which may be a genuine result of the brain dysfunction can be utilized in a manipulative context. The child quickly learns that the behavior occasions specific reactions which he may feel are advantageous; hence, he continues his ineffective functioning. The clumsy child does a poor job of making his bed, cleaning his room, and dressing himself. The parent feels it is easier to do these chores herself. The child realizes that as long as he remains clumsy he can avoid these tasks. The distractible child or child with poor auditory memory forgets to do what he is told. Hence, constant parental reminders are the result. But the parent may decide that it is not worth the trouble to ask the child to do something. Thus, as the child's ability to complete assigned tasks improves, he still may find it advantageous to appear forgetful so that demands are not made of him.

The l.d. child learns that he can interrupt others and be excused on the basis of impulsivity. He finds that he can destroy toys and household objects and awaken his parents at night, having his behavior blamed on hyperactivity. Inflexibility is extremely effective in avoiding tasks, since the parent prefers not to make demands rather than face a battle of wills.

Manipulative behavior frequently is obvious at school. A child who has had difficulty writing refuses to write any of his assignments. A child learns that his disability can be an excuse to avoid any school subject that might prove challenging. Adults who work with the l.d. need to be extremely sensitive, so that they do not make demands of a child that he is unable to execute, and conversely do not allow the child to use his deficits as a crutch to avoid responsibilities.

Regressive Behavior

When Jack is faced with a stressful situation at home or at school, he soils his pants. Unconsciously he may be feeling that babies do not have impossible demands made of them, hence, a return to infancy will occasion a return to a carefree life. There may be an element of punishment in Jack's behavior, since he is creating an unpleasant cleanup job for adults and it is the adult world that has created the unreasonable demands. Jack's parents should examine the demands of home and school. It may be that Jack's message is well taken, that unfair stress has been imposed upon him. It might be appropriate to have Jack rinse his own clothing when he has an accident. If removal of stress does not result in disappearance of regressive behavior, psychotherapy may be indicated. Other types of regressive behavior are urinating, baby talk, and dependency.

Compensatory Behavior

When Cary is under stress he steals money. Unconsciously he may be feeling ineffective and unloved. Money represents compensation and love. Cary's parents should examine the demands made of him, and remove unrealistic expectations. He should be loved and rewarded for that which he can accomplish. If stealing does not disappear with the establishment of realistic expectations and achievement, psychotherapy might be indicated.

He Turns You On By Turning You Off

Sometimes l.d. children learn that the only attention they can receive is negative attention, so they persist in undesirable behavior in order to provoke a response. If we refuse to respond to irritating behavior, but reward desired behaviors, the inappropriateness should diminish. If we ignore negative statements, we do not place the child in a position of having to defend his statement. Charlie says he is not going to join us when we go out. If we involve ourselves in a discussion with him, we consolidate his position. However, if we state the time and condition of our departure, he well may tag along. If he does not, his nonconformity can be dealt with at that point. If we are able to leave him behind, he will learn that we mean what we say.

Let Us Allow Him To Save Face

Bob, the camp counselor, lightly sketched a cartoon for Karl, who then colored it and hung it on the cabin wall. Karl proudly escorted everyone into the cabin to see the picture he had executed. His other counselor told him that she felt that he was deceiving people, stating that he had made the picture, whereas, in reality, Bob had drawn it.

Karl may have needed the esteem of saying to people, "Look at the picture I made." His counselor should recognize his need to feel important and protect this need rather than expose it. Possibly she could have encouraged him to draw an additional picture himself, expressing greater appreciation of his own production.

Parents' Reaction to Behavior

Undesirable behavior is guaranteed to deteriorate if parents react to it on an emotional level. Granted, it is most difficult not to become upset with many of the behaviorisms that are associated with learning disabilities, but parental frustration and verbal and physical anger accelerate the child's reaction. Some parents almost seem to desire such acceleration, since their anger only dissipates after the hitting and screaming has reached its peak. The tantrum or other undesired behavior offers them the genuine opportunity to punish the child who has afforded his parents so much trouble.

The child may be frightened by his lack of inner control. He looks to adults to provide the control he lacks. He needs to receive the message from adults that "I won't let you have an endless tantrum, or be hyperactive indefinitely." The adult who responds to loss of control in the child by losing control himself denies his child needed structure and support. The parental reaction should be: "Your behavior is unacceptable. You can't handle the situation in which you find yourself, therefore we'll attempt to modify the situation, make a more realistic demand, and if necessary remove you from the situation until you can handle yourself acceptably." Certainly the child will realize that the parent does not enjoy his behavior, but he must not be allowed to use behavior as an irritant. He behaves badly because you have asked something of him. If you react emotionally to his behavior, he has succeeded in punishing you for your demands.

Will the Child Outgrow His Behavior?

Some of the behavior associated with a learning disability, such as hyperactivity, seems to diminish in adolescence. Much of the behavior still is discernible in some people in adolescence and adulthood. There may be a residual degree of distractibility, fidgitiness, disorganization, literalness, and inflexibility. However, the extent of this behavior will be dependent, in part, upon the success the person feels that he has achieved academically, socially, and in his general skill development. If he has experienced sufficient success and recognition, he will possess motivation to succeed in social interaction, a job situation, and in recreational pursuits. The person who has "something going for him" is far less likely to become frustrated, or to be inflexible. He will exert the extra effort required to become organized and attentive.

By the child's adolescence the parents should have effected a transfer of controls exerted by outsiders to controls internalized by the young person. He needs to recognize his vulnerability and compensate for it. The disorganized person will have to take the time to prestructure a job or a daily schedule. In an unfamiliar environment, the adult lacking in spatial memory will need to exert a conscious effort to note the direction in which he has walked. The distractible person must always choose a quiet place in which to complete a job. The l.d. adolescent or adult needs to recognize when he is becoming overstimulated or frustrated. He must remove himself from such situations, and choose acceptable releases for his anxiety, excitement, or frustration. One expects a six-year-old l.d. child to stamp his feet with frustration, but that is inappropriate behavior for an adolescent. He may choose to run around the block, punch a punching bag, or throw darts at a target.

It is most important that the child not adopt neurotic compensation for his deficit. The child who copes with disorganization by becoming obsessive and ritualistic, or the child who has trouble expressing himself, and consequently withdraws into his bedroom behind closed doors during all his free time, might benefit from professional help.

L.d. youngsters, being vulnerable, are likely to encounter many unpleasant experiences in their childhood and adolescent years. On Halloween Bob went "trick or treating." His collection of goodies was taken forcibly by a group of older boys. In order to compensate, Bob took the goodies of a younger child. However, this really did not make him feel better; rather, he felt ashamed of himself. The same Halloween Alan spent considerable time making a costume for himself. He misjudged the space that his body would take in the subway turnstile, where he caught and ripped his entire costume. When he arrived at his club Halloween party, he and his fellow members scouted around the "Y" and collected items to concoct another costume for Alan. We involved Bob, Alan, and their fellow club members in a discussion about acceptable and unacceptable ways of dealing with frustration and anger. Similarly, other l.d. youth need to devise adaptive methods of dealing with upsetting experiences.

Part Two / Notes

Chapter 7:

1. Edward T. Hall, *The Silent Language* (New York: Doubleday and Co., Inc., 1959).

2. Doreen Kronick, *They Too Can Succeed* (San Rafael, Calif.: Academic Therapy Publications, 1969).

3. Ibid.

4. Albert E. Sheflen, lecture given at the New York State Branch of the American Academy of Pediatrics, 1970.

5. Kronick, *They Too Can Succeed*.

6. L. F. Kurlander and Dorothy Colodny, "Pseudoneurosis in the Neurologically Handicapped Child," *American Journal of Orthopsychiatry*, Vol. 35, No. 4 (July 1965).

7. Kronick, *They Too Can Succeed*.

8. Ernest Siegel, "The Real Problem of Minimal Brain Dysfunction," in *Learning Disabilities: Its Implications to a Responsible Society*, ed. Doreen Kronick (Chicago, Ill.: Developmental Learning Materials, 1969).

Chapter 8:

1. G. Langdon and I. W. Stout, *These Well-Adjusted Children* (New York: The John Day Co., 1951).

2. Doreen Kronick, "Guidelines for Parents," in *Helping the Adolescent with the Hidden Handicap*, ed. Lauriel E. Anderson (San Rafael, Calif.: Academic Therapy Publications, 1970); Kronick, *They Too Can Succeed*.

3. Kronick, *They Too Can Succeed*.

Part Three

The Family in the Community

Chapter 10:
Relating to the Professional

I HAVE MET MANY PARENTS of the learning disabled who attribute their family's well-being and their child's improvement to the sensitive, knowledgeable direction of professionals. Other parents are bitter and frustrated by their contacts with the professional community. In too many cases the latter reaction is caused by the professional's genuine lack of knowledge as well as an unwillingness to provide the type of information to the family that would lead to pragmatic action. Certainly, parents unknowingly are guilty of compounding their frustration by looking for help in the wrong place. In other words, if you make an appointment with an electrician to fix your plumbing, and phone him whenever you have a question about the plumbing, you are programing for dissatisfaction. If, on the other hand, you consult an electrician for an electrical problem, the probability of satisfaction is extremely good. Additionally, parents' attitudes and behavior, however justified, may antagonize a professional; they must know the preferable approach. In this chapter I will try to catalogue, in part, some of the services the various professions offer, the type of professional to seek at specific times, and for specific concerns, and how best to approach the professional.

Diagnosis

You suspect that your child may have a learning disability. You may, at this early point, be like some parents who think they, or their friends and neighbors, are capable of deciding whether or not their child is l.d. They launch their child into a remedial program and agonize over his future, without first investigating why he is not attaining the expectations of parents and educators. It is important to realize that the human organism has only a set number of behaviors with which it reacts to stress; a child may be exhibiting some of the behaviorisms commonly associated with the l.d., yet suffer from another exceptionality. Or, he may have no exceptionality, and merely be responding to stresses in home, school or playground, or be exhibiting behavior within the "limits of normal development," or have a physical problem. In any case, the task of differentiation calls for professional skill.

First Steps First

A good first step is a visit to the physician who has been caring for your child. He will have observed your child's development throughout the years, and should be in a position to discuss your concerns in view of his observations. Additionally, your child should receive a thorough physical examination including tests of sight, hearing, metabolism, and levels of blood sugar; this is important as it will reveal or eliminate possible physical causes of the dysfunction. Then ask your child's physician to refer you to someone who can determine the presence or absence of an exceptionality and delineate areas of function and dysfunction.

Educational or Clinical Psychologist

If the child's physician suspects the presence of l.d. and does not feel that the child suffers from a progressive lesion, or a primary emotional problem, the best referral often is to an educational or clinical psychologist. He should be in a position to discern whether or not the child is disabled, where his problem lies, and what can be done in the home, school, and community to reduce his areas of difficulty. The psychologist may not be prepared to be consulted over a period of time, unless the family has arranged to see him for extended counseling.

Should I See a Neurologist?

Your family physician always should be apprised of the steps you are taking to investigate and remediate your child's handicap. Although you may initiate some steps without direct referral from your physician, do keep him posted and do not enter into a neurological or psychiatric examination for your child unless your physician deems it advisable and arranges a direct referral. He then can provide the neurologist or psychiatrist with useful background information.

A neurologist is consulted if a convulsive or progressive disorder is suspected, or if drug therapy is indicated. I do not feel that it is meaningful for the parent or physician to request a neurological examination merely to discern the absence or presence of brain damage. No one, at this point, knows the cause of most learning disabilities. Whether or not they are caused by brain damage is not relevant to the treatment, since all remediation is based upon presenting behavior. Consequently, if the parent seeks a neurological examination to satisfy her own concerns as to cause of the l.d., she may be exposing herself and her child to unnecessary expense and stress. In addition, most neurologists do not attempt in-depth assessment of auditory and visual organization and memory, as does a psychologist. Therefore, in addition to seeking services of a neurologist, a psychological assessment still is indicated for purposes of program planning.

In some instances physicians still are referring children to neurologists when the l.d. is suspected, because the physician is unaware of the type of information the parent should be seeking in the diagnostic process. It is appropriate, then, for the parent to explore, in a tactful manner, the physician's reasons for the referral. Generally speaking, a neurologist is not prepared to be consulted over a period of time on the child's behavior, school problems, or changes in program.

Should I See a Psychiatrist?

A psychiatrist is consulted if a primary emotional problem is suspected. If the child's physician feels that the problem in learning or behavior has an emotional base, psychiatric referral is valid. If such a referral is deemed advisable, the parents need not feel that investigation of these factors in any way reflects on their ability to provide a healthy upbringing. Some children become "stuck" at specific developmental stages, requiring professional help to become "unstuck." Some children are traumatized by seemingly uneventful incidents that might have occurred in or out of the home, and must be assisted over this hurdle. Therefore, we look to psychiatrists for this kind of help, but it may be inappropriate, unsuccessful, or frustrating to seek from them a delineation of strengths and deficits, establishment of a remedial program, and ready accessibility whenever a problem arises.

If the stress exhibited by child and parents seems to be the result and not the cause of the learning problem, a psychological assessment might be a preferable first step; it would be followed by psychotherapy to reduce stress, if required, after remediation has been initiated.

Who Can Provide Ongoing Direction?

This is a valid question. It highlights a serious gap in the structure of services for the learning disabled. Often a town or city will be supplied adequately with diagnosticians but have no one who is prepared to offer long-term direction. In some cities such a role has been assumed by some social workers, psychologists, or pediatricians. Often the parent has to consult a variety of persons and use a great deal of his own judgment in program planning. Some parents have found knowledgeable assistance from the consultant in special education of their school board, an itinerant teacher, or teacher of the l.d. class. These people generally are familiar with the child and his difficulties, and know what the school is providing in the way of help. Their suggestions will be most valid, since they can propose a program to complement and augment that which the school is providing. In some instances the local volunteer association can refer the family to a professional who will act as a catalyst and provide ongoing direction.

What Therapies Should I Seek For My Child?

In North America, at this time, there seems to be feast or famine, depending upon the area in which one lives. In some communities there are no services and the parents are in despair. Conversely, in some communities there are special educational services, motor therapy, language therapy, optometric therapy, and private tutorial assistance.

For most handicaps and exceptionalities the medical and paramedical professions offer specific and confident direction as to treatment. Unfortunately, this is not always the case with the learning disabled. The professional community is not in agreement concerning the efficacy of specific treatment procedures. Consequently, situations occur in which an optometrist will suggest that he can effect great improvement in a child and a pediatrician might call optometric therapy "witchcraft." The parent is torn between the tales of great improvement about which she hears or reads, and the physician's negative response to some treatment procedures. Who should she believe and what should be her guidelines?

There is no simple answer to this question. Meaningful establishment of a child's program will occur only when the variety of treatment processes have been adequately researched, and diagnosticians familiarize themselves with the existent treatment modalities and the types of handicaps they help. In the interim, I would like to list a series of general guidelines.

1. If your child is receiving remedial work for his l.d. from the school system, through placement in an l.d. class or itinerant teacher or resource-room program, consult the special education teacher before embarking on any additional remediation. Follow her suggestions concerning additional help. In many instances, the special education program provides the extent of assistance and pressure with which the child can cope, and no additional remediation should be undertaken. Be patient. Do not expect instantaneous miracles, but allow the school program the time it takes to effect changes.

2. If your child is not being helped through the school system, seek remediation that is directly related to the areas of deficit. If the

child has a motor problem, motor or optometric therapy may help. If a language processing problem is discovered, try to find a language therapist (as differentiated from a speech therapist). If the problem is with academic work, look for a tutor who has special training in teaching the learning disabled child. If someone with this training is unavailable, find a patient, flexible tutor (possibly a college student), and have the remedial program set up and examined regularly by an educational psychologist.

3. Only enter a program that is temporally and financially reasonable for you.

4. If your child is the recipient of any form of private therapy, and no growth is evident after ten months, you might question whether continuation in such a program is worth the effort involved.

5. Do not overload your child. Allow plenty of time for hobbies and relaxation.

6. If you react to your child's failures with frustration or impatience, or if you are too anxious for him to succeed, do not do the formal therapy with your child yourself.

7. If he has received formal therapy for several years, think seriously about whether he should continue throughout adolescence.

8. If he is receiving remediation, have him assessed every two or three years to reexamine his needs.

When seeking an appropriate program, parents should be aware that there is not just one type of learning disability. The term describes a multiplicity of brain dysfunctions of varied origins and manifestations that differ with each child. Consequently, a program that will work miracles with one child will be a waste of time and money with another. Additionally, a greater number of practitioners now feel that the acquisition of prelearning skills is not necessarily a guarantee of improved ability to acquire learning skills. Thus, a child who has a language disability may not be able to process language more effectively after participation in a motor program. However, if he shows deficits in motor as well as language functioning, remediation in motor and language might be advisable.

Parents are so overawed by the professional mystique that at times they are too frightened by their supposed incompetency to plan and assess their child's remediation. Nonetheless, until professional agreement is more of a reality, the parent must continue in the pseudoprofessional role, and should trust his own judgment. He is the person who will follow the child through life and must steer him through the professional mixed-message maze. Therefore, he should learn as much as possible about the disability.

The Preferable Approach

Professionals seem particularly vulnerable to the attitudes of parents, and these attitudes will often influence their response and assistance to the family. As unfair and uncomprehending as this may sometimes be, it is a reality, so that the parent who achieves the most, frequently is the one with the approach most acceptable to the professional. Parents, therefore, must call forth superhuman effort to appear relaxed, and not seem anxious about prognosis or availability of services. They should not express their anger at the failings of other professionals, nor demand of the diagnostician that which he is unprepared to offer.

The positive approach will be enhanced if the parent is aware of the types of information that can reasonably be expected from the professional. Some of the professional's findings might be confidential, and his report might be couched in terminology that is comprehensible only to fellow professionals. However, the parents have a right to be informed about their child's current level of intellectual functioning, his emotional health, his areas of strength and deficit. In addition, they should be given information on the approach that can be adopted at home, school, and in the community, as well as the general prognosis for their child's condition. Information on physical illnesses is not cloaked in an aura of secrecy, and I feel that parents have the right to knowledge of their child's exceptionality. If they are confused by the diagnosis, they should ask for simple clarification. Parents are justified in asking why specific remedial techniques have been instituted and what they are designed to accomplish.

Parents Who Program For Failure

Some parents are more hyperactive than their children. They drag their child from one diagnostician to another, and rush him through every treatment center. Many fail to carry a program through to completion, or give a program time to work. One has to question whether their mad dash is not motivated more by a desire to soothe their own concerns by proving that they are leaving no stone unturned, than it is a genuine concern for the child itself. It is better not to initiate a demanding treatment process than enter into one which you are unlikely to see through to completion. You must consider the amount of spare time you have, the extent of your patience, and the other demands on you and your family.

162

At times we parents drop many treatment programs because we lack the confidence that they will create improvement. If they have been prescribed by reputable professionals, we must give them the time to succeed.

Pushing For Services

In most parts of North America there are too few services for the learning disabled. This lack is particularly obvious in the area of educational services. Each parent must fight for his own child, and there is a way of fighting that stands the greatest chance of success. By all means, communicate regularly with your school principal, school board, and elected trustees. Tell them of the demonstrated success of services for the l.d. and the prognosis for a child if he is not assisted. Do not, however, be unreasonable and demanding. Be understanding of the shortage of trained personnel and the other physical problems which might impede enlargement of services. Work with them in devising solutions to their problems. Join or form a parents' group and fight for services for all l.d. children. The voice of many carries greater weight than the voice of few, and asking that all children be helped is more favorably received than fighting for one's own child.

Chapter 11:
Person to Person

Betty Lou Kratoville

COMMUNICATION unquestionably holds a position of high priority on the long list of parental duties and responsibilities involved in the rearing of the l.d. child. At a time when the family may be reeling under the impact of diagnosis, the question unfailingly arises, "What do we tell our friends (or the grandparents, or the other children in the family, or the neighbors)?"

This dilemma has been compounded in recent years since parents have often had to assume an instructional role with professionals. If the child's diagnosis has been psychological or educational, how do you fill in the family doctor, especially if his help is needed with medication or diet? If the diagnosis has been medical, how do you reach the teacher who has no special training in the field of learning disabilities? What does one say to a scout leader, a dancing teacher, or a baby sitter—or even salespeople who are obviously disenchanted with a child who knocks down arrays of merchandise or propels shopping carts into plate glass windows? And, perhaps most important of all, what do you tell other children in the neighborhood who shun or persecute the l.d. child?

Each day, all of these people cut a wide swath through the lives of the l.d. youngster and his family. Their impact can be brutalizing if not downright fatal—or, conversely, it can contribute to the remedial, rehabilitative process. Therefore, no alternative exists. These individuals must be dealt with—effectively and courageously—to the point where simple communication becomes almost an exercise in the art of public relations.

When the parents are first confronted with these responsibilities, their courage is probably and understandably at low ebb. They are, above all else, human beings and must be allowed that period of mourning which follows any family tragedy. Nevertheless, as in any other trauma, grief cannot be prolonged and must be replaced by action, and most parents know this. So often I have heard them plead, "What can we do? Tell us what to do, and we'll do it!" Learning how to deal with the many individuals who will pass through the life of the child is one thing that parents can do. Indeed, no one else can do it for them. And only they can decide how much, how little, and what kind of communication will best shed private and public illumination.

It is difficult to generalize specific communication procedures because of the enormous variation in people and in situations. However, one rule of thumb seems to have merit in most situations: communication in the form of explanation and education IS required if the child is to have an ongoing relationship with his neighbors, friends, doctors, relatives, and teachers. Communication in the form of explanation and education is NOT required if a chance or one-time encounter is involved. For example, a mother and her hyperactive, l.d. six-year-old son enter an elevator. The child squirms, pushes, and eventually comes down hard on the toes of one of the passengers, who with some justification utters a cry of pain and outrage. No good purpose will be served if the mother launches into this lengthy explanation: "Johnny is a brain-injured child, and it is hard for him to be confined in small spaces, and it is hard for him to stand still," and so on. A better way of handling the situation is to say with as much grace as possible, "Johnny and I are very sorry that he stepped on your toes." (If the parent is aware that Johnny cannot tolerate confined spaces, she should head for the nearest stairs or escalator—unless her appointment is on the 18th floor!)

On the other hand, if Johnny is prone to uproot the dahlias in the flower bed of the kindly lady next door, or to smash all of the soft drink bottles in her garage, or to endanger the well being of her favorite cat, then some line of communication must be established. The initial overtures and follow through, while sometimes painful or embarrassing, are minor compared to the anguish of moving to a new neighborhood.

Once the decision has been made that some form of communication is indicated, what is the best way to do it? Circumstances will dictate the appropriate measure and the best approach. One thing is certain: the child should never be present during such an exchange. An optimum setting should be sought, a time that is both convenient and relaxed for all involved. The key word is explanation—not apology. The approach should follow this pattern: *this is the way it is, this is the way it will be, this is what we are going to try to do about it.* Since the printed word is apt to command respect, reading material may be offered, but it should be simple, straightforward, nontechnical, and, if possible, brief. (A list of suitable publications and where to obtain them can be found at the end of this chapter.)

As time passes, parents will learn how to "read" the people with whom they must communicate about their l.d. child. It becomes almost an intuitive thing. One learns to sense if a lengthy description is required or if a more perfunctory one will do the job. If the ear of the listener seems less than sympathetic, it may be better to postpone the conversation, or on some sad occasions the parent may simply have to give up. Indisputably, the whole world is not yet ready to listen or to care about learning disabilities, and parents must be grateful for those loyal, compassionate people who do attend, take heed, and help.

Parents must take care to emphasize that they are not seeking pity for themselves nor their child. Pity is not constructive and can even prolong the initial feelings of inertia, guilt, and frustration. The recommended point of view is one that is upbeat, matter of fact, and optomistic. One can imply, in effect, "Well, now at least we know what the problem is and have begun looking for answers."

As has been indicated, specifics of communication are difficult. However, the following categories with recommendations for constructive action will attempt to deal with "special interest" groups.

Children in the Family

Seldom does a learning disability appear overnight. Therefore, children within the family group have gradually been tuned in to the fact that a problem exists. They have been witness and party to the dilemma and confusion. Perhaps they have already learned to cope with some of their l.d. brother's or sister's behavioral problems. Perhaps they are aware that mother or father or both have been summoned to the school on a number of recent occasions. At any rate, they know that something is up, and the sooner they know the truth, the better.

Communication, of course, is a great deal easier with older children. A family conference can be scheduled, and the facts made known. "You are aware that we have been having some problems with Johnny and that we haven't exactly known why he was behaving the way he was nor what to do about it. It would be wonderful if when one became a parent, one automatically became wise about all things, but this just isn't the case. We've had a number of tests run on Johnny, and the results are now in. The best opinion that we have been able to get is that he has a learning disability, and this is why he is having trouble in school. We've also learned that children with this kind of problem do not always behave in the same manner as other children, and this is why Johnny sometimes creates such a rumpus at home. Luckily, there are things that can be done to help such children, and we are going to start learning about them at once."

Time and opportunity should be made for questions which should be answered as truthfully as possible. Children can be very perceptive, and their questions are not always easy to answer. In such cases, a parent should feel free to say, "I don't know the answer to that question," and, perhaps, to add, "I'll try to find out."

A debatable point is whether or not children within the family group should be called on for help with the l.d. child. Circumstances alone can dictate the answer to this. Nevertheless, it is perhaps wiser that the matter of their assistance (which conceivably could involve some sacrifice) not be dealt with in detail during the first family conference. "We are all going to work together to help Johnny" should suffice until the brothers and sisters have had time to adjust to their new concept of Johnny as a human being with diagnosed problems rather than just a "troublesome brat." When the time does arise to call on older siblings for help, it is wiser to start with small doses, ten or fifteen minutes, and work toward gradually increasing the amount and substance of their contribution.

It would seem better for all concerned if younger children in the family are not involved in long, easily misinterpreted explanations until they are actually old enough to sense and inquire about the problem. Occasions may conceivably arise when the l.d. child's behavior will cause them grief or pain. Even at such times, the offering of immediate, on-the-spot solace and sympathy is the best approach. "You must feel very bad because brother knocked you down. I know it hurts, and I am very sorry it happened," is much more comforting to a howling child and will assuage hurt feelings or a skinned knee much faster than tedious explanation of Johnny's compulsive behavior. This does not mean that the l.d. child's unacceptable behavior should be tolerated or that it should not be dealt with appropriately. It should! But that is quite another subject. A good general rule to remember is that any child in a family who is hurt, ill, or in a crisis situation deserves top priority at that point in time.

It should also be recognized that children have a way of accepting bizarre situations that adults do not, that they often devise their own methods for coping and are, perhaps, stronger and wiser for the experience. If they can rely on their parents for honest information, frank answers, and an equitable relationship among all the members of the family, they will respond with rare insight and nobility.

Children in the Neighborhood

Nothing in this world can more intensely arouse the primitive emotions of anger and pain than a child who has been injured, physically or emotionally, by another child in the neighborhood. At such times parents are apt to lose all objectivity and perspective. It seems almost unnecessary to point out the futility of such reactions, and in the case of the l.d. child, where the parental anguish and indignation are apt to be intensified, inept handling of such situations can result in long-term isolation for the child. To further complicate the matter, other precarious factors exist. First of all, it may be the l.d. child who, through disruptive behavior, has triggered the incident. Secondly, the l.d. child may be honestly unaware that what he is doing is intolerable or unacceptable. Thirdly, he may be trying to compete or engage in an activity for which he lacks the skills.

It would seem, then, that the first job of the parent is to make a proper assessment of the situation before any action is taken. However, before dealing with a crisis event, attention should be directed towards prevention of just such crises. The l.d. child needs instruction in the important area of socialization, and this can best be done in the home environment by inviting one other child for a period of play, by seeing that there are sufficient and suitable materials on hand to enjoy, by being ready to step in if intervention is needed, and to terminate the session when signs of boredom or restlessness are evident. A young guest who has had a good time is likely to want to come again or to return the invitation.

If proper facilities, such as a well-stocked playroom or a large backyard, are available, the home of the l.d. child can be a gathering place for other children of all ages, and in such an informal setting the child can learn much about the give-and-take of social situations. Although it involves considerable time and ingenuity on the part of parents, such free and easy social intercourse does much to provide the proper climate for communicating with the young people who are important in the child's life, with or without the l.d. problems. If the parent has been hospitable, friendly, and interested, it will be infinitely easier to gain the attention and cooperation of neighborhood children.

Sometimes, with older children, a tactful invitation for a chat becomes necessary. A soft drink or a home-made cookie will do much to promote a good exchange, for if a child is treated like a guest and a worthwhile human being, he will respond in kind. Typical remarks from a parent might sound something like this: "I know Johnny is not always easy to get along with because I live with him. Do you know what a learning disability is? Well, it is a condition which keeps a child from acting or learning as other children do. Johnny has a learning disability, and we are working with doctors and his teacher and other people who have studied such children, and we are all trying to help him as much as we can. No one is quite sure yet what has caused the condition, and, really, that isn't important. The important thing is that

Johnny, who down deep knows he has these problems and is fearful of them, can have a normal, happy life, just like any other child. One of the things he most needs is friends, and that is why I am so grateful that we live in this neighborhood where we all care about one another and come to one another's aid in times of crisis. Do you remember when Mr. Jones died and everyone rallied around to help Mrs. Jones? Your mother kept her children for several days, and I know you helped at that time. That's how come I'm sure you know what caring is all about . . . . Now I don't want to ask too much of you. If you are all playing outside, and Johnny is creating a disturbance, feel free to come to me. I'll be there in a flash to help. If you are all playing a game, and Johnny is slow to learn the rules or to catch on, it really isn't his fault. He's trying as hard as he can, and a little patience would mean so much to him." Once again, the parent should provide an opportunity for the youngster to ask questions. On some occasions, it might be better to deal with two youngsters at a time to lessen embarrassment or anxiety on the part of a single young guest.

In the matter of a crisis confrontation, the parent must be prepared to use his wits and his humanity. In such emergencies, it is of little consequence who is to blame. The effective approach is action, quickly and resolutely taken, with a minimum of hurt feelings and damaged pride for all concerned. If the l.d. child dashes into the house screaming, he needs comfort, not questions. He quite literally needs the sanctity and safety of his home, and he needs time to pull himself together. Indeed, on many occasions, this is all he will need to rise above the situation or to forget it. If he has been abused, the parent may need to resort to the kind of scheduled conversation described earlier or, all else failing, to limit his outside play activities. An alternate measure might involve an older child within or without the family group who can be hired as a kind of roving baby sitter with the function of simply keeping an eye on the l.d. child while he is wandering about the neighborhood. In such an arrangement, the child does not need to know he is being watched, and the parent can enjoy a few moments of well-being, secure in the knowledge that the child is in no danger of physical or emotional injury.

When a neighborhood child comes to the door with the complaint that Johnny is doing this or Johnny is doing that, his grievance should be treated with utmost respect. Children will usually put up with quite a lot before they risk an encounter with an adult. Therefore, such a complaint generally indicates that the playmate has reached the end of his rope. At this moment the l.d. child may have to be removed from the group for a cooling off period, and the best way to handle this is an attractive bribe, even if the parent has to reschedule his or her activities. "Johnny, come on in and help me bake cookies," or "Johnny, come take a ride with me to the store," will circumvent many a neighborhood or family storm.

In summary, kindness, common sense, courtesy, consideration, and a pinch of humor are prime ingredients for good relationships with children in the neighborhood.

Friends and Neighbors

Bad news still travels fast, and in the area of communicating with adults, the problem is generally one of clarification. The first item of business will be the elimination of confusion between mental retardation and learning disabilities. The importance of this cannot be underestimated because, undeniably, information on this critical aspect will filter down from adults to children in the neighborhood, and it may do much to stamp out the painful labels often affixed to l.d. children. The point must be clearly made and clearly understood that the l.d. child has normal or above normal intelligence and that his behavioral or learning problems stem from a disability quite as real and debilitating as blindness or deafness. Emphasis must be placed on the child's inability to grasp or deal with his own problems, on certain characteristics of the disability such as low boiling point, perseveration, hyperactivity, and spatial problems.

Language should be forthright and nontechnical, and sometimes a salient example will make a telling point: "Do you remember the day that Johnny blew up and threw stones at the children when they were playing ball? On the surface, that seemed inexcusable and, of course, in a sense it was. No one can be allowed to hurt people. On the other hand, Johnny had been trying to take part in the game and simply couldn't catch the ball. One of the symptoms of his disability is that his eyes and hands don't work well together. He became angry at himself, and he exploded. Once out of control, he couldn't turn it off—that's another symptom. What he did cannot be tolerated, but it can be understood. And if you remember, after that day he threw stones we worked with Johnny in the back yard for weeks until he could finally catch a ball, and there hasn't been a similar incident since then."

Adults, like children, need to be reassured that the parents are seeking help in professional areas and that there is every hope for Johnny's ultimate rehabilitation. The stock phrase, "You know this problem didn't develop overnight; therefore, we can't expect it to disappear overnight," does much to put the entire subject into perspective. Again, a modest amount of help and support can be solicited: "If you see Johnny in an impossible situation, please call me at once. His judgment is not always sound, and I don't feel at all threatened by phone calls which alert me to signs of trouble. On the contrary, I am very grateful."

Once communication has been established with friends and neighbors, there is no need to belabor the subject. If further questions are forthcoming, of course they should be dealt with in honest and forthright fashion, but learning disabilities, like other family concerns, are more interesting and vital to the involved family than to anyone else and should not be dwelt on to the point of saturation or boredom. It should also be noted that sometimes one friendly ear in the neighborhood or circle of friends can be called on to do the required public relations job with other neighbors or friends, thus eliminating the need for the parent to explain the subject over and over again. The inherent danger in this approach lies in the realization that facts often get twisted in the telling, no matter how good the intentions, so perhaps first-hand transmittal of such critical information is, after all, the best course.

Doctors

How do you tell the family doctor that you know more on a specific subject than he does? This is often the case in the matter of learning disabilities, and the average parent who has been indoctrinated from childhood with awe of the medical profession often finds it difficult to proceed. Since doctors, like other people, tend to respect the view of their contemporaries within their profession, a well-written, informative article written by an M.D. may be the best answer. (See bibliography at the end of this chapter.) On the other hand, since one cannot always be sure that the material will be read, some eye-to-eye exchange is probably necessary. At such times, the parent may have to cultivate a thick skin and ignore the fact that there are fifteen people in the waiting room—not an easy thing to do!

Information put in the form of a question is sometimes easier for the professional man or woman to tolerate. Examples: (1) "Did you know that some doctors have been getting good results with (such and such a drug)?" (2) "Have you read the studies that show that most of these children do not outgrow their problems without specific remediation?" (3) "Knowing the other children in the family as well as you do, do you really thing that my husband or I are the cause of Johnny's problems?" (4) "Based on what you have observed, would you be willing to write an excuse to have Johnny excused from P.E.?" Of course, the parent must have done his homework and done it well so that he can present facts and figures if necessary.

If the doctor simply refuses to listen or to learn or to move with the problem, then it is time to look for another physician. Happily, in recent years the medical profession has become and is becoming more aware of the subject of learning disabilities. Yet pockets of ignorance still exist and will continue to exist, and the parent must be prepared either to enlighten or, if rebuffed, to seek services elsewhere. In dealing with any professional, if the parent will consider the fact that the ground-work he does with this person may bear fruit for other l.d. children who will follow, perhaps it will become easier for him to persevere in this important area of communication.

Doctors can also be alerted to relevant meetings, workshops, and conferences sponsored by groups of good reputation. They may not be willing to attend such meetings, but at least they will be made aware that attention is being focused on learning disabilities by dedicated, aware, intelligent people who are convinced that the problem will not disappear through maturity or benign neglect. Also, asking a doctor to serve as professional advisor in a group concerned with learning disabilities will help to bring him or her into the fold and establish strong lines of communication. It should be mentioned before leaving this precarious subject that should an encounter be made with a professional person who has an l.d. child in the family, the parent can do much to make contact and to disseminate useful information in the hope that it will be proliferated, resulting in substantial gain for increasing numbers of l.d. children.

Teachers

Communicating with teachers is an enormously complicated subject, encompassing as it does the broad spectrum of educators, including principals, superintendents, counselors, coaches, and school nurses. The parent can expect to encounter a wide span of awareness on the subject of learning disabilities—from enlightenment and eagerness to help and participate, to complete disavowal and disinterest. As a further complication, the situation may vary from year to year as the child moves from teacher to teacher.

The first premise which the parent must hold firmly in mind is that the child's progress or lack thereof in any academic year is in direct relation to the skill and understanding of his teacher. Each year is precious, and not a single one can be wasted. Therefore, it would seem inexcusable for a parent merely to wait out a year and hope that the next teacher will bring more insight to the problem.

The second premise is that parents must be willing to place in jeopardy their own reputations. Parents hate to be stigmatized as meddlers, and yet meddle they must. Parents hate to be categorized as complainers, yet complaints must be made. Parents hate to be labeled as troublemakers, but the trouble already exists, and what they are actually trying to do is "unmake" it. However, if meddling, complaining, criticizing, and suggesting are beamed toward the larger issues, and the parent is able to overlook minor matters, the net and long-range gains will be better and more quickly accomplished.

The total reeducation of an individual teacher or a faculty cannot be realized overnight. Indeed, this kind of comprehensive awakening may be better left to an organizational effort or to the teacher-training institutions. Nevertheless, the parent can stay alert to opportunities for pragmatic suggestions and in this way accomplish gradual philosophic inroads. The latter can once again be handled by providing suitable reading materials. (See bibliography.) The former depends on the needs of the child, although it is recommended that a positive approach be employed and that, when necessary, names be dropped or leverage be used. Examples: (1) "I noticed that Johnny's desk is in the back of the room. Dr. Smith has diagnosed auditory problems which means that Johnny needs to be as near to your desk as possible. Would you like me to have him call you about this?" (2) "We have just learned that Johnny suffers from hypoglocemia. Do you need a doctor's certificate to allow him to eat a midmorning snack?" (3) "Dr. Black is treating Johnny's visual problems and feels that for a time he should not be required to copy work from the chalkboard. Would you like my help in making duplicate copies of chalkboard assignments that he can use at his desk?" (4) "Dr. Jones feels that much of the physical education program is beyond Johnny unless he can work in a less competitive, less pressured environment. Can you manage that or would you like me to have him excused from physical education?" (5) "With Johnny's reading problems as acute as they are, it is embarrassing for him to have to read aloud in class. Is it necessary for me to get permission from the principal in order to have him read such assignments orally to me at home each evening?" Approaches such as these indicate credibility, reliability, determination, good preplanning, and confidence in the teacher to make a proper choice.

Once again, a private conversation with the teacher, carefully scheduled and planned, can break down many communication barriers. Frequently it is better to manage such a meeting away from the teacher's area of authority. Invite him or her to lunch at your home or at a pleasant restaurant and be sure that the tone of the conversation is authoritative without being overbearing. For example, "The subject of learning disabilities is enormous, and I don't pretend to know all about it. But I have been studying and reaching out in all directions for many months now and am fascinated by how much can be done for these children. Have you had time to read much on this subject yet? I've brought some books and articles which have been written by or for educators, and if you find them helpful, I hope you will pass them along to some other members of the faculty."

The parent must accept the fact that occasionally, for one reason or another, he will be rebuffed. Teachers feel threatened by this kind of intervention and may react with hostility. The best course of action in such cases is to resort to a higher authority and insist that the child be moved to another class. No popularity contests will be won when such strong measures are invoked, but that is of small consequence, and the ill will can be held to a minimum if the parent handles himself well. For example, "I know that what I am asking may be difficult and inconvenient, but every day, every week, every year is critical for Johnny. He is not happy in his present class placement because he realizes that he is not making progress, and it is my responsibility to insist that he be given an opportunity to succeed in another class. I have heard that Miss Green is interested in and works well with children with problems like Johnny's, and I should like to see Johnny placed in her class." Such comments must be altered to fit the individual predicament, but the parent must be careful to emphasize what is needed at this point rather than to criticize the personality or methods of Johnny's present teacher.

Eternal vigilance, positive recommendations for change, and a willingness to overlook minor mishaps of the same caliber as those shrugged off for "normal" children will stand the parents in good stead in dealing with educators at all levels.

Other Persons

Attention cannot possibly be given to all of the individuals who will pass through the life of the child, but a few examples may serve as a guide.

One of the problems likely to beset the family of the l.d. child is that of a suitable baby sitter. How do you find an individual who can handle several children, including one that is hyperactive, disruptive, and prone to temper tantrums? Few such paragons of virtue exist. The alternative is to hire two sitters, one to keep an eye on Johnny, his needs, and foibles, one to attend to the siblings. The sitter should be clearly informed as to what is required of Johnny and what is not: "Johnny finds it hard to get to sleep at night and may make several trips for a drink of water. Don't make an issue of it, and you will find that after half an hour or so, he will settle in for the night." Or "Johnny cannot yet cut his own meat. We do it for him in the kitchen before bringing his plate to the table." Or "If Johnny seems to be getting excited and strung out, ask him to pick out a favorite story and read to him for a few minutes. You will find that he will calm down at once." A little flattery (as well as an occasional small bonus) will work wonders toward holding on to a capable sitter: "We are so glad that we have you. Few people can handle Johnny as well as you do!"

As a rule, leaders of scout troops and other organizations need only to be advised of the nature of the handicap and concomitant behavior to insure their willingness to cooperate. However, if they seem baffled or incapable of handling Johnny at certain troublesome times, and if it seems important that the child be a member of that group, the parent can volunteer to serve as an assistant, at least for a time until the leader feels more comfortable. Within clubs, other children sometimes need to be called on for help and support, and the recommendations made for dealing with children in the neighborhood earlier in this chapter can be employed.

This, then, is what communication is all about—the need to cultivate the ability to open doors and minds and hearts to the plight and the problems of the l.d. child and his family. It will be helpful to take the long view, which holds the conviction that light focused on specific problems of specific children will add to the general knowledge and will serve all children well. Such an attitude on the part of parents is bound to increase their dedication, to stiffen their determination, and, quite simply, to ennoble the cause.

SUGGESTED READING LIST FOR FRIENDS, NEIGHBORS, AND RELATIVES

Ellingson, Careth. *The Shadow Children*. (Source: Topaz Books, 5 N. Wabash Avenue, Chicago, Illinois 60602.

Golick, Margaret. *A Parents' Guide to Learning Problems*. (Source: Quebec Association for Children with Learning Disabilities, P. O. Box 22, Cote St. Luc Postal Station, Montreal 29, Canada.)

Gordon, Sol. *The Brain Injured Adolescent*. (Source: New Jersey Association for Children with Learning Disabilities, 61 Lincoln Street, East Orange, New Jersey 07017.

Kratoville, B. L. *Death of Dilemma, Birth of Decision*. (Source: Texas Association for Children with Learning Disabilities, Resources and Publications, 430 Rose Arbor, Houston, Texas 77037.)

Kronick, Doreen. *They, Too, Can Succeed*. (Source: Academic Therapy Publications, 1539 Fourth Street, San Rafael, California 94901.)

Lewis, Richard S. *The Brain Injured Child*. (Source: The National Society for Crippled Children and Adults, 2023 West Ogden Avenue, Chicago, Illinois.)

_____. *The Other Child*. (Source: Grune and Stratton, New York, New York.)

McDonald, Eugene. *Understanding Parents' Feelings*. (Source: The National Society for Crippled Children and Adults, 2023 West Ogden Avenue, Chicago, Illinois.)

Olds, Sally. *Is There a Tornado in the House?* (Source: Today's Health, Nov., 1969, published by the American Medication Association.)

Smith, Bert Kruger. *Feelings are a Family Affair*. (Source: Texas Association for Children with Learning Disabilities, Resources and Publications, 430 Rose Arbor, Houston, Texas 77037.

Smith, Bert Kruger. *Your Non-Learning Child, His World of Upside-Down.* (Source: Beacon Press, Boston, Massachusetts.)

Woodward, Dan and Norma Biondo. *Living Around the Now Child.* (Source: Charles E. Merrill Publishing Company, Columbus, Ohio.)

SUGGESTED READING LIST FOR DOCTORS

Baldwin, Ruth et al. *The Doctor Looks at the Neurologically Handicapped Child, Diagnosis and Treatment.* (Source: California Association for Neurologically Handicapped Children, Resources, P. O. Box 1526, Vista, California 92803.

Bennett, E. Muriel. *The Pediatrician's Role in Evaluating the Child with a Learning Disability.* (Source: Academic Therapy Publications, 1539 Fourth Street, San Rafael, California 94901.)

Boder, Elena. *A Neuropediatric Approach to the Diagnosis and Management of School Behavioral and Learning Disorders.* (Source: Write the author at Special Child Publications, 71 Columbia Street, Room 320, Seattle, Washington 98104.)

Conwell, John. *The Role of Drug Therapy.* (Source: Texas Association for Children with Learning Disabilities, Resources and Publications, 430 Rose Arbor, Houston, Texas 77037.)

Dunn, Paul. *Child Development and Reading—a Pediatric Viewpoint.* (Source: Dallas Academy, 321 North Pearl Street, Dallas, Texas 75201.)

Hoffman, M. S. *Early Indications of Learning Problems.* (Source: Academic Therapy Publications, 1539 Fourth Street, San Rafael, California 94901.)

Sheve, Edward. *Some Factors of the Neurological Examination Indicating a Deficit and Interference Toward Learning Processes such as Reading and Writing.* (Source: Academic Therapy Publications, 1539 Fourth Street, San Rafael, California 94901.)

Solomons, Gerald, Anthony Davids and Harry Novack. *The Role of Medication in the Treatment of Learning Disabilities and Related Behavior Disorders.* (Source: California Association for Neurologically Handicapped Children, Resources, P. O. Box 1526, Vista, California 92083.)

Chapter 12:
Telling It Like It Is!

Betty Lou Kratoville

HELLO! Perhaps you are wondering why someone, probably one of your parents, has suggested that you read a chapter in a book which seems to have been written for adults. Usually books are written either for adults or for young people. Seldom are they written for both.

Books are written for many different reasons. Sometimes there is a story to be told; sometimes there is information to be given; sometimes there are experiences to be shared; many times people are just hoping to make money, and there is nothing wrong with that. Writing books is a very honorable way to make a living. You may want to try it some day!

This particular book has been written for a very special group of people—parents and teachers who live and work with young people who have learning problems, people like *you*. The people who wrote this book are parents who have lived with their own children with learning disabilities for many years and who have found that there are ways to help. Now they are eager to share their knowledge and their experience with other families— with *your* family!

When plans were being made about what to include in this book, one wise person said, "Why shouldn't we write a section for the young person? Maybe we can help him, too, and that would be beautiful because he is the most important person of all."

And that is a good place to start. Have you ever stopped to think that you are a very important person? You are! Not only are the people in your own family vitally interested in seeing that you have a happy, meaningful life, but there are adults throughout the world who are tremendously concerned with persons who have special problems. They believe with all their hearts that every human being in this world is important because every one of us has a shining contribution to make, each of us in his or her own way. These adults also know that some of the most famous people in the world began with handicaps or problems. Please believe this because it is true! Somewhere during the lives of these outstanding people, however, someone had confidence in them, someone helped, someone believed. And finally they learned to believe in themselves, and then there was nothing that they could not accomplish.

Of course, you have wondered why you, out of everyone in your family, happen to have learning disabilities. It doesn't seem fair that many things which seem easy for most people are so difficult for you. Perhaps you should stop to think just a moment about blind people or deaf people because they probably have exactly the same thought—why me? This is not really a very good question to ask because there is no answer and because even if there were, it wouldn't be helpful in solving any problems.

You have also probably wondered about *how* you happen to have learning disabilities. What caused them? Many different things can cause learning disabilities, but one fact is most important of all, and that is: YOU didn't cause them; it wasn't YOUR fault! And neither did your parents. Well, then, what did? Sometimes learning disabilities are caused by an injury to the brain before a baby is born or even during the time it is being born. Sometimes the lack of certain chemicals in the body can cause learning disabilities. Sometimes the reason for learning disabilities is that certain parts of the body do not work as well as they should—a pair of eyes that do not see things properly, a pair of ears that do not receive information properly, eyes and hands that do not work as well together as they should. Sometimes a serious childhood illness with a very high temperature can cause learning disabilities. But, once again, how it happened really isn't important. What is important is how we feel about ourselves. Right?

Many people with learning disabilities feel that they are dumb or stupid. Well, it just isn't so! Persons with such problems are just as smart as anyone else, sometimes a lot smarter, often a lot more talented. But it is true that such persons have to work harder than other people to learn, and sometimes special methods and materials have to be used to help them. There is nothing wrong with this either. Blind people have to use Braille in order to read, and deaf people often have to use hearing aids. These are simply special tools to aid in learning in spite of a handicap. How wonderful is this world where people have bothered to design or invent these special materials in order to help others.

Youngsters tend to call one another unfriendly names. They have done this for thousands of years, all over the world. When angry or upset, kids tend to lash out with words like "dummy" or "stupid." This is usually because they can't think of anything else to say or do, and because at that moment they are not in control of themselves. Such name calling is always hurtful, and in the case of a boy or girl with a learning disability, it is even more painful because they already have doubts about their own mental abilities. But just because someone says it doesn't make it so. As a rule, even the kid who says it knows it isn't so. The important thing is not to believe any foolish statements or labels that are hurled in the middle of an angry quarrel.

You will know that you are truly growing up when you begin to wonder about the kind of job you will be able to find when you become an adult. This is very normal. At an early age, little children begin to say things like, "When I grow up, I'm gonna be a fireman—or a nurse—or an astronaut." Most of the time, however, people do not choose a job or a profession until they are out of high school, many times until they are well into college or vocational training school. There is really no rush about this because the longer one waits, the better the decision is likely to be. People with learning disabilities, of course, are likely to be more worried than most. "What can I do when I grow up?" or "Who will want to hire me?" are questions that pop in and out of the mind at regular intervals. These words are written to be sure that you understand that you will certainly be able to find a job, and if you are prepared to put your heart and determination into it, you will be able to fill exactly the job that you want.

"What can I do when I grow up?" The answer is: many, many things. People with learning disabilities are often above average in artistic ability. Perhaps you can write, or paint, or create some kind of lovely music. Learning disabled persons are also often highly skilled in mechanical occupations of all kinds. It has been discovered that they also work very well with children, for they know how important it is to be a warm, understanding teacher. These are just a few examples, but it must be clearly understood that a learning disabled person, like everyone else, can do exactly what he wants to do if he is willing to work hard for his goal. Truly, the only serious limitations in this world are the ones we put on ourselves. If we think we can do it, we can!

Have you ever wondered about whether or not you will be able to marry and have children? Of course you have! The answer to this is, "Yes, most likely you will." It will, of course, depend on many things, such as your ability to give of yourself, to be unselfish, to stand fully on your own two feet, to be aware of all that marriage and having children involve. But when that time rolls around, you will have read much on the subject, you will have been counseled by teachers, doctors, and your parents, and you will be able to judge if and when you are ready for one of life's giant steps. (For a very good book on sex and marriage, we recommend *Facts About Sex for Exceptional Youth* by Dr. Sol Gordon.)

180

It is very unlikely that any of your children will be learning disabled. On the other hand, it will be wise to get the opinions of the medical profession before you decide to have children. This is a procedure that many adults are now following, whether or not there is a history of learning disabilities in the family. You should also be aware that it is the opinion of many experts that having been a learning disabled child makes one a wiser, more sympathetic human being, and hence, a better parent.

The fact that you are reading this chapter means that you have been a part of this world long enough to realize that there are many kinds of people. Some people are brilliant, others are slow and plodding; some are athletic, others are clumsy and uncoordinated; some are short and fat, others are tall and thin; some are warm and understanding, others are intolerant and quick to judge. You must be willing to recognize the fact that many people will make allowances for learning disabilities, will understand that not everyone can do everything equally well, will try to help in large and small ways. But you must also be ready to cope with those people who will not make allowances, who will not try to understand, who will make harsh judgments.

What can be done about such people? Sometimes not one single thing! At other times, an explanation may help. You should never feel that you have to make an apology, because you do not! An apology implies that you have done something wrong. An explanation, on the other hand, may help a person not only understand you a bit better but understand other children like you. It is perfectly acceptable to say, "I cannot do that very well because I have a learning disability. My parents and teachers are helping me, and I hope some day that I will be able to do it." Such a statement could cover many things: reading, writing, throwing a ball, swimming, dancing, sewing, or roller skating. Just be sure, however, that you do not use learning disabilities as an excuse for not trying a new or difficult activity.

Sometimes making friends and being with other young people is difficult for youngsters with learning disabilities because they are unsure of themselves. It might help you to know that almost everyone in this world is unsure of himself in certain situations. Even the cockiest youngster who always seems to know what to say and how to act has moments of uncertainty which he has learned to cover up. The best advice we can think of is this: be yourself, don't try to imitate other people, be natural, be as relaxed as possible, and don't try too hard. If you fail in some kind of social situation, as everyone does, you will probably feel bad for a while. That is perfectly natural. But don't let this keep you from trying again. Be interested in what other people have to say and do, be willing to praise and express admiration (not flattery), and, above all, use your sense of humor. It is not always easy to laugh at ourselves but it helps, and young people tend to warm toward other young people who can laugh and say, "Boy, I really messed that up!" or "Wow! I seem to have two left feet today!" In addition, they admire the person who is willing to try and try again to master a skill or activity. So hang in there and enjoy yourself!

It's wonderful to have friends, but much can also be said for solitary activities which give us time to think, dream, and get to know ourselves. If you like to read, grab a good book now and then and enjoy the pleasures to be found. If reading is not your thing, there are many hobbies which are exciting, and you may also make friends with people who enjoy the same hobby. Walking, bike riding, and exploring can also be very enjoyable pursuits when one feels like being alone.

We sincerely hope that this article hasn't sounded too "preachy." Nobody likes to be preached to—we certainly don't! We have written these pages because we really care, because we are convinced that you are a very special human being, and because we want to help. Everyone in this world needs help at one time or another, everyone needs to know that someone cares, everyone needs to feel worthwhile. Some day, we are sure, you will be the one who is giving the help, the sympathy, the advice.

In the meantime, remember, please, that you have much to do, much to enjoy, and much to give. Take each new day, each new experience, and try to drink deeply of the beauty, the fun, and the joy of just being alive. Never forget, you are you, there is no one else in the world like you, and that is the most beautiful thought of all!

Chapter 13:
Maximizing the
School Experience

THERE IS a little girl in your classroom who is quiet and well behaved, but she does not learn. You have a little boy in your room who squirms, falls out of his seat, fidgets, calls out when he should be quiet, and also is doing poorly academically. You have students who forget class assignments; when you give them homework, they forget to do it or take home the wrong books. You have students who experience difficulty relating the rules they have learned from one assignment to the next. There are youngsters in your class who cannot print or write neatly, who draw primitively, and who are clumsy. You have pupils who repeat themselves, youngsters who will not try anything that they feel is difficult, children who become easily frustrated, who lose interest quickly, who answer questions beautifully yet cannot write them on paper, students who spell poorly, read poorly, or have trouble with arithmetic. You have pupils who are friendless and students whose clothing never looks neat.

When I attended school it was assumed that these children were stupid, disturbed, unmotivated, had a poor home life, or needed more discipline. These factors may be behind the behavior of a few of your students; however, others may not learn because they never have found a reason to learn. Whatever the etiology, we do know that from 8 to 20 percent of the children in our classrooms experience specific problems in learning.

But we should not be eager to label these problem learners in the classroom as "disabled." Many of these children are neither slow learners nor emotionally disturbed. They are products of every conceivable home environment. Their problems range from mild to severe, and since many of us experience the same deficits that affect these children, it is arbitrary to suggest the point at which a "normal" person ends and "learning disabled" person begins. In addition, we should consider the fact that a child who is handicapped in one environment may function adequately in another setting. Perhaps your problem learner has encountered poor teaching at some stage of his school career, or spent a year with a teacher whose techniques suited some of the students well, yet failed to meet his needs. Perhaps he was expected to sit at a desk and execute fine-motor work before he was ready developmentally. Whatever the reason for his current difficulties, it is more important to *isolate his areas of deficit functioning and work with them* than it is to saddle him with a label which will follow him throughout his school career.

Labels may not only divert us from discovering the child's real needs, they also create tremendous anxiety in parents and isolate the child as being different in the community. Children model themselves to our expectations, and if we supply the child with the message that he is handicapped, he will live up to our expectations and be handicapped.

Why, then, have I written this book about the l.d. and set them apart as different? Unfortunately, our institutions are structured on a premise of conformity rather than individuality, and unless one has a "tag," one rarely receives the help he requires. However, no lay person is in a position to "tag" a child as being learning disabled—or with any other label. It is a skilled diagnostic procedure, usually requiring the services of an educational psychologist.

Similarly, you, the teacher, cannot be expected to differentiate between emotional disturbance, learning disabilities, lack of motivation, or poor home life. What you can do is handle the presenting behavior without being judgmental. You also can ask yourself what the child is attempting to tell you by his behavior. When does Gary become hyperactive? Is it when he is expected to handle a seat-work assignment at which he feels inadequate? Is Jane withdrawing because she cannot understand or remember what you have said?

One of the most effective methods we can utilize towards helping children with learning problems is to discard our preconceived notions of how things have to be done, or what must be accomplished in our classroom. If it is compulsory that a child complete three units of arithmetic in the academic year, Paul may remain in the same classroom forever. That would be a pity because he knows everything about snakes and the life histories of the composers of nearly every symphony that has been written. If Mark must sit quietly in his seat for three hours every morning and two and one-half hours every afternoon, he may never progress past grade two.

Many children with learning problems understand the history or science lesson you have taught—and you are aware of this understanding by their questions and responses—yet they fail their tests because the quality of their written answers is poor, or they have not comprehended the questions or understood which answer you wished for those questions, or their spelling, language usage, and organization were atrocious. A child may have difficulty expressing himself orally, and even more trouble expressing himself on paper, yet understand the content of the lesson you have taught.

Some children are penalized for their sloppy writing or printing, yet you are aware that they cannot write more neatly.

Some children cannot work as quickly as others, yet teachers seem to think that allowing more time to complete an assignment would constitute preferential treatment.

Educators tend to gauge progress by class or grade expectations rather than individual progress. Therefore, a child might be showing considerable gain in terms of his own development, yet the school classifies him as a failure.

We expect a child with a five-minute interest span to complete a half-hour assignment. Would the world fall apart if we gave him four five-minute assignments instead of one twenty-minute assignment to which he could devote only five minutes of concentrated effort?

I realize that most of you teachers have classes of thirty or more children, that you are hampered by demands from many quarters, and additionally handicapped by the scarcity of diagnostic and remedial help. You cannot be expected to, nor should you, diagnose and establish a remedial program on your own. However, the reality of the situation is that the majority of l.d. children spend some or all of their school years in the "normal" classroom, which is as it should be, and virtually every classroom in North America has one or more l.d. students. It is the teachers of the "normal" classrooms who will make or break these children. Either you can continue to try to fit the l.d. child into the standard educational molds and he will continue to elude them, or you can individualize your approach and begin to reach the child at his level.

The first step is honesty. I do not know why we have been frightened of being honest with kids. Perhaps you need to say, "I'm sorry John, I think that I have been approaching you the wrong way. Let's try this." He should know that you are human and fallible.

The next step in individualizing the approach is to analyze the areas in which the child is failing or running into difficulty. Warren became unmanageable each time the children lined up to leave the classroom. His teacher was beside herself until the consultant suggested that Warren leave a few minutes before his classmates. The l.d. child generally does not possess the flexibility to find a way around his difficulties, so he continues to bang his head against the brick wall. The adults who work and live with this child must supply the alternatives. When the environment offers no alternatives, the child is in trouble. Then you, the teacher, would have to ask yourself why you are unable to be flexible. The following suggestions may be used in providing the child with alternatives and will be helpful in individualizing the approach.

Individualize His Space

Perhaps you have a student who always is misbehaving. He does his best work when you put his desk in the hall or send him to the principal's office to work. He is telling you that he cannot handle seatwork in your classroom under the present structure. You may have to modify his working environment. Perhaps he could bring a pillow or throw rug from home and leave it at the back of the classroom. Whenever he feels that he would work better sitting or lying on the pillow or rug, he would be free to do so. Possibly he could work more comfortably if he were shielded from the other distractions in the room by a screen. Discuss the various possibilities with him and determine the method he would like to try.

Individualize His Time

With another child it might be necessary to determine *when* he learns best and reserve his most difficult assignments for that time. If he is restless when he enters the classroom each morning, each afternoon, and after each recess, that may be a good time for him to sharpen your pencils or run errands. You know how some of us are morning people and some of us function much better in the evening, well children are the same way, and we have to respect their body clocks.

Help Him To Understand The Temporal Organization of The School Day

If he can be helped to feel when recess, lunch time, and the end of the school day arrive, he will be more comfortable functioning within a familiar structure. Tell him the sequence of activities the group will undertake in each of those time blocks. Structure the day for him in terms of events instead of hours of the day.

Structure Changes

On days when your class routine will be changed, describe the change to him. Take the time to explain to him what is happening, and why you have made the change. If you are embarking on an outing, describe the forthcoming event to him step-by-step. If a guest is coming to the classroom, tell him about the person, where he will sit, and what he is likely to do.

Establish A Relationship With Him That Will Be Conducive To Learning

The l.d. person has suffered assaults to his self-esteem from early infancy, so that continued negative reinforcement will cause him to resist or withdraw. If he is to learn, you must provide him with activities at which he can succeed, however elementary, and proceed to more difficult ones until he is sufficiently secure to risk some small failures. If he feels good about his accomplishments, and feels that he is competent and skilled at some things, he will be prepared to invest himself in greater challenges.

Remember: Success Generalizes and Failure Generalizes

If you have him succeeding, he will continue to do so, and conversely, if he feels he is a failure, he will program for failure.

Determine The Best Way He Learns

Some of us learn better by seeing, some by listening, some by feeling, and some by a combination of approaches. You know that some people can attend a lecture and remember the contents well, whereas others are more able to remember the things they read. Does the child remember the pictures he has seen, the contents of the material he has read, or how the words he has seen are spelled? Some children reinforce their weaker sensory channel by utilizing a multisensory approach, whereas others are overloaded by this system and do better if they learn through their most functional sensory system, that is, functional in terms of organization and memory.

Many of these children do well if they are provided with short assignments with immediate feedback. If your student concentrates well only for three minutes, provide him with a series of three-minute tasks with a break between each. If he can do only one arithmetic question correctly, give him one only, and after he has succeeded at that for several days, increase the number to two, and so on. If he does only the first one or two questions on a page correctly, it may be that his attention is caught by all the material on the page and he would do better with a series of individual questions, each on its own page. The extra work in preparation probably would be tackled gladly by the child's parent the night previous to the assignment, or, failing that, a classmate, older student, or volunteer could undertake the mechanical preparation.

Initially establish only a few modest goals, academic or behavioral. Develop with him the ways you will attempt to reach those goals and involve him in ideas on how he would like to approach his learning tasks.

Make Learning Worthwhile for Him

Some children never learn because they have not found any reason for learning. If they are to learn, there must be a payoff. Whether the payoff is reinforcement of correct answers, rewards for genuine effort or improvement, or material that is relevant and exciting to them, we must find a way to involve them. Whenever Ian associated the letter *b* with the "b" sound, we shook his hand and that was his payoff, immediate and fun. Another child's payoff might be a star, verbal appreciation, a special privilege, or acquiring knowledge in his special area of interest.

Help Him To Feel That You Are On His Side

He needs to feel that you are aware of his difficulties and are prepared to involve him in ways to overcome them. You need to be realistic in the demands you make of such a child, but once the demands are made, you must be firm and consistent. He may test your demands initially, but he needs the security of knowing you can be counted upon. You should not be judgmental about or overreact to his behavior. The l.d. child is particularly sensitive to others' reactions to him, and he needs to feel that although his personal control is flimsy, outsiders will not lose control in response to him. He needs the security of knowing that you will not allow him to remain out of control.

If he has become too upset or overstimulated, he needs a place in the school where he can retreat in order to calm down. Initially you may have to take him there, but you should work toward helping him to recognize when he is becoming overloaded and to make the retreat himself. This should not be viewed as punishment; rather, it is a recognition of his needs, an accommodation to his sensitivity to stress, his propensity to become overstimulated by auditory and visual stimuli, and his low frustration point.

An Answer Is An Answer

Rather than react to the *way* the child has organized his written or oral response, your one criterion in marking him right or wrong should be whether or not he knows the answer. Thus the child who writes 6 + 6 = 21 or 5 − 2 = Ɛ knows the answer and should be appropriately awarded. His reversal problems should be dealt with as a separate issue, and since one can safely assume that no child would reverse numbers or words if he realized the direction they should go, we should not penalize him when he does.

The child who gives a garbled oral or written response still may demonstrate that he knows the answer, and that should be acknowledged. Then you can work with him on organizing his spoken and written language. Sometimes a child will converse more effectively on a topic if he is looking at the object, or holding it, or looking at a picture of it. Help him structure his oral language by asking him what happened first, next, and so on. Perhaps he could give himself the required structure by taping the events of an outing sequentially or writing them in diary form. Teach him what you want in a written answer, project, or assignment. Help him structure it on the page, discuss content and, with his help, draw up a homework schedule, being very specific about the amount of time he will spend on each assignment, and the time of day he will tackle it. Inform the parents of the schedule that you and the child have drawn up so that they can help him abide by the system.

Determine The Complexity Of Tasks He Can Handle

If you sat your class group in a circle and rolled a ball to each child randomly, most could roll it back adeptly. Then if you asked each child to say his name before he rolled the ball back, a few would fumble. If you then asked each child to state his name and the name of the child two removed from him, several more would fumble. Or, if you gave a child a simple arithmetic question, he might provide the correct answer readily. However, if you asked him to clap his hands and touch his head before answering, the complexity of the demand may have rendered him inoperant. Perhaps you have noticed how some of your students cannot tie their shoes and answer you simultaneously.

Have you realized the multiplicity of task development required before a child can write a composition? He needs to develop an idea, remember it, organize it sequentially, and write it neatly, which is a complex fine-motor demand, as well as translate the thought from his mind into a symbol system which is executed by an extension of his hand, and employ accepted spelling, language usage, and punctuation. If he is failing at the assigned task, simplify it until you have found the level at which he can cope. If he cannot handle an essay, perhaps he could write a few good sentences. Failing that, perhaps he could write one good sentence, tape a story, or tell it orally. Allow him to use concrete materials for mathematics as long as he needs to, even into secondary school. The child who counts on his fingers needs that reinforcement, as does the child who reads with his finger under the word.

The latter child might do well with a piece of cardboard placed under the line he is reading.

Provide Him With Materials On His Level

If you expect him to cope with the same materials as his classmates and he cannot, you are encouraging him to copy and cheat. Being forced to work with materials with which he cannot cope creates the most devastating feelings of incompetence, impotence, and fear of the consequences, so that the child resorts to subterfuge. Since he already knows that he is different from his classmates, providing him with material on his level does not make him aware that he is different. Conversely, it tells him that you are aware of his needs and are prepared to accommodate them. Select material that does not have a grade level printed on it.

Don't Say, "You Can Do The Work If You Only Try"

Avoid this and other equally unproductive comments. Although the child may be highly intelligent, at this point in time he cannot produce more efficiently. He and his parents have been the recipients of countless such comments throughout his school career, just as they have been victims of the "red pencil treatment." Let's work on helping him feel organized and confident enough to do a bit better, and cease talking about his supposed potential.

Don't Talk Too Much, He May Tune You Out

Many of these children experience much difficulty processing and remembering ongoing language. In addition, they have lived through years with nagging parents and other adults, so that in order to preserve their sanity, they tune out on volumes of language. Some experience difficulty separating critical and noncritical words from speech, and many do not comprehend a number of the words in our language. Speak simply and briefly. Try to determine whether his difficulties with mathematics stem from problems in computation or the language surrounding the questions. Simplify the language of some questions as much as you can, and see how he then handles his math.

Teach Him To Read If You Possibly Can

Some children learn best phonetically, some visually, and some with a combination approach. Some relate best to meaningful material and some respond to nonsense material. He needs to feel that it is worthwhile for him to read; write "fun" notes to him and notes about coming events. Have his parents encourage him to read the slogans on television, in magazines, on packages and billboards so that he will realize how much he already can read. Have him make a list of the words he can read, such as "Coca Cola." Have him hang the list in the kitchen at home and add to it as he learns new words. If he learns to read, he will have acquired the single most critical academic skill, and he also will have a tool which you can utilize to encourage further teaching by way of written assignments and programed learning.

Allow Him His Props

If he needs to fidget or chew gum in order to establish a rhythm whereby he can work or release energy and anxiety, we should allow him and his classmates this expression of individuality.

Establish A Tutorial Community

Possibly some of his classmates or older students in the school can work with him in his deficient areas, and he, in turn, can assist others in his areas of strength. Possibly he could teach a lesson about snakes or composers.

Be Honest With Him

Acknowledge his reality. If his output is poor, do not praise it. If his behavior is inappropriate, do not reward it. If he has tried, acknowledge his effort. If we relate to kids with honesty and sensitivity, neither denying their problems nor penalizing them for that which they cannot help, they will respond to our acceptance and honesty.

Don't Destroy Him In The Peripheral Subjects

In anticipation of the impossible demands they will face in the gym, the shop, or the sewing room, many l.d. children dread the entire school day. Their poor spatial organization, memory, and coordination mean that they cannot hit, kick, or aim the ball with accuracy, cannot read a blueprint or sewing pattern, cannot hammer a straight nail or sew a straight line. However, they desperately need the exercise and practice in coordination that a physical education program can provide. The demands in all these subject areas should be geared to the child's level.

The physical education program should be geared to individual development rather than be focused on competitive teams. The latter provide practice for the athletic students who do not require such practice, and they exclude the uncoordinated and the unfit who could benefit from the program, and who need the esteem of inclusion. Children who experience difficulty learning written symbols also may have trouble with decoding musical notes. Allow them to participate in a music program on their level. They need practice in rhythm, concepts of high, low, loud, soft, and the spacing and timing of music.

Sit Him Near the Front of the Classroom

This will reduce distractions and allow the child who has trouble processing ongoing speech to look at the teacher, or the child who has trouble processing visual material to be near the blackboard. When you speak to him, make certain that you are standing directly in front of him and that he is facing you and attending to what you have to say. If attention is a problem, hold his face in your hands or place your hands on his shoulders while you are speaking to him. When you talk to the class, stand in front of his desk as much as possible.

Include the Parents In Your Planning

Parents of the l.d. feel very threatened by the school. School may be the place where their child's problems first appeared. They have been the recipients of report cards, notes, and phone calls, all containing bad news about their child's progress and behavior. They live in constant fear that their child will be removed to the slow-learner stream or the class for the disturbed.

The parents are probably just as baffled, thwarted, and ashamed at their child's behavior as you are. If you assure them that you want to work with their child without deciding that all his problems are caused by his parents and former teachers, which you will rectify, chances are that you will find the parents more than cooperative. Share with them the approaches that you and the child have evolved to tackle his difficulties, and solicit their assistance. Plumb them for insights into the child which would assist you in planning for him. Tell them the techniques that you have found have worked with their child and how they might apply them to home management.

Encourage the parents to reinforce formal learning with nonacademic learning. This learning can come about through assembling models, cooking, and outings. Teach the parents the areas in which the child requires reinforcement and how that can be incorporated into everyday life.

Teach Parents How to Simplify Activities and Demands

If the child cannot remember several commands, perhaps he can remember and execute one or two. If he cannot tie his shoelaces, perhaps he can begin by learning to tie a large knot using a rope or sash. Teach them how to break down the negotiable skills the child needs to learn in order to socialize with the neighborhood children—skills such as baseball, ice skating, and bicycle riding.

Encourage Him to Join Social Groups

If he is a loner, he may do best within the structure of a non-competitive club or group organized around a special interest. Steer him and his parents to resources such as this. If he is socially happy, he will be more receptive to learning.

Establish the Mood

Your nondisabled students can participate in a noisy, exciting game, or share a raucous joke, yet follow this stimulation by quiet seat work. However, the l.d. child tends to have difficulty changing moods and may continue to be active and noisy after his classmates have settled down. You may decide to limit his stimulating class activities to just before recess or noon and after school breaks. Work moods can be established by using a quiet voice, soothing music, and putting an arm around the child.

Plan His Time and Keep Him Busy

Many l.d. children do not use their time productively and will require your assistance in planning what they are to do throughout the school day. You may have to keep him personally busy rather than allow him to listen to or observe the work of others. At times his hyperactivity or noise may signify boredom or confusion concerning what he is supposed to be doing. Encourage him to tell you what is bothering him rather than leave him to withdraw or act up when he becomes anxious or confused.

There Is No Simple Cure For a Learning Disability

The technique that works miracles for one child will be a disaster for the next. A variety of approaches must be attempted before you discover the ones which are workable. The l.d. child will be able to master a task one day, yet not comprehend it the next. He may demonstrate periods of rapid growth along with plateaus. If he is well-motivated because he feels good about himself, he will work very hard to succeed. The l.d. person possesses areas of adequate to superior intelligence, and his deficits generally respond well to remediation, though they remain the weaker areas of functioning throughout his life. If he is not coping well, the problem may be his mode of learning, your mode of teaching, or a combination of both. However, it is pointless to expend energy looking for someone to blame; rather, it is critical to attempt to find ways whereby he can learn.

Before l.d. children were diagnosed and understood within the schools, they were the illiterates, the semiliterates, the dropouts, the unskilled, the unemployed, and the disturbed. Now that many of them are receiving the remedial assistance and the flexible educational approach that they require, they are progressing through secondary school and, in a number of instances, on to post-secondary education. Every one of their teachers plays a critical role in their development; they tend to blossom under an understanding teacher and wilt under those who are rigid. Remember that the achieving student generally will prosper regardless of the teacher's approach, but if you can reach the nonachiever, you may have altered the direction of his life.

SUGGESTED READING LIST FOR TEACHERS

Anderson, Lauriel. *Helping the Adolescent with the Hidden Handicap.* (Source: Academic Therapy Publications, 1539 Fourth Street, San Rafael, California 94901.)

Ashlock, Patrick, and Alberta Stephen. *Educational Therapy in the Elementary School.* (Source: Charles C. Thomas, Springfield, Illinois.)

Kephart, Newell. *The Brain Injured Child in the Classroom.* (Source: The National Society for Crippled Children and Adults, 2023 West Ogden Avenue, Chicago, Illinois.)

McCarthy, Jeanne McRae. *How to Teach the Hard to Reach.* (Source: Teachers Publishing Corporation, Darien, Connecticut 06820.)

Schloss, Ellen. *Educator's Enigma: Adolescent with Learning Disabilities.* (Source: Academic Therapy Publications, 1539 Fourth Street, San Rafael, California 94901.)

Siegal, Ernest. *Special Education in the Regular Classroom.* (Source: John Day Company, New York, New York.)

Waits, Lucius. *Specific Dyslexia and Related Language Disabilities.* (Source: Texas Scottish Rite Hospital for Crippled Children, Dallas, Texas.)

Wearne, Carol. *Tips for Teachers.* (Source: Association for Children with Learning Disabilities, 2200 Brownsville Road, Pittsburgh, Pennsylvania 15210.)

Woodward, Dan and Norma Biondo. *Living Around the Now Child.* (Source: Charles E. Merrill Publishing Company, Columbus, Ohio.)

Part Four

Recreation and Camping
for the Learning Disabled

Chapter 14:

For Recreation Administrators and Leaders

IT IS ONLY in the past few years that we have seen the beginning of diagnosis of l.d. children. Previous to that time it was assumed that they were disturbed, retarded, lazy, or underachievers. Now that we know who they are, we have devoted our energies to finding ways to assist them, and it is now known that recreation can play a central role in the rehabilitation of such children.

Learning-disabled persons are those who possess areas of adequate functioning along with areas of deficit functioning. However, the latter tend to respond to specific remedial assistance and, in many instances, improve considerably. Learning-disabled persons have normal or above intellectual capacity although, because of their disabilities, may experience much difficulty handling academic work, difficulty in small and large muscle coordination, and in processing language. They may be hyper- or hypoactive, easily frustrated, have a short interest span, be inflexible, illiterate, disorganized, repetitive, and overrespond to stress, excitement, or stimuli.

Recreation agencies have found that they can provide effective services to this population, and I have written this section of the book to make an initial attempt to deal with some of the issues involved in serving the l.d. in this context.

Recreation is essential for all persons and a critical need for the l.d. Nondisabled persons generally can develop their own recreational pursuits, finding their own friends, activities, and hobbies. Conversely, many of the l.d. do not know how to make friends or avail themselves of community facilities. They have suffered failure in school and on the street, so they need very much to feel that they are successful, contributing members of a group. Recreation can provide them with opportunities wherein they can become proficient in skills and develop satisfactory relationships with contemporaries and adults. The acquisition of adult social skills is built upon the sequence of social experiences the l.d. child acquires from his peers from early childhood onward. He needs to be part of the games, secrets, tasks, interests, patterns of dress, and habits of his contemporaries. Recreation can begin to satisfy some of these basic needs.

When an administrator of a recreation agency is approached by a parent or other person to start a program for the l.d., he should consider the following questions.

Should You Start a Segregated Program?

Sometimes persons in the community are so desirous of starting a program that they may not have considered whether there is a real need for such a program. You should determine what programs for the l.d. already are in existence in the city, how the recreation needs of the l.d. currently are being met, and whether the existing programs are functioning to capacity. You need to determine whether the population you are being asked to serve requires a segregated program or whether they would function adequately in an integrated setting. You must ascertain whether the proposed program is the one that the intended population desires.

There are several issues involved in deciding whether a program should be segregated or integrated, some of which deal with the agency's resources and some of which center around the child.

Agency Considerations

1. Staff-child ratio, staff age, maturity, previous experience, expertise.
2. Possibilities of augmenting the staff-child ratio through use of volunteers, paid staff, parents.
3. Competence of supervisory staff and frequency of supervisory sessions.
4. Flexibility of program in provision of alternatives to ensure success.
5. Commitment of supervisor to succeed.

Serious consideration must be given to the possible detrimental effects of operating a segregated program in a general recreation agency. Are we once again repeating the "dummy" class model by setting these youngsters apart in a special group?

Considerations for the Child

Some children, in different stages of their development, will function at one time better in a segregated setting—at another time in an integrated setting. One child might need a segregated program to develop social and behavioral skills to handle his interaction with nonhandicapped persons. Another child might cope with nondisabled friendships until, with age, his social demands become increasingly complex and he needs to return to a more sheltered experience. Most typically, l.d. children can handle integrated interaction throughout their life-span, with the provision of a few safeguards. The following points should be considered before you decide whether the child should be in a segregated or integrated program:

1. Appropriateness of his social and behavioral skills.

2. The disparity between his age-related expectations and actual functioning.

3. The amount of neighborhood street play in which the child participates and the extent of other nonhandicapped friendships.

4. His attention span—how long can he remain with an activity?

5. His ability and willingness to follow directions.

6. His ability to comprehend organized and unorganized games and his skill in playing them.

7. His ability to delay gratification.

8. The extent to which he is outgoing and self-assured.

9. Whether he enjoys new experiences and handles himself well at those times.

10. His motivation—whether he will attempt something he perceives as difficult and remain with the task.

A general rule is that a child who is likely to function in nonhandicapped society in adulthood should join an integrated program, or, if he enrolls in a segregated program, his placement there should be viewed as transitional. Most l.d. children will function in nonhandicapped society so that any efforts made toward building their social skills with their nonhandicapped peers will provide them with the building blocks for "normal" functioning. Agencies should consider offering a continuum of services from segregated to integrated, with the former feeding into the latter.

Parent Expectations of Recreation

Parents of exceptional children are so anxious for their youngsters to be cured that they have expectations of great improvement, even from a recreation program. That is why they try to encourage recreation agencies to institute gross- and fine-motor programs.

Parents also expect that their children will act normally in each new situation and they are afraid to tell recreation personnel about their children lest they be excluded from the program. Thus they tend not to share much information on their children with the agency, so as not to prejudice their opportunities for enrollment or for being treated like "normal" people. In addition, they often do not have much information on their offspring because some medical and paramedical practitioners do not share such information with parents. The parents, in turn, are unaware of what kinds of information they should share with a recreation agency, so they may not be too helpful.

The agency has a responsibility, then, to clarify for parents the type of information that they would find helpful. They also should tell the parents the number of times they will be contacting them about their child's progress, and whether this will be alone or with a group of parents. Tell the parents your ground rules as well as your expectations of them.

Should the Program Have Therapeutic Elements?

Throughout the U.S.A. and Canada gross- and fine-motor groups have been started for the l.d. in hundreds of recreation agencies. Generally speaking, the population that enrolled in these groups had not been preassessed to determine whether gross- and fine-motor therapy would be of benefit to them or whether, in fact, they already were receiving such therapy. Rarely are their specific motor disabilities predetermined so that a differentiated program directing itself to their deficits could be established. Most typically, a very general gross-motor group is initiated, the children are enrolled solely on their parent's stated need for the group, the program is not coordinated with the other therapies the child is receiving, and it is staffed partially or only by volunteers who have minimal background in such therapies. Whenever a program has a title which implies therapy, the parents have expectations that the disability will be alleviated, and they also have expectations that the program will provide companionship and social learning for their lonely children. Unfortunately, a program that does not have a well-planned remedial or social rationale is likely to do a minimal job of meeting either expectation. Agencies have to ask themselves whether they morally wish to be responsible for programs that hold out the promise of therapeutic improvement.

Before an agency embarks on a therapeutic program, it should take the same steps that I suggested precede the establishment of a segregated recreation program. They must determine whether there is an actual need or whether it is merely presumed, generated by the parents' anxieties. Are the children uncoordinated? Are they receiving gross-motor therapy in their school program or elsewhere? Are they so handicapped that even if their motor skills were improved, there likely would be no improvement in academic or overall functioning? Does the agency have the resources to run a quality therapeutic program? Should the children use their recreation time receiving therapy or are there other ways in which the time more profitably could be spent?

Leslie is a brain-injured retarded boy who attends a special education class. Every Saturday he attends a remedial program for three hours where he receives academic remediation and motor therapy. Additionally, Leslie's mother and two other mothers of multiply handicapped children convinced their local "Y" to initiate gross- and fine-motor groups for their supposedly l.d. children. This meant that Leslie and several other children were involved in at least three lengthy therapeutic sessions weekly, in addition to the special education assistance they received in school. Two occupational therapists and one physical education teacher were hired to run the gross- and fine-motor groups, presumably for l.d. children. They were left to their own devices in rooms each of which held twelve youngsters whom they had not previously met, and who displayed relatively severe degrees of mental illness or mental retardation. Needless to say, the programs were off to a rocky beginning.

When a recreation agency determines that there is a genuine need for a therapeutic program and they are able to benefit the recipients by filling that need, the agency should:

1. Have on their part-time staff a psychologist or consultant in special education who will be able to obtain detailed diagnostic information on the child, peruse other programs the child is receiving, and devise an individualized program that complements his current program or fills in some gaps.

2. Examine the child's current program to determine whether he is receiving enough and the right kind of remediation, and whether his spare time would best be spent this way.

3. Maintain contact with the child's home and school to ensure that the program is part of a total approach.

What Type of Recreation Program Should We Initiate?

Ask for a meeting of the parents whose children will be participants in a proposed program and, if the prospective clients are eleven years of age or older, meet with them as well. Determine what the parents and children would like to see in a program, and what periods of the week the children have free to devote to the program. Tell them the resources your agency can offer and determine how they can augment them (by their own time, money, facilities, etc.). Talk about the needs they feel that such a program will meet, and, if their expectations are too high, share with them your goals for the program, for example, companionship, acquisition of independence skills, and fun. It is best to underplay your goals rather than create expectations which you might not fulfill. Tell the parents your criteria for enrollment and for remaining in the program.

In my experience the desired social learning is most readily acquired in a club program or a group organized around a specific interest. Whatever program you decide to run, it should be well structured, with minimum competition and the maximum involvement of each member.

Should The Segregated Program Serve Only The Learning Disabled?

If your agency's prime orientation is that of recreation, you probably do not have a psychologist or special education teacher on the staff. Consequently, you will not have access to psychological information so that you will have no method of determining whether the population you intend to serve are l.d. in the strict definition of the term. Many parents think that their children are l.d. when, in reality, they are other-handicapped.

If your group has therapeutic goals you may want to select a relatively pure population of l.d. children and then will have to make provision to obtain diagnostic information. However, if your program has recreation goals, you likely have no choice but to establish social and behavioral requisites for attendance rather than restrict your intake to a specific exceptionality. If the proposed program aspires to a fair degree of sophistication, you may wish to establish a base line of functioning so that children who cannot maintain the pace are referred to less demanding programs. Your agency will have to deal with the issues of whether there is validity in offering a recreation program only to the l.d., whether inclusion of other exceptional children would harm the self-image of the l.d., and whether or not children suffering from other exceptionalities could derive equal benefit from the program. If you decide to opt for behavioral criteria rather than serving a specific label, you likely will have to deal with the parents' concerns that children suffering from other exceptionalities are in the group.

Intake

Whether you are screening children for a segregated or integrated program, the leader and the supervisor should have an opportunity to meet the child before the program begins. This allows the staff an opportunity to become acquainted with the prospective clients, to develop an idea of the children's needs, developmental level, interests, and aspirations. It allows them to redirect the occasional child who is not ready to handle the proposed program to a less demanding or more protected setting, rather than enroll him and have him fail. It provides the child with the opportunity to meet the adults with whom he will be interacting, and to familiarize himself with the building and the meeting room. The leader should describe some of the intended activities to the youngster as well as structure the first meeting in detail for him.

Ask the child and parents about the things the child does well, the things he enjoys doing, and what he would like to do. Determine whether there are any medical conditions requiring special care, such as epilepsy, hypoglycemia, asthma, or allergies. Ask the parent and, if necessary, the physician, about the child's diet, whether the child should ride bicycles, horses, etc., and whether there is any danger of seizures in other specific recreational activities. Determine whether there are any physical limitations on the activities of any of the children. If there are any children with medical conditions of a serious nature, it is a wise precaution to obtain the telephone number of the home, father's office, one or two relatives, the physician, and hospital. Inform your insurance agent of the type of child you are serving in your program and the professional persons you have on your staff who are skilled in handling such children.

Staffing

Therapeutic programs in recreation agencies should be staffed by one or two persons who are intimately familiar with the therapeutic techniques used with the l.d. They can be augmented by less well-trained staff or volunteers. Segregated or integrated recreation programs can be staffed by untrained persons, but there should be an advisor who has a thorough background in l.d. and recreation. The leaders should be sufficiently mature that they do not feel that the children's behavior is a reflection of their ability as leaders, and sufficiently young that they are energetic and flexible without preconceived ideas on how children should behave. They should be good models for the children to emulate. The staff should make a commitment to attend sessions regardless of other conflicting demands such as college exams, and to remain with the program for the season or the year.

Supervision and Support of Staff

The leaders who work with the l.d. will be functioning under a degree of strain so that they should receive supervision on a regular basis from someone who is familiar with learning disabilities, with recreation, and with the particular children you are serving. This supervision should have a heavy emphasis on support and direction. Persons who are faced with handicapped individuals initially may react with fright. Their concerns about their ability to cope and their feelings of rejection need to be recognized rather than denied. If they receive sufficient support to continue working with the child for several sessions, once they learn to know him, their fears usually dissipate. The leaders should be apprised of the availability of crisis personnel and the resources they can mobilize if the child requires additional assistance, becomes upset, or needs to be removed from the group.

Volunteer and Leader Training

The following are some of the points which you might cover in leader training:

1. Provide a general background in l.d., its manifestations, a description of the l.d. child, his problems, his strengths, and what we might do for him in a recreation program. This orientation should be concerned only with the knowledge that the leaders will need in order to provide a good experience for the children and therefore should avoid issues such as etiology and complex psychological guesses as to why the children act the way they do. Similarly, the leaders should be discouraged from playing the "Freud game" themselves.

2. Goals for your program and how these goals might be implemented.

3. How to structure, how to break down a task.

4. What behavior tells us and how we can deal with it.

5. How to establish realistic demands and expectations without under- or overestimating the child's capabilities.

6. Support versus overprotection.

7. Honest interaction with the l.d. and nondisabled children in the group.

8. How to make the child an integral part of the group rather than peripheral. How to provide the child with a role that is within his capabilities and tolerance, yet will make him a contributing member of the group. How to assess tolerance for specific tasks.

9. How to determine the length of session a child can handle.

10. The need of the l.d. to be kept busy because they tend to become bored and hyperactive as observers.

11. How to encourage the child to problem-solve rather than receive answers from the leader. How the group can effect learning in the child.

12. How to deal with deficits in organization, language, and memory.

13. Setting individual goals with child and parent. Sensitization to parents' needs, hopes, and concerns, and the leader's role in dealing with parents.

14. When the program does not work, how to provide modified or alternative programs.

15. The needs of the l.d. to feel important, liked, and wanted, and how these needs can begin to be met; for example, the leader telephones the child midweek to chat, to remind him about the next program and things he will need to bring. Encourage the children to telephone one another or give them the "job" of phoning another child. Involve the child in planning and preparation. Give some prestige roles.

Before the program begins, staff orientation is important. However, the meaningful training will occur after the staff have begun working with the children. The training then can revolve around specific children, staff practices, and concerns. Encourage the staff to read the following chapters in this book: "Dealing with Behavior," "Parents' Attitudes are Important," and "Program Ideas and Games."

The supervisory staff should consider the following:

1. Are they keeping the needs of normal children in mind and redirecting the program to those goals?

2. What do they wish to accomplish with the program?

3. How many people will the program effect?

4. Have they utilized all local resources, physical and human?

Assessing Progress

We may have misjudged the child's capabilities upon enrollment, he may change, or the group may change. There is a continuing need to consider whether the current group best meets both the child's needs and those of his clubmates. If we should decide that the group is not adequately meeting his needs, we have to assess whether the child has been misplaced or whether it is because alternative approaches have not been tried. When the child is experiencing difficulty, you might ask the following questions:

1. Is his difficulty generalized or specific?

2. If generalized, can we modify the demands to aim for more productive, comfortable functioning; for example, shorter period of attendance, simpler tasks, briefer instructions, have an extra volunteer in the group, orient other children to the child's difficulties?

3. If his difficulty is specific, how can that area be modified to obviate failure?

4. Is the difficulty more a problem of the child's or the leader's? Is the leader programing for failure by his demands?

5. What benefits has the child offered to others within the group?

6. Have his behavior, social, and independence skills improved or deteriorated since entry into the group?

7. Is his participation in the recreation program part of a larger program that has specific goals? Can others who live or work with him suggest possible ways of programing for success?

8. Is he able to function as a participating member of the group?

9. Is he upsetting the group unduly? How do they show their upset?

10. Are one or two children leading others to reject the child?

11. Is much of his behavior bizarre or grossly inappropriate?

On the other side of the coin you frequently must assess whether his behavior, social, and general skills have improved sufficiently to graduate him to a carefully selected, integrated program. Recreation agencies tend to opt for the easier road of enrolling children in segregated programs. They then tend to keep children in such programs after they are capable of functioning in an integrated group. Certainly, arranging success in an integrated program requires creativity, flexibility, and support, but it provides the child with the experiences he requires to function in society.

Chapter 15:

A Parent's Guide to Camping

THE LEARNING-DISABLED CHILD has experienced such frequent failure in formal learning situations that he may reject efforts to teach him in such a setting. Therefore, there seems to be validity in promoting learning and the development of the cognitive process in a less tense and demanding environment. Camp can play an important role in this context. Camp can also do much to improve the social skills and create desired behavior in the l.d. child. The long-term, intensive living situation provided at the camp allows the staff continuous opportunity to encourage the acquisition of appropriate behavior patterns. The child is anxious to relate well to his peers, and generally is prepared to exert the effort required to bring about change.

Many l.d. children who have been overprotected at home can benefit from a sojourn at camp, since it teaches them a wide variety of skills in independent living. They learn to set and clear a table, gauge the amount of food to eat, make a bed, sweep and mop a floor, fold clothes and place them neatly on shelves, choose appropriate clothing for the weather, and make decisions. Cultural deprivation, overprotection, or the uncertainty of how the child will behave in a strange environment often inhibit the child's exposure to new learning situations. Camp can play an important role in exposing the child to a multiplicity of new experiences, from catching a fish to visiting a mill.

Camp also provides a setting wherein the child can maintain the gains he acquired during the school year, and in some instances continue to habilitate his deficit areas. The emphasis on language and motor development and cognition, through informal and formal teaching experience, means that the summer will be a time of growth and consolidation rather than two months of wasted time, which the l.d. child can ill afford. The routine of camp provides a comfortable structure wherein the child can feel sufficiently secure so that he can begin to make decisions, grow, succeed, and feel better about himself.

Is Segregated Camp for the Learning Disabled Valid?

Many l.d. children are sufficiently well organized and socially adept to handle themselves in a camp for nonhandicapped children. The child whose problems are specifically academic should do well in a nonhandicapped camp. Most l.d. children who do not suffer from other handicaps, such as mental retardation or emotional disturbance, attend a segregated camp only until they have acquired the social skills which would enable them to attend a "regular" camp. I feel that the only consideration in having the socially adept l.d. child attend a segregated camp would be the child's need for the remediation and therapy available at the camp, which is otherwise inaccessible to the child in his community.

However, some l.d. children are not ready to cope with the confusion, demands, and competition of a nonprotected setting. They require an interim period of approximately one to three years in a specialized setting wherein there is understanding of their difficulties, and the specialized staff and program are specifically designed to create change and growth. This is particularly vital at this time in history when l.d. children do not yet receive the understanding and accommodations in our schools and communities to the extent that they should.

What is the Difference Between a Specialized Camp and a Regular Camp?

A specialized camp is just that. It "specializes" in serving one or more specific problem areas. There is every conceivable type of camp, from camps for obese girls to camps for the learning disabled. In the latter, one should look for a senior staff with a background in normal and abnormal child development. There should be staff with comprehensive training and experience in special education. The counselor-camper ratio should be high, with approximately one counselor per three campers. (Do not confuse this with staff-camper ratio.) The counselors should be mature, empathic, and have a background in camping, recreation, and work with exceptional children. The program should de-emphasize competition, and possess a fair degree of structure. The physical, health, and general staff standards should meet the American Camping Association requirements.

A specialized camp should offer the camper a high degree of protection. Demands are not made of him that are beyond his capacity to meet. His inability to handle a specific situation should be quickly recognized, so that he is removed from the frustrations, stress, or excitement that have overwhelmed him, and introduced to an activity with which he can cope more readily. The camp functions as part of an ongoing program, so that close contact is maintained with school, home, and clinic before and after the camp season. This allows for maintenance of precamp gains and post-camp capitalization of strengths acquired during the camp season.

Some camps for the l.d. primarily are summer schools with the major program emphasis on formal habilitation. Some camps combine habilitation with recreation, and other camps strive to achieve remediation through recreation. Some camps serve a variety of exceptionalities, with a major emphasis on one or two exceptionalities. It is important for the parents to acquire details of the camp program, and choose a camp specifically suited to their child's needs at that period of time.

A "regular" or integrated camp has one or more l.d. children and possibly children with other handicaps or exceptionalities as living, participating members of a cabin group and camp population of other children who are nonhandicapped. A nonspecialized camp gears its physical plant, staffing, and programing to children who fall within the normal range of mental, physical, and emotional development. When a camp director decides to enroll l.d. children into his camp, either he can enroll children whose needs can be met by his present structure or modify his structure to meet the special needs of his prospective campers. Thus, a camp enrolling l.d. children who have considerable difficulty with coordination or behavior might hire an extra counselor for the group, or hire a more mature counselor, or place fewer children in the group. Generally speaking, a regular camp does not offer the extensive protection, employ the mature staff, or have the high staff-camper ratio that is provided by the specialized camp.

Some regular camps have initiated special l.d. units within their structure. There are advantages and disadvantages to such units. They can serve as a transitional step between specialized and nonspecialized camping for the child who cannot yet cope with the physical, emotional, and social demands of a "normal" group. This affords him the additional protection he might require while allowing him to take advantage of the comprehensive facilities of a regular camp. Semi-integrated camping can provide children with opportunities to develop alternating identification, both with "normal" and l.d. children, with less stress than is experienced by the integrated camper. Many children will be able to graduate from the special unit without the additional adjustment of changing camps.

However, I am opposed to the special unit concept. If a child requires specialized assistance he should be in a setting wherein he is not exposed to the competencies of the nondisabled. In the segregated camp he realizes that his fellow campers all experience difficulty in performance. The supportive encouragement of the staff permits him to succeed without having to weigh his progress against that of his more adept contemporaries. A special unit tends to perpetuate the separation of the different child from his non-disabled peers, as we do in our communities. Thus we encourage ostracism, discomfort of the nondisabled with the child who is different, and scape-goating. When a special unit is available, l.d. children tend to be enrolled there because it does not require the necessary adjustments that are made to accommodate them in the regular groups. Similarly, directors keep the child in the special unit after he could integrate because it is easier to plan for and handle a special placement.

How Do Parents Choose an Integrated Camp?

The most important criteria should be the readiness of the camp to accommodate l.d. campers and its demonstrated success in providing such children with an enjoyable summer. Your local volunteer association likely will have a list of such camps and can refer you to parents whose children have attended, or the camps themselves can refer you to camper parents.

The camp should meet American Camping Association requirements for staffing and for the physical plant. Discuss the camp's standards with your state camping association. A registered nurse should be on the staff, and if a physician is not part of the camp staff, one should be readily available. As I have mentioned, it is preferable for the director and some of his supervisory staff to have a background in child development, and the counseling staff should be emotionally mature, preferably in their late teens or twenties.

The director must be prepared to be flexible about cabin placement, program, and approach. His willingness to attempt a variety of possibilities will be communicated to his staff who, in turn, should be encouraged to be flexible in their approaches, demands, and programing. Since there are no set rules whereby one can be guaranteed a successful experience, the staff must be prepared to try a variety of possibilities before the most acceptable solution is found.

What Type of Program Orientation is Best Suited to the L.D.?

A group-centered program, where the competitive aspect of living is kept to a minimum, where there is close supervision of campers and staff, and time for the child to pursue some individual interests, often is a good choice for l.d. children. Such an approach provides the kind of structure that the l.d. seem to require. The occasional child who is particularily skilled in a specific area of endeavor does well in an activity-centered camp. Mark attended a specialized camp for two years. At the end of that time he handled himself much more adeptly than he had previous to his camping experiences.

210

However, his coordination still was so poor that he would be unable to participate in any athletic program with "normal" children. His parents sent him to an arts camp where he could further his interest in music. Mark now has enjoyed two summers in that setting. A work camp or outward bound type of program often is well suited to the older l.d. youth.

Avoid camps that pit one camper against another so that there is pressure to make a wrinkle-free bed and to excel athletically so that one's team won't lose. Steer away from camps that have color wars and best-camper awards, or permissive program structures where, for most of the time, the campers choose what they want to do, or do nothing if they wish. This is a superb structure for some children, but rarely for the l.d. Choose a camp that offers structure without rigidity, and whose philosophy and standards are compatible with your mode of life. Do not expose the l.d. child to a camp whose religious or cultural orientation is alien to him, or where his background will stand out as being different.

All the parents in one state should not attempt to enroll their children in the one or two camps that are receptive to inclusion of the l.d. in their programs. A large influx of children with special needs places a considerable strain on the camp staff which may dampen their enthusiasm for further ventures in integration. Also, a large number of exceptional children within one camp changes the camp from an integrated program to a specialized one, with the resultant loss to the l.d. of the benefits of integrated camping. If there is a shortage of camps that are willing to include some l.d. as campers, the volunteer association should plan a program for the camp directors in the state. This program should deal with issues such as:

1. What is a learning disability? In what ways are the l.d. child's problems apparent in camp? What benefits do the l.d. derive from "regular" camping?

2. How have l.d. children successfully been integrated into other non-specialized camps?

3. What type of program orientations work best for them?

4. When is the l.d. child ready to attend a nonspecialized camp?

5. What special resources will their camp need in order to accommodate the l.d.?

6. The ways in which the parents and the volunteer association are prepared to assist. (For example, films, literature, or lectures for staff orientation, arranging to have the counselor observe the child in special education class, approaching colleges to place students at the camp for practicum or work-study placements in order to pro-

vide extra coverage, arranging to have a service club underwrite the cost of extra staff, or arranging for parents to underwrite the expense.)

Parents' Role

If the child is ready to attend a nonspecialized camp, the parent must be prepared to comply with the camp's rules on telephone calls, gifts, and visits. If you are relaxed about your child being away from home, he too will be relaxed. Write him frequent, newsy letters, but avoid telling him how much you miss him, how much you wish he were home, and all the fun he is missing at home. Do not be concerned if you receive a few homesick or unhappy letters. The l.d. child is not the world's most speedy adjuster, and it may take your offspring a couple of weeks to feel comfortable in the new situation. Anyhow, by the time you receive the unhappy letter, chances are the precipitating incident has long passed. If you are concerned, telephone the director and trust his judgment. Rarely do camp directors attempt to keep unhappy campers in their camps.

Exert every effort to make your child feel as much like the other campers as possible. DO NOT send special remedial equipment to camp or ask that he pursue his remedial program there. Send the same kinds of clothing and equipment as the other campers will have. You may want to read my chapter on camping in *They Too Can Succeed* which deals with how to prepare your child for camp.

Tell the director any information that he should have in order to make your child's stay more comfortable, and allow him to use his judgment on which information he wishes to share with the counselor and when. Obviously, the director should know of any major immediate family problem such as death of parent or sibling, or a divorce. Inform him, as well, of any physical or medical problem, how it is handled and how the child feels about it. Tell him whether your child has any difficulty writing or reading letters, whether he is embarrassed about this and what assistance he will require from the counselor. The director should know how the child feels about his disability and whether he knows what is the matter with him. Tell him whether the child is disorganized and what the counselor will need to do in order to help him organize his time, his belongings, and his language. If he is clumsy, describe the assistance he might require tying laces, folding clothes, making his bed, and cutting food. If he becomes easily frustrated, overexcited, or perseverative, suggest to the director what might be done in those instances.

Whatever intervention you do suggest, always remember that the counselor may have from eight to ten campers in his charge and is responsible for their well-being while dealing with your child. Be certain that you share with the director what the child does well, likes to do, would like to do, and has difficulty doing. Tell him whether your child attempts things which are too difficult for him or whether he shies away from activities that are within his ability level.

How Long Should a Child Attend Camp?

Specialized camps that have a therapeutic orientation typically enroll their campers for an extended period of time, from four to eight weeks. If a child is going to derive any therapeutic benefit from that type of camp, he should expect to remain at the camp for the entire period. Specialized camps typically employ a careful intake process and hire a select staff. Consequently, they rarely find themselves with a child who they have to send home because they cannot cope with him. This means that when the parent orients the child to a camping period of a prestated number of weeks, the specialized camp is likely to be able to fulfill the obligation to keep the camper.

When a child is enrolled in a nonspecialized camp, encourage the director to make a committment to try to keep the child in camp for a prestated period of time, two weeks or more. Similarly, encourage the child to allow the camp the same period of time so that he gives it a fair chance. After the predetermined period has elapsed, either the camper or director might terminate the stay without considering that one of them has failed. However, when we consider that the l.d. generally are slow to adjust, we must settle on a sufficiently lengthy period to allow the child the time to settle in. Another factor in determining the length of stay at camp would be the typical length of attendance of the other campers. If it is the child's first summer at a nonspecialized camp or at this particular camp, the parent should tell the director where he can be reached during the summer.

Chapter 16:

For Directors of Nonspecialized Camps

A MERE FEW YEARS AGO we readily enrolled children into our camps who were considered to be clumsy, lazy, disorganized, dreamers, overactive, slow moving, late bloomers, or underachievers, and they became integral members of our camper groups. Now they are labeled "learning disabled" so that many directors suddenly become hesitant to include such handicapped children amongst their camper population.

The problems of some l.d. children become apparent only when they are faced with academic tasks, so they are as adept at being campers as any of their peers. Others have more global difficulties, but they, too, generally can enjoy happy, productive camping experiences if they are treated with some understanding. The majority of l.d. children attend classes for "normal" children throughout their school career. We now realize that we have wrought an injustice on many others by placing them in self-contained classrooms and separating them from their contemporaries when, with some assistance and flexibility, they could and should have remained within the "normal" stream. We can carry this analogy to camping. These intelligent, basically functional children need to experience the give-and-take of peer and adult interaction which will equip them to handle themselves in society at large.

Will Enrollment of L.D. Campers Alienate the Other Camper Parents?

Dr. Phyllis Ford, in her booklet, "Your Camp and the Handicapped Child," (see the Reading List at the end of the chapter) deals with this issue:

As camp director, one may feel limited in accepting certain children because of suspected opinions or open remarks of the parents of other campers. This limiting factor can be overcome through educating the parents in personal conversation or by use of a printed statement which openly discusses the philosophy of the camp. It is believed that the parent who would refuse to choose a camp which admitted slightly handicapped children is a rare one, particularly if that parent realizes and understands that the program of his own child will not be changed. Most parents favor a camp which gives attention to the fact that all children are different and are respected as individuals.

To my knowledge there has been one law suit (Massachussetts, 1970) in which a parent claimed misrepresentation by the camp because the camp's brochure or literature did not mention that it served exceptional children. The parent claimed that the presence of a retarded child in the camp was psychologically harmful to her son. Consequently, it seems to be a wise precaution to mention in your literature the fact that you serve some l.d. campers. However, you should realize that the above mentioned lawsuit is atypical because hundreds of camps have served handicapped and exceptional children without being sued or without losing campers.

How Do I Decide That a Child is Ready to Attend My Camp?

The following list of criteria for establishing whether a child is ready for your camp is not meant to be comprehensive; rather, it includes the basic questions that you might consider:

1. Is the child socially aggressive, self-assured?

2. Is he able to be involved in most camp activities?

3. Does he have reasonably good self-care and independence skills?

4. Has he spent time away from family?

5. Has he had some successful previous camping experience, perhaps day camp?

6. Has he been part of a nonhandicapped recreation group such as scouts or community center, and functioned as an integral member of the group?

Sources of Information on the Child

Information obtained about the child not only will assist in determining readiness, but will be of value in grouping him with compatible cabinmates and ensuring the likelihood of an enjoyable experience. If the child has been the client of a mental health clinic, or family service agency, their departments of social service often can provide a comprehensive report of his functioning. In smaller communities the public health nurse may assume this role. An additional source of information is the child's school. Its staff has been in a good position to observe his independence skills, social skills, and general behavior. In some instances, parental knowledge of a child's handicap may not be as comprehensive as that of the physician, psychologist, or agency. The parent may not be in a position to determine how the handicap will be affected by the camp environment, and, at times, the professional or agency can provide a more objective picture of the child's functioning. The camp director may need a signed release from the parents in order to secure information from the pediatrician, psychiatrist, psychologist, school, agency, or clinic.

Information the Director Might Seek from the Physician

1. Extent and implications of child's learning disability.

2. Is the l.d. congenital or acquired? If acquired, what is the cause and time of acquisition?

3. Does child have seizures, cerebral palsy, behavior disturbances, asthma, other allergies, good bowel and bladder control, enuresis?

4. Does he fatigue easily?

5. Does he have special medical or dietary restrictions? (Obtain details.) Should the camp have a supply of specific medications for emergency use? (If child is on behavior modifying medication, suggest that it not be discontinued for first part of summer.)

6. Are there specific or generalized medical procedures we should follow with this child?

7. What is his physical, social, and emotional functioning?

8. How dependent is he on the family? What is the general family functioning?

9. When did the physician last see the child?

10. What other sources of information should be contacted?

Information the Director Might Seek from the Psychologist or Psychiatrist

1. General behavior of the child.

2. Specific problem areas and suggested handling procedures.

3. Is he hyper- or hypoactive?

4. Family functioning.

5. What are the results of screenings, assessments?

Information the Director Might Seek from the School

1. How does the child function behaviorally and socially? (Individual and group adjustment.) Does he make friends easily, give-and-take?

2. Is he hyper- or hypoactive? Does he have a long interest span? Is he easily frustrated?

3. What are his interests and aptitudes?

4. Is he independent, aggressive, self-assured, shy, withdrawn?

5. What is he able to do in physical education, art?

6. What is the parental attitude?

7. What are the results of screenings, tests?

Assistance the Director Might Seek from Agencies and Clinics

If the child has been under the care of a family service agency, learning center, or mental health clinic, some of the following information might be sought.

1. What is the child's background, limitations in functioning, strengths, degree of independence, social skills, and ability to function as a member of a group? Is he reserved, withdrawn, outgoing, or aggressive?

2. What are the parental attitudes?

3. If the child attended the agency's camp in previous years, how did he function? Was improvement noted in self-care, independence, and social skills?

4. What are the short- and long-term goals that the agency has for the child and what can the camp do to build toward these goals?

5. Will the agency assist the precamp and inservice staff orientation? Can they provide a staff member who will assume this role as well as provide films and literature?

6. Will the agency be on call for consultation should a problem arise during the summer?

7. Will the agency work with the family, interpreting camping to them, preparing them for separation, and "running interference" during the summer? In instances of limited family finances, can the agency provide a campership?

8. What information about the child's camp experience would the agency like to receive at the end of the summer?

The home interview is a productive source of information. The responses of child and family to the interviewer's comments and questions, the family interaction, the child's behavior and general ability to handle himself, provide the interviewer with considerable information and valuable impressions for planning the child's summer.

Many l.d. children and their parents will not have a well-defined idea of what camp is all about. They may be anxious about the impending experience. A home interview can relieve much of this anxiety if the interviewer takes the time to discuss the concerns expressed by parents and child, and encourages the "untying of apron strings," if the child seems ready to take this step. The interviewer should describe the sleeping accommodations at camp, (tents, cabins, canvas bunks, mattresses, screened buildings or open, etc.), and the availability of toilets, washing, and bathing facilities. He should describe a typical day at camp, some typical meals, some special programs, and explain the step-by-step occurrences of the first day at camp, from the time the child leaves the house. Show pictures to the child, possibly leaving them with him. Explain visiting and telephone procedures, rules about cancellation of registration, and charges if the child leaves camp before the period is ended. Tell them the ages of the staff, the counselor-camper ratio, and where the counselors sleep. Paint a verbal picture of the physical plant, swimming facilities, etc.

The interviewer should be careful not to express hopes for the camp experience that are beyond the child's reach. Parents, child, and interviewer can establish realistic goals for the summer together. The family should be told exactly what will be expected of the camper if he is to attend the camp.

If the camp intends to take pictures of the l.d. child, or identify the child in any publicity, brochures, or camp literature, it is wise to obtain a release signed by both parents.

Each camp has a format which they normally use for a home interview. The same format can be utilized with the learning disabled. Listed below are some suggested questions and observations on the child's social relationships and emotional development. The comprehensiveness of the list is not meant to be frightening. Rather, it is designed to provide camp administrators with the kinds of information that will assist them in determining readiness, deciding upon appropriate placement in a group, and plan handling procedures and program modifications so that the child and his cabinmates can maximize their experience.

1. Who decided that the child is ready for placement in a non-specialized camp? (Parent, teacher, clinic?) What was the basis for that decision? What made you feel that this camp is best suited to your child?

2. Does the child have friends? Many or few? Do they seek him out or does he approach them? Does he play with contemporaries, older or younger children, l.d. or non l.d.? Does he play with children in the neighborhood? Is he a leader, follower, or both? Does he relate to peers with ease and discuss topics of mutual interest? Does he always want to have his own way? Is he competitive, shy, outgoing, aggressive, or withdrawn?

3. Describe his activities after school and on weekends. Does he plan his free time well or need you to plan it for him? How much television does he watch?

4. How old are his brothers and sisters? How does he relate to them? Do they tend to give in to him or protect him?

5. How does he relate to his parents?

6. Is he always looking for praise? Does he argue a great deal? Cry easily? How does he react to discipline? Is he dependent or independent?

7. When asked to do something that he doesn't wish to do, what is his reaction? (Submissive, stubborn, aggressive?) How does he adjust to a sudden change of plans? Does he enjoy new experiences? When faced with a task that he feels is difficult, what does he do? (Attempts task, becomes frustrated, defeated?)

8. Does he like to help others? Does he willingly do his share of household chores?

9. How does he handle disappointment? How does he convey the fact that something is bothering him? Does he verbalize concerns easily, bottle them up, show that he is anxious through other behavior? Are his feelings easily hurt?

10. Does he express himself well or become frustrated when others have difficulty understanding him?

11. How has he handled formal experiences with nonhandicapped children in recent years? (In nonspecialized class, recreation program, camp.) How does he react when he can't do some things as well as his peers?

12. Does he know what is the matter with him? Do his parents discuss his l.d. openly with him? How does he feel about it?

13. When he is told to do a number of things, does he remember what he has heard? Is he compliant or resistant?

14. Is he disorganized, leave his belongings around, never remember where he has placed anything?

15. Does he become upset by an unexpected change in plans?

16. Does he forget what time of day it is? Does he know the days of the week, months of the year? Can he tell the time? Does he know denominations of money? Can he read? Write? Will he need assistance reading letters or writing them?

17. Is he well coordinated both in gross and fine-motor skills? If not, what self-help chores can't he do well? Which sports has he mastered and which cause him difficulty?

18. Has he been away from home and family before? For how long and in what setting? How did he react? How did the parents feel about his absence? Was he ever at camp? What kind of camp? When was he there and for how long? How did he function?

19. What do the parents feel are his main problems and successes at home, in school, and on the street?

20. What does he like to do, and hope to be able to do? What can he do well? Will he attempt things that he can't do well? Does he have a good attention span? Is he easily frustrated? How does he express frustration? What does he do when he tires of an activity?

21. Is he in a self-contained or regular class at school?

22. What do his parents hope to have him get out of the camp experience?

23. Ask the child if he wants to go to camp. Was enrolling at camp his idea or his parents'? Ask him how he feels about leaving his parents for a period of time.

24. What does the child hope to get out of the camp experience, do and learn?

25. Has the child received psychotherapy? If so, why, and for how long? Was it helpful, and if so, in what ways?

26. Are there any special handling procedures that the parents wish continued at camp?

Interviewer's Observations

Observations of Parents

Are the parents prepared to be separated from the child for the period of time that he will be at camp? Are they prepared to accept the camp's rules on telephone calls and visits? Are they overanxious? (This may be expressed by concerns about food, weather, and cleanliness.) Are the parents realistic about the child's capabilities and limitations? Does the information that the interviewer has from the physician, psychologist, and school relate closely to the information received from the parents?

Some parents may verbalize realistic expectations yet expect the camp to effect miracle cures and achieve pronounced improvement in general functioning. Conversely, many parents overprotect their l.d. offspring and underestimate their child's capabilities.

The interviewer should note whether both parents participate in the interview and whether the child is interested or allowed to be present. Are father and mother in agreement about the disability and handling procedures? Do they discuss the handicap furtively and with difficulty or in a relaxed fashion in the child's presence? Have either parent or any of their children attended a camp?

Observations of Child

1. How does he interact with interviewer?

2. How does he relate to parents and siblings?

3. Can he maintain interest in the discussion? Is his articulation clear? Does he understand what he hears and is his use of language adequate? How does he react if you can't understand him? Are the quality of his responses to you bizarre or inappropriate?

4. Is he hyperactive or lethargic?

5. Does he seem interested in or excited about going to camp? Fearful? Does he have specific concerns? What aspects of camp life appeal to him?

6. Does he know his age, birthday, how many months removed his birthday is from the present?

Physical Considerations

1. Does the child have any bowel or bladder difficulties? Does he wet his bed? How have the parents handled these situations?

2. Can he dress himself, choose appropriate clothing to wear for the weather?

3. Can he cut his food? Does he have any dietary restrictions?

4. Can he find his way around a strange place without assistance? Does he follow directions? Does he tire easily?

5. Does he fall asleep with ease? If not, what does he do? What time does he generally fall asleep? Does he sleep through the night? What time does he awaken? If early, what does he do?

6. Does he have any specific medical problems?

Period of Enrollment

It is preferable to have the child begin his period of camp at the beginning of the camp season. Thus he will be able to adjust to camp and make friends at the same time as his bunk mates are doing so. Alternatively, if he attempts to join a preformed group in mid-season, he faces a potentially more difficult situation.

Some of the variables in deciding on an optimal period of enrollment are:

1. How ready does the child seem for attending a nonspecialized camp? How suitable is the camp that the parents have selected for the child?

2. What is the average duration of enrollment for a child in the camp?

3. Settle upon a minimum period of time as the target for which the child and camp staff would aim for his stay at camp, and the director should attempt to keep the child in camp for that duration, and longer if the experience is a positive one.

4. Is this the child's first time away from home?

5. How well has the child adjusted to other nonspecialized situations?

6. How demanding is the camp program?

7. Finances of parent or agency enrolling the child.

What Kinds of Staff Will I Need?

In an integrated camp, l.d. children often do well when placed with a counselor whose previous record indicates that he is mature, flexible, and generally accepting of differences in his campers. Counselors should be asked whether they want a child with special needs in their group rather than have it thrust on them.

A "float" or spare counselor can be important in providing relief for the regular counselor by handling the l.d. camper, on occasion, so that the regular counselor can spend time with other campers.

The counselor should receive regular supervision that is practical and supportive. The supervisor should spend time with the group so that his suggestions will be based on actual observations.

Is Extra Staff Needed—If So, How Are They Paid?

Whether or not extra staff is needed will depend upon the camp's staff-camper ratio and the number and type of handicapped children that will be enrolled. Generally speaking, if the child feasibly can be accommodated in camp without assigning an extra staff member to him, it is preferable. The presence of his own personal counselor serves to accentuate his difference and decrease the possibility of his becoming an integral member of the group.

If additional staff is required to provide individual attention, staff relief, and coverage, it is preferable to assign the staff member to the total cabin group rather than to the individual child. Possibly extra coverage might be needed only at specific times of the day. This need might be met by the oldest campers.

If full additional staff seems advisable, the cost can be met in a variety of ways. If an agency, church, service club, or industry is sponsoring a campership for the child to attend camp, the campership could include the salary of an additional staff member. A number of colleges now have work-study programs from which mature staff can be recruited. A student in education, psychology, social work, occupational or physiotherapy, or speech pathology might receive credit for field study course requirements as a member of the camp staff, if the camp is prepared to provide supervision and evaluation. The salary of the additional counselor could be interpreted as an "extra" paid for by camper parents who could afford this expenditure, just as other optional extras are offered by some camps. If the child needs his own counselor, he should spend several days with the counselor before he comes to camp.

Staff Training—Precamp and Inservice

The following factors will determine whether the entire staff should be sensitized to the presence of the l.d. child in camp:

1. Number of l.d. children who will be attending camp.

2. Degree to which they will require special handling procedures or to which their behavior will occasion anxiety.

3. Size of staff and amount of contact they have with camper in question. In essence, then, if several campers are l.d., the entire staff may attend a precamp session devoted to the general considerations involved in l.d., whereas a child with a similar disability may attend another camp and have only the director, nurse, supervisor, and child's counselor aware of his problem.

In a group-centered camp, where the counselors are with their campers all day, the cabin counselors can interpret some of the camper's special needs to staff members, as the occasions arise. In an activity centered camp, where children do not remain with their cabin groups, the staff members might need a more comprehensive interpretation. Similarly, in a decentralized camp, where age groups live in self-contained villages with little mingling, the orientation might be limited to the staff of the village concerned, as well as to the specialty people, maintenance and kitchen staff.

Precamp sessions can be conducted by a discussion leader provided by the local volunteer association or a member of the camp staff who is knowledgeable about l.d. and who can explain what it means in terms of the child attending camp. Although brief mention might be given to the cause of the handicap, prognosis, and other issues of general interest, the emphasis of the sessions should be on manifestations and handling procedures, reasons the child is attending camp, and goals and creative methods of program adaptation. This material can be augmented by films and pamphlets.

In precamp and during the course of the season, meetings about individual children often prove extremely helpful. These meetings can be attended by the child's counselors, section director, and, if relevant, specialty staff, medical staff, and staff member from the clinic the child attends. This can be a good vehicle for developing handling procidures, clarifying concerns, and designing program modifications. Optimally, such a case conference also should be held at the conclusion of the child's stay at camp, in order to provide a comprehensive picture of the child's functioning and achievements. This can be recorded and shared with the family, school, and clinic.

How Much Information Should be Given to the Staff?

In order to assure the best care for the child and protection for the camp, the director and medical staff must possess *all* the pertinent information on a child. It is not necessary or even desirable in many cases to convey the totality of information to the counselor. Too much material may cause the counselor to form a damaging image of the child before he arrives, to be prejudiced toward the family, or create anxiety on his part. Provide him with the details necessary for him to exercise the requirements of safety, care, comfort, and participation. As additional questions arise, provide ready access to a senior staff person, the director, supervisor, or nurse. Use non-medical terminology in describing the child and limit information to that which is relevant to the camp experience.

Be certain that the counselor knows the few special handling procedures that may make the difference between a comfortable experience or an anxious one.

Illustrative Incidents

Harry became very anxious when he could not find one of his belongings, or when an activity changed. His tantrums at these times were upsetting to staff and campers. His counselors were taught how to help Harry organize himself and to prepare for changes. Before he went to the washhouse, the counselor would check with him whether he had his soap, toothbrush, towel, etc. Five minutes before a change of activity, the counselor would prepare Harry for the change; for example, he would tell Harry that as soon as the arts and crafts material was cleared up, or the horses taken back to the barn, the group would go swimming.

Karl also tended to forget his schedule, and since he attended an activity centered camp, his counselor was not with him to help him organize his day. Therefore, he made Karl a bracelet of elasticized string on which sturdy discs were strung. Each disc was numbered on the one side to correspond to the period of the day, and the activity was printed on the other side. Staff members who found Karl wandering around or attending the wrong activity would check his bracelet with him.

Barry's paralyzed left side made him a slow dresser. Because his counselors were aware of this ahead of time, they had him begin dressing himself several minutes before his cabinmates.

Ian was ashamed of his poor ability to read or write. When letters arrived from home, the counselor would read them to Ian during free activity period and Ian would dictate his letters home while sitting with his counselor on a rock, away from the other campers.

Adjusting the Child to Camp

1. If possible, have the child travel to camp with fellow campers.

2. Have the counselor-in-training or regular counselor stay with him on the first day until he feels comfortable. Be certain that he knows the first day's routine in detail.

3. If the camper has seizures, a noticeable behavioral problem, or severe motor disability, it may be advisable to give the cabinmates an orientation before the l.d. child joins the group. This might involve a brief description of their cabinmate's disability. Tell them the things that the l.d. camper enjoys and does well. Encourage them not to baby him or offer help when it is not solicited.

4. Make twice-weekly letters from home a requisite for attendance at camp. The type of news that is helpful or harmful to include in a letter should be spelled out to parents.

5. Keep the family posted on the child's progress. Write a letter home at the end of the first week, commenting on the child's adjustment and activities. Plan to spend a few minutes with the parents on visitor's day. They might be quite anxious about the separation from their child and need periodic assurance that their youngster is well and happy.

Grouping

There is no ironclad procedure for grouping. Generally speaking, children's self-esteem is best served if they are grouped with agemates and, if possible, with friends. However, if the child is immature and physically small, he may do well with a younger group. Conversely, the l.d. have done well when grouped with mature, understanding, and accepting children who are prepared to include the different child in their group.

Try to group the child with cabinmates whose interests and physical abilities are compatible with his; for example, an uncoordinated child may not do too well in a group of athletic children.

Social Interaction

The admission of the l.d. child into a "normal" group of campers is not necessarily analogous with acceptance of the child by counselors and cabinmates. Some l.d. children who lack the social skills, maturity, or self-acceptance, function on the periphery of the social structure. Children who present such a picture are more likely to be rejected by the group. Some relevant considerations are:

1. Any child, l.d. or not, will experience more difficulty joining a group after subgroups have formed. It seems preferable to have the l.d. child join the group at the beginning of the camping period, and be placed in a group that does not consist of campers who have all bunked together previously, or been close friends in the city.

2. If the camp serves children primarily representing one ethnic or financial background, introducing a child from a very different background creates an additional degree of adjustment. For example, if the children at camp are almost exclusively upper middle-class Protestants, a Jewish child from a modest home will have fewer commonalities with his cabinmates than a child from a background similar to theirs.

3. The child with a visible handicap may be more easily accepted by cabinmates than the child who "looks like everyone else" but is different.

4. The counselor should have a clear idea of his role in fostering interaction of the l.d. child with his fellow campers. He should have guidelines for modifying activities so that the l.d. child can participate. It is important that the counselor view the child as a full-time member of the group to be rarely exempted, rather than a "sometimes" member, to be left behind at the least suggestion of inconvenience.

5. The director should be prepared to arrange placement in another group if the child is not interacting positively with his bunkmates or counselors after a reasonable adjustment period.

6. Interaction may have to be viewed as a give-and-take process at the child's level of functioning, rather than a mutual sharing of interests.

7. The l.d. child's road to acceptance will be eased if his counselors capitalize on his interests and skills. Cabin projects might evolve from his skill or hobby. He might take a leadership role in the activity he enjoys doing.

8. Do not hold the group back from participating in activities because of the presence of an uncoordinated or unwilling camper. Modify the camper's role in the activity, having him contribute on his level, or provide alternative arrangements that will be enjoyable to him. It is questionable whether activities should be modified for the group as a whole.

9. Guard against the child manipulating bunkmates and counselors, capitalizing on their lack of knowledge of his capabilities to elicit sympathy and to do things for him that he is capable of doing himself. Beware of preferential treatment of the camper, such as overprotection and reinforcement of undesirable behavior, as when the child is allowed to interrupt the counselor and claims his attention when he is busy with another child.

Dealing With Rejection of Fellow Campers

If the counselor can discuss the child's handicap with his campers honestly and without shame or embarrassment, it will lose its aura of mystery. Avoidance of discussion of the l.d. perpetuates the environment of many homes. It makes the l.d. child and his peers feel that the problem is too shameful to be discussed.

The l.d. child tends to be vulnerable and the staff needs to guard against scapegoating by bunkmates and other campers. The children will take many of their cues from the staff, and if the l.d. camper is accepted and appreciated by the staff, the possibility of rejection is lessened. The following considerations may prove helpful:

1. Rejection is less likely to occur if the camper is placed in a group that is not tightly knit and unreceptive to inclusion of an outsider.

2. Happy campers whose individual needs are being met are less likely to reject a cabinmate.

3. Rejection may be an expression of fear on the part of the non-disabled campers. They may feel that the presence of the l.d. child in the group might result in less enjoyment for them during the camping period.

4. Rejection of the l.d. child basically is the same phenomenon as rejection of any child and can be dealt with in the same fashion.

5. A discussion of differences in people and the fact that we all have deficits and strengths might prove helpful.

6. Ascertain that the l.d. child is not seeking rejection by making himself the scapegoat.

Rejection should diminish if:

1. The rejection is not rewarded by fellow campers or staff.

2. The children become familiar with the child and the manifestations of his disability.

3. The campers are able to discuss their own concerns, anxieties, and feelings with the counselor, and those feelings themselves are not minimized or denied.

4. Campers realize that the presence of the l.d. child in their group will not deter them from enjoying a full program.

5. The l.d. child participates in group interaction.

6. The counselor attempts to meet the needs of *all* the campers in his group. If rejection continues, alternate placement should be considered.

Dealing With Problem Behavior

It is common for many handicapped children to be somewhat immature and insecure. Some may be angry at being handicapped and lash out physically or verbally. They may feel that they have been handicapped as a punishment for bad thoughts or actions. Therefore, it is important that the discipline that they receive be related directly to the undesired action so that it is less likely to be viewed as punishment for being handicapped. The consequence should immediately follow the act, and be a consequence, rather than punishment. For example, if you come late for meals, you miss the part of the meal which preceded your arrival; if you are becoming too stimulated by the activity, you return to the bunk to relax.

L.d. children have a hazy idea of time so that they tend not to relate their current demands or behavior to past or future events. Many do not comprehend innuendos, sarcasm, or subtleties; they will take what you say or do completely literally and be unusually direct in their response to you. Consequently, you will have to say exactly what you mean in dealing with them as well. If they live in the stark reality of the here and now, you will have to deal with them on this level.

The staff members should be able to discriminate between the behavior of a child who does not remember what demand has been made of him, does not know how to organize himself to carry out the demand, feels that the demand has been too difficult, has indeed been faced with too difficult a demand, behaves inappropriately because he has not had the opportunity to learn the required social skills, and behaves in an undesirable fashion even though he has the ability to control it.

One child in every ten is learning disabled. Most of these children can and should attend our camps, and indeed, would make fine campers. If our camps are to provide a service to our communities, we must then serve the l.d. children in those communities to whom camping would be of such great benefit.

Suggested Reading List for Camp and Recreation Personnel

Canadian Red Cross Society, Water Safety Service. *Swimming for the Handicapped—Instructor's Guide.* (Source: 460 Jarvis Street, Toronto 284, Ontario, Canada.)

_____*Teaching Swimming to the Disabled.*

_____*Water Games and Individual Figures for the Handicapped.*

Cohen, David C. *Camp Recreation for Children with Perceptual Learning Disabilities.* (Source: The Summit Camp Program, 12 Alpha Lane, Monsey, New York 10952.)

Dibner, A. S., and S. S. Dibner. *Report on Studies of Integrated Camping.* (Source: Easter Seal Society for Crippled Children and Adults of Massachusetts, Inc., 9 Newbury Street, Boston, Massachusetts 02116.)

Flax, N., and E. Peter. *Retarded Children at Camp with Normal Children.* (Source: Jewish Community Centers Association, 11001 Schuetz Road, St. Louis, Missouri 63141.)

Ford, Phyllis M. *Your Camp and the Handicapped Child.* (Source: American Camping Association, Bradford Woods, Martinsville, Indiana 46151.)

Gordon, Sol, and Risa S. Golumb. *Recreation and Socialization for the Brain Injured Child.* (Source: New Jersey Association for Children with Learning Disabilities, 61 Lincoln Street, East Orange, New Jersey.)

Information Center, Recreation for the Handicapped. *Diversified Games and Activities of Low Organization for Mentally Retarded Children.* (Source: Southern Illinois University, Carbondale, Illinois.)

Kronick, Doreen. *Regular Camp, Special Camp or No Camp.* (Source: Academic Therapy Publications, 1539 Fourth Street, San Rafael, California 94901.)

Miles, Nancy R. *Swimming Techniques for Children with Learning Disabilities.* (Source: Developmental Learning Materials, 3505 North Ashland Avenue, Chicago, Illinois 60657.)

Mondschein, Diane. *They Can, Camping.* (Source: Academic Therapy Publications, 1539 Fourth Street, San Rafael, California 94901.)

Chapter 17:

Establishing a Special Camp

F EW CAMPS in North America are designed specifically for the learning disabled, and many of the private camps exceed the financial range of families who wish to enroll their children in a special setting. Some communities are beginning to create solutions to this dilemma by organizing nonprofit or residential camps for the l.d. Typically, such camps have been organized by the local or state volunteer association.

If you are considering the possibilities of operating a residential camping program, you could start by borrowing the facilities of a church camp, or a camp for crippled or other handicapped children, rather than incur the capital indebtedness of building or buying a camp. Sometimes these facilities are not used the entire summer, so that the owners are pleased to accommodate other groups. If they will provide you with kitchen and maintenance staff, that will solve another of your problems. This will enable you to have a "dry run" at operating a camp. If a day camp is being considered, it may be feasible to obtain space gratis or at little cost from the board of education, the city department of recreation, a local university, or the State Parks and Conservation Authority. If they are reluctant to give you the facilities, perhaps they would like to be your partners in the camping venture.

The Towhee Story—A Successful Model of Specialized Camping

"I was exsided when a was caming to camp. It has good food but the lundery is bad because it loses to mooch lundery. I like were they made the camp because you get frash air and it is away from pepole and cars. They have a good swiming arey and all the cancerlers are good to me. But a think we shoud have a biger boat becaus a like to go water sking and a like horse back riding." (Comments by a Towhee camper.)

I have been on the directorate of a foundation that was established to provide direct services to the l.d., and our first project was Camp Towhee, a six-week residential camp founded in 1968. Our land was donated by the director of a nonspecialized camp. Our buildings were funded by three foundations, private donations, and a bank loan. Two camper cabins and the infirmary were built by the Toronto Junior Chamber of Commerce. The first three summers we rented mobile homes to use as sleeping space for non-counseling staff. In our second summer we purchased a barn which we divided into sleeping quarters, remedial rooms, and a recreation hall.

Camper Fees

The camper fees were based on a sliding scale, with the maximum fee of $950.00 for a six-week period. (Every camper had to attend for the entire six weeks.) A campership committee consisting of two camp directors, an accountant, and a businessman, determined the fee expected of each family, based upon the income, number of family members, and extenuating circumstances. Since 1971 we have been designated as a government-funded treatment center, so that no fee has been charged since that time.

Camper Selection

The purpose of Camp Towhee is to train practitioners in the field and students studying in one of the professions concerned with the diagnosis and treatment of learning disabilities. We also serve as a demonstration project and a vehicle for research. Our staff, who follow the campers subsequent to their stay at camp, attempt to teach the families, schools, local professionals, clinics, and recreation services how they can serve our campers and other l.d. children more effectively. It is for this reason that we select campers who meet a specific criteria. Camps that have different raison d'etre than ours may develop different but equally valid criteria for enrollment.

We serve l.d. children as defined by the United States Office of Education. Before processing a camper application we require a completed questionnaire from the child's physician, teacher, and a copy of the child's psychological assessment, with the breakdown of subtest scores. These are processed by a selection committee consisting of psychologists and special education personnel. A home visit completes the intake process. Our camper population does not possess the social and behavioral skills to attend a nonspecialized camp. As soon as they acquire these skills, we refer them to carefully selected "regular" camps.

Camp Staff

The following list comprises the staff of Camp Towhee:

Professional Director
(Ph.D. Psychology)
Business Manager
Director of Remediation
Program Director
Secretary
Kitchen Staff (5)
Maintenance Staff (3)
(one part-time driver)
Language Therapist
Crisis Counselor
Counselors (30)

Consulting Psychiatrist
Pediatrician
Physician (on call)
Gross-motor Specialist
Physiotherapist
Drama Counselor
Nature & Campcraft Counselor
Music Counselor
Arts & Crafts Instructors (2)
Swimming Instructors (2)
Nurse

The children are grouped according to age and each cabin group of six children is staffed by three counselors. One counselor is a practitioner involved in the remediation of l.d., and the other two are students in one of the related professions.

Philosophy

We function on the premise that children are people of dignity and worth. The camp attempts to create an environment in which the children succeed, in which they begin to organize their lives, thereby thinking of themselves as persons with competencies, as learners. Camp Towhee strives to provide a remedial and a camp experience. Remediation, in our terms of reference, incorporates a child's total functioning—social, behavioral, and academic.

Staff Training

The camping season is preceded by several training weekends in the city, and we have seven days of training in camp before the campers arrive. We include some select staff from other day and residential camps in both of these training sessions. The training is very pragmatic, with emphasis on camping, nature study, and out trips. The staff orientation occurs at the activity areas, such as the arts and crafts room, swimming area, and hiking trails. We deal with such questions as: What kind of structuring is meaningful and how do you do it? How do you simplify activities and gradually introduce complexity? How do you teach children to handle problem-solving tasks? How do you create a mood for rest hour, bedtime, meals? We found that the following procedures were particularly helpful in the staff training sessions:

1. Movies of the previous summer's remediation experiences were used as a teaching aid. We also used video tapes in which a camper was followed through his day's activities during cabin cleanup, specific remediation tasks, and meals. The rationale for his program was discussed, and suggestions were made for additional intervention.

2. The previous summer's counselors taught the new counselors how to structure wake-up, cabin cleanup, and other activities.

3. The staff was taught the kinds of learning that can occur while campers are dressing and washing, and during cleanup, table setting, and meals.

4. Demonstrations of how all campers in a group can participate in one activity on a different level.

5. Discussions and demonstrations of how remediation can be achieved through the general camp program.

6. Discussions of the mechanics of three persons functioning as counselors on an equal level.

After the camping season has begun, the inservice training consists of regular supervision of staff, individually and with their co-counselors, and excellent training is accrued from the case conferences, movies, books, and tapes. In addition, we invite several experts each summer who observe the camp in action and then deliver a critique. Along with this, an interdisciplinary workshop is held in the camp each summer.

The Campers' Week

Monday thru Friday

7:30—8:00	Wake-up (dress).
8:00—8:30	Jogging. The campers were not in the best of physical condition, so jogging was part of the program to get them in shape. Each day they logged their collective miles run, with the goal to run the equivalent of the number of miles around Lake Ontario.
8:30—9:00	Breakfast. A different cabin group set the tables every day.
9:00—9:30	Cleanup.
9:30—10:10	First remedial period*
10:20—11:00	Second remedial period*
11:00—11:40	Third remedial period*
11:50—12:30	Fourth remedial period*

*Each child had one instructional swim in one of these blocks. The other three are scheduled according to a child's areas of deficit.

12:30—1:00	Each day a different remedial group set tables. This was particularly good as an opportunity to make table setting a learning experience.
1:00—1:30	Lunch.
1:30—2:30	Rest hour. During each rest hour a case conference was held on one or more children.
2:30—3:30	Cabin-planned, group-centered camping activity. Boating and canoeing instruction was given twice a week for each cabin in one of these periods.
3:30—3:40	Snack.
3:40—5:00	Second cabin activity period.
5:00—5:30	General swim.
5:30—6:00	Table setting or supervised free play.
6:00—6:45	Supper.
6:45—7:00	Free play.
7:00—8:00	Interest clubs three days a week, cabin activity or campwide program on other nights.
8:00	Camper snack and then bedtime.

Each Wednesday we had a campwide program. Wednesday morning the children were involved in learning about the theme, making costumes, table decorations, and decorations for the dining hall. At lunch, short presentations on the theme were made in the dining hall. After rest hour, we had a campwide game such as "capture the flag" or a series of games such as log chopping or apple bobbing, depending upon the theme. Then general swim, free play, and supper. The foods reflected the theme. In the evening we would have a campwide program related to the day's theme.

We found that the themes, such as "Natives of Canada," "People of Other Lands," and "Our Holidays" were excellent learning experiences for the children. They went to the town library to obtain reference books, researched the costumes, foods, and habits of the theme in question, and had discussions around the problems experiences by our native population, and so on.

On Saturdays the campers went horseback riding and ice skating. The program had a heavy emphasis on teaching the children the skills that they would need in order to play with their contemporaries on their return home. This included riding two-wheel bicycles, skipping rope, skating, and baseball.

Remediation

Our formal remediation period each weekday morning offered the following: special education (reading, spelling, language, and mathematics), gross-motor training, arts and crafts (fine-motor and visual organization), music, speech and language, nature, campcraft, and drama.

Each evening the three counselors of each group would meet with the senior remedial staff to design each child's individualized remedial program for the following morning. Augmented by the senior remedial staff, the remediation then would be implemented by the child's own counselors.

The child's counselors and all remedial and specialty staff would attend the daily case conferences. At this time, as well as discussing behavior and interaction, combined remedial approaches were designed. Thus a child's language and mathematics deficits would be worked with in the gross motor, drama, or arts and crafts periods, and similarily, his motor deficits would be remediated in his language period. All his deficits and strengths would be taken into account in his daily routines and camp program periods. The participants in the case conference would suggest ways whereby counselors and program specialists could help meet the remedial goals for each child through camp activities.

We attempted to create an environment that was conducive to the acquisition of motor and language skills. We encouraged physical problem-solving tasks by surrounding each cabin with wooden horses and ladders, and making the inside of the cabins into one big jungle gym. We set the camp grounds and woods into ever-changing obstacle courses. Campers took polaroid pictures of their programs, pasted them on poster board and told the other campers in the dining hall about their program. They made logs of their canoe trips and read them to the others in the dining hall; they joined the radio club, interviewed staff and campers for the camp newspaper, made up plays on tape, worked on the announcements for the campwide program, wrote recipes for other groups to use, went on treasure and scavenger hunts, followed Indian trail signs, wrote invitations for staff to join them in their programs, read the words in their song books, read the day's menu so they would know which utensils to set on the tables, and read the instructions for sorting the cutlery.

When the counselors cleared the following day's program with the program director each evening, he would make certain that they knew how to break a program into its component parts and start at the simplest level. He taught them how to structure programs and have the campers repeat the structure at the end of an activity by drawing a map of the program or "rehashing" it at the campfire by playing "I baked a pizza, and the first thing I did was . . . ." He taught them how to plan individual cabin group theme programs and include in them elements of remediation and education.

Just as the morning remediation periods were "camping through remediation," the afternoon cabin activity periods were "remediation through camping." Toward this goal the remedial staff helped the counselors devise ideas whereby a program would contain general and individualized remedial components. Each of the senior remedial staff were assigned to specific cabin groups. They joined the groups during activity periods to further this goal, as well as to assist with behavior and socialization. The following are examples of how the remedial components were utilized in the camping activities.

1. If a child had a poor auditory sequential memory, while on a hike the group might play, "I touched a tree, I touched a tree and then a leaf," and so on.

2. If another camper in the same group had difficulty with gross-motor coordination, on the hike the group might walk across logs, step on stepping stones, squeeze through small spaces, hop, skip, jump, crawl, walk backwards, walk on tiptoe, and so on.

3. The child with expressive language problems might describe to the group what they did after the program.

4. The poorly organized child might plan what equipment the group would need to take, where they would go, in what order, and who would carry what.

5. The child with writing and spelling difficulty might keep the log of the trip.

6. The child with mathematics problems would figure out the amount of snack the group would need to feed nine people and how much money they would need to buy a special treat.

7. If one of the campers had a problem with visual memory, the entire group might close their eyes while in the woods and tell the things they have seen and their location. Then, while their eyes are closed, they might describe all the sounds they hear and guess their source and direction, describe the smells and conjecture on their origin, tell

what they feel against their skin, such as the sun or a breeze, and describe the sensation, and feel objects from the woods that the counselors or fellow campers place in their hands, then describe the texture, size, weight, and other attributes such as symmetry, assymetry, and softness, then guess what it is.

Three nights a week we offered interest clubs in which children could select an activity of particular interest to them. However, we encouraged them to select a club which might benefit them, such as knitting for those girls who had fine-motor and spatial organization problems. Each child was expected to remain with a club for a minimum of three sessions.

Routines were viewed from a context of skill development and problem solving. Remedial staff were utilized heavily to improve skills in dressing, toileting, bathing, cabin cleanup, table setting, and bedtime. Many techniques were utilized. For example, if a child persisted in placing the narrow side of the sheet on the wide side of the mattress, the counselor might have the child feel both sides of the mattress to determine which was longer and do the same with his sheet, then lie down on the bed to determine which part would accommodate the long part of his body, draw the outline of his mattress on the sheet, and so on. Or, a remedial teacher would sit beside a child at mealtime, several days in a row, to teach the child the skills of cutting food and holding eating utensils. If the child's skills were so deficient that he required very intensive assistance, or if the help proferred was drawing too much attention of cabinmates, the child and remedial staff member would have a few meals at a separate table at which time skill development would be intensively stressed.

Remedial goals were established with each child at the beginning of the summer and reviewed with him throughout the course of the season and at summer's end so that he could be involved in post-camp planning. In establishing remedial goals for the summer, we considered the child's age, the parents' aspirations, the areas of deficit that created the greatest problem in functioning, and the kinds of program to which he would be returning. We considered, as well, the goals of school and referring clinic.

A crisis counselor moved into cabins in which there was a problem, either with the behavior of a camper or staff member, or difficulties in counselor interaction. In the course of working with the group he was able to suggest ways whereby the children could be handled more effectively, or that the counselors could interact more effectively. He would meet with the three counselors involved and devise a more effective plan of action.

Structure for Staff

Any time we had an impending period of stress or change in routine, the change was planned with the staff and then carefully structured for them. This is the method whereby we ensured comfortable functioning on the first day of camp, during the campwide programs, visitor's day, final banquet, and parents' weekend. We provided the staff with mimeographed sheets on which every step was delineated. This meant that every detail of a special program had to be carefully planned in advance to eliminate the expenditure of time and energy on last minute plans.

Involving the Parents

There was a two-hour parent visiting period on a Sunday half-way through the camping period. At that time the parents had an opportunity to meet their child's counselors, remedial specialists, and the specialty staff. However, the indepth involvement occurred during the parent weekend on the last two days of camp. A stipulation of the child's attendance at Camp Towhee was the parent's attendance at the final weekend, from after supper Friday until Sunday after lunch. They slept at local motels and the camp provided meals and snacks. Friday night the parents attended a general orientation session which dealt with the goals for the summer and the director's assessments of accomplishments followed by an informal coffee hour with the staff.

On Saturday the parents went with their child for the entire day, observing the independence and social skills he had acquired, his progress in remediation, and how he handled the camp program. At some point during the day, each set of parents had a personal meeting with the professional director or senior remedial staff member so that they could share their observations of the child, the extent whereby the child met the goals which had been established for him, and suggestions for post-camp follow-up at home, school, and in the community.

Saturday supper was a weiner roast for each cabin group and parents, and Saturday evening a casual skit night by campers for parents. On Sunday morning, while the counselors helped the children pack, the parents were involved in discussion groups.

Early in September a detailed report was sent to the parents, the psychological services and special education departments of their school boards, as well as to the referring agency or clinic. This report dealt with the child's ability to handle himself as a member of a group of peers, his general behavior, self-care skills, level of achievement, progress, and current problems in each specialty and remedial area. We stressed the ways whereby the child did respond and learn. Very specific follow-up suggestions were included.

These suggestions were consolidated by visits in the autumn of our community liaison staff to the home and school, where once again, the report was discussed in light of current functioning. This outreach team also encouraged local mental health centers and professionals to acquire the techniques of providing for the l.d. in their home communities.

Impact

Camp Towhee serves sixty boys and girls ages eight to twelve; therefore, as a direct service, it is limited in scope. However, its primary orientation is to effect change in the provision of services to the l.d. in Ontario, so that all of our activities have this goal in mind. Our staff orientation sessions include staff of other services. Our professional and program staff give workshops to recreation and camping personnel in various parts of the province, as well as the interdisciplinary workshop held at camp. We educate non-specialized camps and recreation programs on how they can provide a positive experience to Towhee graduates. Senior professionals from clinics, school boards, universities, and education regions are invited to observe the camp in action. Our staff is selected from all parts of the province and they return to their locales better equipped to serve the l.d. or prepared to initiate new programs, with our assistance. Our outreach team is oriented to educating parents, teachers, and other professionals and agencies in a child's home area, with the resultant improvement of services for our clients and other l.d. children.

A project such as Camp Towhee utilizes considerable human and financial resources so that, if it merely served sixty children, one would have to question its validity. However, its impact on the province has been of considerable consequence so that we feel that it is more than worthwhile.

What Happens to Our Campers

At the time of this writing, we have had a community liaison worker for nine months, so that children served previous to this past summer received only minimal follow-up. Some of our children come to us from remote rural areas where no one knows what a learning disability is, and some come from sophisticated urban areas where they receive highly specialized remediation. They come from supportive homes and they come to us as state wards. Their IQ's range from low normal to very superior; some converse beautifully whereas others are aphasic. A few are athletic and many are clumsy. None of them have the social or behavioral skills to function in an integrated camp and that is why they attend Towhee.

242

During the course of the summer some make remarkable gains in reduction of deficit areas and some show minimal improvement. However, all grow discernibly in confidence. They are noticeably different in the way they feel about themselves—they are competent swimmers, can ride a bike, a horse, build a raft, skate, and so on. In their ability to live with others they have made gigantic strides. They take others into consideration, take turns, defer gratification, have begun to develop empathy with their peers, and relate warmly to adults. They are more competent in organizing themselves and their time.

Predictably, when they return to the city, a few children do not maintain their gains, some do for part of the year, and many, with our help, continue to grow. The most fascinating result has been that children with whom we did not feel that we had made a remedial "breakthrough" returned to school, graduated from special class shortly after camp, and attributed their improvement to Camp Towhee's program. I only can conclude that their improved self-esteem and expectations of improvement were the decisive factors.

What Can We Learn from a Project Such as Camp Towhee

Whatever the reasons, l.d. children are turned off by school. However, when we transport them to an exciting environment, rich with stimulation such as camp, we can find new ways whereby they can be reached and learn. We can develop methods whereby every aspect of living is a potential learning experience. We can research and begin to document material such as how social learning occurs, how we deal with the feelings of the l.d. child, and the value of a twenty-four hour therapeutic environment in effecting change in the l.d.

In the course of my involvement with Towhee I have made some fascinating observations, a couple of which are: (1) the hyperactivity of all but one or two campers disappears after two weeks of camp so that, what once may have been an organic hyperactivity seems to be anxiety-based or secondary in the child of eight years of age and older, and (2) l.d. children seem to be able to direct their attention despite copious auditory and visual distractions if they are not anxious, know what is happening, and realize that unreasonable demands are not being made of them.

"At Camp Towhee they love you even though you don't do always good."

/s/ Helene
Towhee Camper

Chapter 18:

Program Ideas and Games

AN INCREASING NUMBER of special education programs are being transported to the informal settings of camps and ranches. As well as providing new and exciting ways of learning, these settings provide the students and teachers with opportunities to relate on an informal level, to become friends, and begin to know one another. Thus, it was the coordinator of special education of a school board who asked me to make certain that I included program ideas in this book that could be utilized in the camp setting.

DRAMA

Drama has endless possibilities for developing body and verbal expression, acquiring a sense of time and space, becoming sensitive to people's feelings, learning how to express and control emotion, developing concentration, and improving sequential memory systems. I am particularly indepted to Helen Porter for her endless supply of ideas, many of which have been incorporated in the following activities.

Tell the children a sequence of activities which are part of their daily routine and have them pantomime them. Have the other youngsters comment on how realistic the pantomime was, and which actions were omitted.

Tell them a situation and have them act it out. The others discuss whether people in those circumstances would act that way, whether they were portraying how the people would feel, and how they would feel in that situation.

Have each child express a greeting, goodbye, or other commonplace act, and the others guess his mood and tell which cues they used.

Show the children a picture and have them tell what the picture conveys to them, what preceded it, and what is likely to follow. Then have them act out the sequences.

Tell them a phrase and have them develop a skit around it.

Tell them two random words and have them develop a skit around them.

Give them several random objects and have them develop a skit.

Tell them a story. Then each child takes on the role of one character, thinks about how that character feels, the mannerism he is likely to have, then acts it out, or pantomimes it. The other children discuss whether the acting is realistic. The counselor stops the actors periodically to ask them how they feel at that particular moment. Sometimes the children switch parts during the course of the story.

Have the children act out one scene from a story and do as above.

Have them act out an event which occurred at a different point in history, in America or in other countries. Discuss the customs of that time and country, and try to portray them realistically.

Have the children make up stories and act them out.

Have a child pantomime an activity and others guess what it is; for example, peel a banana or be a banana being peeled, open a can or be a can being opened, be a bottle being capped, and so on.

Make finger puppets, papier-mache puppets molded over greased light bulbs, paint-stir stick puppets, or puppets on a stick with divided fastener limbs. Make up a puppet show and act it out in a theater made of a carton or inverted bridge table set upon an upright table. Have the children take turns being leader of the skit teams.

Develop a number of possible situations that would take place in a telephone conversation and have one of the speakers express his viewpoint while being allowed to use only one word such as "no" or "yes" in his speech.

Set up a situation where two children participate in a pretend phone conversation or skit in which each has a different viewpoint and tries to convince the other person of the validity of his viewpoint. Get them to ask the other person why he thinks that way and have him try to see the other person's point of view. Set up imaginary situations and also situations similar to their real problems in interaction.

Exercises in Movement

Relaxing exercise—bend from head to toe and back up very slowly.

Pretend you are an ice statue that is melting.

You are lying on the floor of a strange and frightening room. You wake up to find that there are no doors or windows and the walls and ceiling start to move in on you. You must push them away from you with all your strength. They finally defeat and flatten you.

Move in a heavy, confined way.

Pretend you are bouncing a ball (Indian rubber or a basketball). Bounce high and low, all to the beat of music.

Walk down the street in an open, free, and carefree manner, to the music of "Feeling Groovy."

Play a pretend game of tennis in slow movement using all positions and levels.

With a partner be the mirror of the other person. Do whatever he does, in slow motion, light and fantastic, angrily, drowsily.

Divide into teams. The leader does the movement which the second person follows. The third person follows the second, and so on down the line.

Each team designs an unusual machine using team members as "parts" of the machine. Each person has a noise that he makes up to go with the action. Homemade musical instruments can provide the music for the machines. (Liquid around rim of glass rubbed by finger, comb covered with tissue, etc.)

Take a list of words and make their sounds and actions in a pattern of movement. Categorize them into groups. (Plop, burst, swim, fly, slither, twist, freeze.)

Curl up into a little ball and on the beat of the drum, unwind and stretch out in all directions. On the beat, curl back up in a snap.

Run through your movements from the time you wake up until you go to work. Now run through them after having awakened from a nightmare that still haunts you.

With a partner plan a scene in which one person is the "aggressor" and the other, the "victim." Music: Prokofiev, *Romeo and Juliet*.

Using a poem such as "Jaberwocky," divide the campers into groups and have each group act out a different idea or character, with one person narrating.

Play a jungle rhythm dance record and have everyone respond to the beat using every part of their bodies. Encourage them to *feel* the rhythm.

With a partner create an individual processional march to a god before whom you must bow. Make it stately and proper with variations. Music: processional with steady beat.

Pantomime the funeral of a Russian Grand Duchess. Everyone must play a significant role: mourner, priest, pallbearer, or townspeople. Music: funeral scene, *Dr. Zhivago*.

Create a tribal ceremony in a primitive African village with everyone participating in a human sacrifice ritual to the god. Children can be priests, priestesses, villagers, dancers, or musicians. Use homemade instruments to create a pulsating beat. Make a tape recording and play it back to the children.

Be a leaf blown by the wind, a tightrope walker, Noah with the dove flying out of the ark. (Release the dove, follow with eyes, etc.) Pretend to write names with blow torches, paint brushes, etc. Be on a crowded bus. Pretend to be walking on stones, mud, or cement. Pull a man up over the side of a cliff. Pretend you are: trees in a storm; cleaning the stars; on the torture rack. Partners together pretend they are the wind blowing. Pretend you are passing a hurt bird, a case of explosives. Be a butterfly.

Move like words sound.

Move different parts of the body to fast and slow music.

Pretend you are: a flower growing into a monster; tearing up the earth; a jack-in-the-box; snake charmer; playing in slow motion in the schoolyard; climbing stairs.

Pretend it is Christmas morning and you didn't sleep all night. You sneak out to look at the gifts with a mixture of anticipation, fear, and excitement. Pretend you are opening the gifts.

You are a sad old man selling balloons in the corner of a park. You sell a balloon to a little girl, a nasty lady, and a drunk sailor.

Pretend you are a snake.

Be a three-speed toy moving very quickly, moderately, slowly.

Improvisation

Walk down the street after a bitter argument with your lover.

Wander by mistake into a dangerous area of the city.

You are working in a steel foundry and hate your job and your boss. The job demands back-breaking work. Show your feelings about this as you do your job, emphasizing all parts of the work and all parts of your body. (Counselor acts as angry foreman pushing the workers.)

Draw faces on the blackboard and divide the children into groups. Each group designates a personality and other characteristics to the face. Spokesman from each group tells what their group saw in the face. Next, each child picks one of these personalities. He answers the phone saying only "yes" the way his character would. He repeats the action, now saying only "no."

Children talk about different ages in time and different events, deciding which would make the best setting for a play. Decide on course of action and assign characters. It should have three parts: beginning, climax, and ending. For example, "Mine Disaster" characters: miners, wives, mine officials, television commentator, bystanders, doctors, nurses, workers for relief. Pretend to be at the movies watching: a scary one, a funny one, a boring one. one.

Improvise a spaceship trip to the moon—taking off, checking controls, acting out eating, walking around the ship, sighting earth, landing, finding rocks, weightless walking, planting a flag.

Two brothers save $2.00 to buy their mother a gift. The money has been lost on the way to the store. Dilemma: the one who loses it discovers that the money is gone after they have chosen the gift. Act out variations on the resolution.

Act out: an old man lighting lamps at night, a teenager walking downtown, a child skipping over the pavement.

Tell the story of David and Goliath and then act it out. Act out scenes from *Kidnapped*. Pantomime a store robbery, old ladies visiting Rome and being robbed, Daniel fighting in the lion's den, a shipwreck.

Move like these words sound: growl, fly, slurp, bubble, and boil.

Improvise from these statements: "We won!" "I didn't mean to hurt him." "How silly you are!" "What is he doing?"

Prepare a skit to act out in the dining hall based on what happens at camp: "Clean up this cabin!" "Where's your buddy?"

Pantomime a burglar on the job and an old man going out to sea.

Improvise a baseball game—commentator, players, spectators, popcorn boys. Be a slow moving baseball.

Listening. What do these sounds make you think of? How would they fit into a movie sound track? Listen to this record of a movie sound track.

What do you think was the mood of the movie? The plot? Do the same with portions of the sound track.

Looking. Pass an object around the group. What could it be used for? Make up a story about it. Look at the room: like a cat would, an artist, a tall person, short person, happy person, sad person, as if you could see only black and white.

Smelling. Talk about smells and what they convey. Make up a story concerning smelling, for example, a forest fire. Walk around camp to see how many odors can be detected, and their message.

Touching. Do the same as for "smelling."

Breathing. Take a deep breath. Hold it while you count to "4" in your head. Exhale, saying "ah." Keep throat and jaw relaxed. Breathe in to the count of "4." Hold to "4." Count aloud to "5." Increase to 6, 7, 8, 9, 10.

ARTS AND CRAFTS

Remediation in every area of deficit can occur in the arts and crafts program.

Fine-motor and Spatial Organization

Following simple patterns for purses, moccasins, wallets, and toy animals, teach knitting, sewing, lacing, beadwork, and braiding.

Macrame—make a loom on trees with sticks and nails.

Draw a design on paper, translate the design onto a piece of wood, hammer nails in at strategic points, and wrap yarn around to make a picture.

Draw a pattern for a wooden toy boat, animal cage, etc. Translate pattern to three dimensions onto wood. Saw wood and assemble.

Using local reeds, make baskets.

Cut a doll house out of a cardboard carton and make furniture out of wood scraps, egg cartons, paper cups, tomato and strawberry boxes.

Carve eating utensils from pieces of wood.

Use popsicle sticks or coffee stir sticks stuck together to make objects or designs.

Wind colored string around a tin can covered with glue to make a pencil holder.

Cut pictures from a magazine and paste in a scrapbook to make your own catalogue, then write a description and price for the items.

Make papier-mache jewelery, with beads made from triangles cut from magazine pictures rolled tightly and glued.

Hammer nails on a piece of wood. Twist rope around the nails and drop at points for a rope sculpture.

Make animals out of styrofoam, plastic bottles, tubes from tin foil. Make people out of the above as well as using pipe cleaners or twisted stove-pipe wire.

Draw a map of the camp. Draw a map of a special outdoor program. In what part of the field was the booth from China? Where was the log-rolling activity?

Make a miniature Japanese garden in a box or a small plot of land.

Visual Organization

Mold a clay square or rectangle. Using index finger, make one indentation. Look in the woods and find a fern or other plant which would look attractive in the indentation. Change the plant periodically.

Paste stones on wood to make a pattern, then paint.

Cut hollow rubber balls in half. Place an object from nature (stones, ferns, etc.) in a visually attractive arrangement on the concave (underside) of the ball. Pour plaster of Paris in the ball and when hard, cut the ball away. If you wish, paste several of these different-size plaster semicircles on a piece of wood, in an interesting arrangement. Give the child a series of the same or different shapes and he pastes them into a design.

Gross-motor and Spatial Organization

Build rafts, docks, cabins, lean-tos, tree houses, soap-box racing cars, bird houses, pottery kilns, an aquarium, etc.

Sequencing

Make murals for a program. Make a map of a hike and draw pictures of what the campers did on the map at the locations where they saw a bird, etc.

Draw sequential scenes in a story on a long sheet of paper. Then make a shoebox theater with pencils inserted at each side of the narrow end, the paper fastened to one pencil, rolled around it and attached to the other pencil. The lid then is replaced on the box and the opposite narrow end of the box is cut out so that the children can watch the story as the camper narrates it. This can be done on a larger scale with a carton.

Body Concept

Sew gloves, slippers.

Press your hand or foot in the sand. Pour plaster of Paris in the depression for sand casting.

Lie on craft brown paper and have a cabinmate trace the outline of your body. Turn around, face down, and repeat. Then cut out the back and front of your body, glue together, and draw in the clothing and features. Hang it beside your bed. Make other paper people in the same fashion. Cut them into puzzles or use them to play "Pin the foot (hand, head, arm, leg) on a person."

Pose while your cabinmates draw you.

Translate a three-dimensional person or animal to a one-dimensional sheet of paper. Translate a picture to a three-dimensional clay or plasticine object.

Language

Print different letters on slips of paper at intervals. Weave them cross and lengthwise and pull different strips to see what word you can make.

Paste pasta letters on a circle of wood to make a special message and varnish or paste them on a cardboard dressmaker's cone and spray with glitter paint.

Random Ideas

Stones painted into animals or people. Paste them onto each other.

Kite making.

Egg carton stone collection.

Leaf rubbing.

Sanding and varnishing driftwood.

Decorating the cabin. Paste pictures on a large tin can and shellack. Make tie-dye curtains or potato prints. Make nameplates to hang beside each camper's bed, and mobiles (learn to balance the sides equally). Make a duty chart, duty tree, or duty wigwam, and wall hangings painted or sewn to look like hangings in an old castle. Paint the cabin theme on windows. Present the plaque to the dining hall.

Music

These activities are offered with special thanks to Nancy Minden for her endless ingenuity.

Have the children clap to language, then tell whether a word is a one-, two-, or three-clap word. Then print the word on the chalkboard, separating it by syllables. Child says the word and claps it again. Child writes notes on the board in the same rhythm as the word. Child suggests one-, two-, and three-clap words, spells and writes them on the board.

Counselor says a sentence and child writes notes on board which correspond with her sentence. For example, "I am going for a swim." (♩ ♩ ♩♩ ♩ ♩ ♩)

Counselor plays a song, then child leads her in the song by pointing to the notes on the note ladder so she will know which notes to play. (Graduated series of notes: ♩ ♩ ♩ ♩) Child learns to play musical instrument and another directs him by pointing to notes.

Children make a rhythm band and keep time to classical music.

Children listen to music and discriminate between concepts of "higher, lower, highest, lowest, louder, softer, chord, discord, major, minor."

Children guess the mood of the music.

Teach half, quarter, and eighth notes to assist with mathematics comprehension.

Children close their eyes and guess the direction from which the music is coming.

Children draw to music, telling a story that the music reminds them of, then telling it while the music is playing, or they pantomime a story to music.

Concept of Time

Each evening when the children are in bed, talk about what will happen the next day. The following morning, mark the day off on the calendar and circle important days such as special programs and visitor's days. Write the date on the cabin chalkboard and draw a picture of a special event that will occur that day. Draw a time-line and mark it off in spaces related to the time blocks allocated to the daily events. Write the days of the week on a piece of poster paper with a picture beside each day of the special event that occurs on that day.

Set the hands of the cardboard blocks in the cabin to the times for meals, general swim, and activity periods. Give each child a bag of candies and a paper plate. He is to place one candy each in the same position as the numbers on the clock. When the counselor calls out a time, the camper sets his candy clock to that time, using licorice sticks as hands. Each time he gets a correct time he is allowed to eat the number at which the big hand is pointing. Have the campers time some of their routines and activities, guess how long they will take, then set the stopwatch.

WATERFRONT ACTIVITIES

These activities are presented with special thanks to Diana MacKay.

Water Safety

Use water safety posters to illustrate lessons. Develop figure-ground discrimination by asking the campers what the poster is trying to say. Ask them to imagine variations on the poster's theme, and what they would do in each situation. Have them read the poster. Have them visualize the situations in their minds and ask them the sequence of events.

Practice the distance you would have to throw the buoy or extend the reaching pole in order to assist a person in distress. Have the children organize the response and sequence of events. Figure out how thick the ice must be before one can walk on it. Hold up your hand to show "six inches." Dig a hole in the sand six inches deep.

Put on a mask and open your eyes under water. Counselor holds up a specific number of fingers and child has to say the number and write it in the water or hold up the same number of fingers. Make shapes with your body or hands in the water and child has to make the same shapes. Hold up fingers in sequence and child has to hold up the same fingers in the same order. Do a series of movements and child has to repeat. Throw colored rocks into the water and child has to pick them up according to a specific sequence. Vary by numbering the rocks or writing the alphabet on them. Pick up rocks that when added up make "six" or when subtracted make "four" or that spell your name, etc. Touch left toe with right hand while underwater and repeat with other body parts. Sophisticate this exercise by holding up instructions written on a cardboard sheet and covered with plastic film. Submerge an instruction card in the water. Child has to read instructions and follow them. Work up from one instruction to several. When child is proficient, flash the instructions and hide the card. An example of such tasks are: "bob six times," "dive for rock," "read the number on your rock and clap your hands the same number of times." Have children swim while following the instructions on a "road sign" that you hold up. Number the buoy lines. Have children swim to each buoy and add the total of all the numbers to which they swam. Draw clocks on the buoys and say, "Swim to five o'clock," etc.

Tape the swim instruction session; play it back and have the children monitor their responses. Video tape the swimming lesson; show it to the children and have them see and talk about the way they use their bodies in swimming.

Diving

Establish a target and aim for the spot. Verbalize the sequence of body movement in the dive—hands go first, head next, then shoulders, back, and legs. After the dive, analyze and then have other campers analyze. Teach child to recognize when arms and legs are bent or straight. Teach diving in steps while sitting on the ladder. Practice in shallow water. Use hula hoops as diving targets.

Body Concept

Give instructions of what they are to do with their bodies while in the water, for example:

Put your knees against your chest and your forehead on your knees. Wrap your arms around your knees.

Put your hands behind your back and find the stone on the dock behind you.

When you are floating or I am supporting you in the water, what parts of your body are on top and what parts are underneath? What parts of your body are above water and what parts are below?

Place your hand on top of your head. If your hand becomes wet, then your head is wet.

Do somersaults and handstands in the water. How does your body feel under water, heavier or lighter? Practice submerging objects held in the hands to determine whether they feel heavier or lighter under water. Discuss why. For example, a hollow foam buoy becomes heavier under water because the trapped air is drawing it towards the surface. Why do people float? What is the difference between air and water?

Skin Diving

Skin diving is particularily beneficial for beginning swimmers who are afraid of water. It gets their head under the water and eliminates the fear of getting water in the eyes and nose. Have them figure out the size of their faces and which masks will fit their faces, then the size of their feet and which flippers would fit. Children learn how big their heads are when they adjust the mask, which is, in itself, a fine-motor task. Flippers make them more conscious of their feet and their movements. Involve distractible children in observing details underwater. Play such games as, "Take five steps to the right and two steps backwards and let's see what you can find." Many of the games that were mentioned for swimming can be utilized in skin diving. Have the children collect items underwater. Later they can look them up in the encyclopedia, categorize them, etc.

Boating

Rowboating is an excellent method for teaching upper body coordination, left-right orientation, and concepts such as forward, backwards, push, and pull. In canoeing the children learn how to cross the midline, how to paddle on either side of the canoe, the names of the parts of the paddle and canoe, and where to sit in the canoe. In sailing they learn the names of the parts of the boat, and which parts are on the right or left (you can remember "port" because it has four letters just like "left" and both end in "t"). They learn to gauge the wind and which direction to swing the sail.

Other Water Games

Hit the Deck. Each child pretends he's a boat with a bow, stern, starboard (right), port (left). Counselor calls, "bow" and they have to move or swim forward, calls "stern" and they have to swim backwards, etc. Other commands are: "Captain is coming"—everyone salutes; "Scrub the deck"—everyone underwater; "Hit the deck"—everyone flops hard onto the water; "Parade the deck"—everyone marches.

Newspaper Relay. Swim or run with paper in hand, keeping paper dry. Touch buoy, run or swim back and give paper to next person on team.

Wheelbarrow Races. In water or sand.

Egg-on-Spoon Relay. This can be varied with legs-in-burlap-sack relay, orange-under-chin relay, all carried out in water.

Water Polo. Excellent for children who have poor eye-hand coordination, stamina, and distance perception. Use Frisbies for tossing. Have children calculate the distances.

On the Beach

1. Have the child walk large shapes in the sand: circles, triangles, squares, straight lines, crosses, wavy lines, then walk numbers and letters.

2. Bury the hand in the sand and wiggle the fingers up, one at a time.

3. Child closes eyes while adult puts different textured things against soles of his feet, palms of hand, and back. Child guesses what they are. Use sand, stone, water, grass, towel, and shovel.

4. Child closes eyes and adult places different objects in his hand. Child guesses what they are. Use right and left hands. Describe how object feels.

5. Bury different objects in sand. Child puts hand in sand, has to find objects and guess what they are.

6. Bury stones of different sizes in sand. Child has to find smallest, next small, etc., then bring to surface and line up in order of size. Use right and left hands.

7. Draw three shapes in sand. Child looks at them, closes eyes, and says what they are in left-to-right sequence, for example, circle, square, cross. When child is able to do that, increase number of shapes. Then progress to numbers, letters, and words.

8. Have child draw shapes, numbers, letters, and words in sand with index finger. Use both dry and wet sand. Draw same things using sticks.

9. Have child pick up small stone using thumb and each successive finger. Use right and left hands.

10. Bury adult or other child in sand. Have child guess where parts of body are under sand; for example, "Here's my chest, thigh, knee, elbow, shoulder, hands, feet, arms and legs, legs end here."

11. Place different amounts of sand in tin cans. Child feels cans and places in order of weight from left to right. Use right and left hands.

12. Place stones in one can, and water in one can. Decide which is heavier. Place as above using left and right hands.

13. Using plastic measuring cups, pour stones from 8 oz. cup to 16 oz. cup, trying not to spill. Learn at same time that one cup = 8 oz., 2 cups = 1 pint. Now pour stones from 16 oz. cup to 3 oz. cup. Learn 4 cups = 1 quart, 2 pints = 1 quart. Repeat with sand and water.

14. Make the same number of sand piles as your age. Write your age and name in the sand.

15. Fill large, empty plastic bottle with sand and water and try to hit circle in sand with bottle.

16. Do same as number 13 with empty cardboard milk cartons. Pour from pint carton into quart, then into 3 quarts.

17. Bake a sand and water cake using measuring spoons, large bowl, and measuring cups. Learn measurements on measuring spoons, assemble and stir. (Good motor-movement training.)

18. Fill glasses with various levels of water. Assemble in order of fullness from left to right. Tapping a stick against glasses, play a tune.

19. Turn bucket upside down. Tap rhythm on bottom of bucket. Child repeats rhythm. Graduate from a three-tap-rhythm to more taps, then introduce stick taps, palm taps, and shovel taps in same rhythm.

20. Stand behind child and tap bucket. He has to tell where you are standing. Tap rhythm from behind him and have him repeat on his bucket.

21. Kick beach ball, catch beach ball. Catch ball with plastic scoop.

22. Hold bucket in front of child at different distances. Have him stretch arms first, then feet, to reach bucket and tell whether it is too far or too near.

23. Walk through dry sand, wet sand, grass, then water. Describe how it feels to walk through various media, then pretend to walk through same media. Do we have to exert more effort or less?

24. Throw a stone in the bucket, first from one foot away, then two, etc. Use right and left hands. Make a hole in sand, throw stone in hole from various distances.

25. Hop various shapes in sand. If child can skip, skip shapes in sand.

26. Make obstacle course in sand using rocks and cardboard cartons. Child pretends he is a snake and has to wiggle on belly through obstacle course.

27. Draw a long line on sand. Child has to walk on the line, one foot after another, forwards, backwards, sideways. Place buckets along line. Child has to walk on line and throw stones in buckets.

28. Play "Angels in the Sand."

29. Have child wet hands, make several hand prints in sand, and then see whether he can place correct (right or left) hands on prints already made. Repeat with footprints. Have adults make some prints. Child has to match his right hands and feet and left hands and feet with prints made by adult.

30. Adult wets feet and walks across sand using short steps, long steps, steps to the side. Child then walks on adult prints. If you miss stepping on a print, you are out.

31. Play sand hopscotch. Child is not likely to hurt himself if he falls.

32. See how many sounds we can hear while on the beach: wind, birds, ducks, seagulls, waves, people. Describe sounds.

LEARNING THROUGH THEME PROGRAMING

Every theme that a group or the entire camp chooses has endless possibilities for remediation and learning. Suppose a cabin group chose "Natives of America" as their theme for a period of time. Some suggested projects might be:

Make a life-size Indian out of craft brown paper, paint front and back, name body parts. Make another and cut it into a puzzle.

Make Indian moccasins from a pattern. Make headbands, headdresses, costumes, bead work, eating utensils, totem poles, tom-toms, and peace pipes.

Learn Indian songs, dances, and stories. Sing and dance for other campers and tell the story with actors or pantomime it. Accompany on the tom-tom.

Learn to make a fire and cook Indian foods for other campers to taste.

Play "Follow the Indian" and "Indian Chief Says" ("Simon Says").

Learn how to pitch a tent or make a teepee.

Develop your own Indian language using rhythms on the tom-tom, smoke from the campfire, and your own written symbol system. Send each other messages.

Make a diarama of an Indian village.

Learn about the Indian before the white man came and the Indian of today. Obtain reference books from the library.

Talk about how Indians used to feel in specific situations and how they feel now in specific situations. Have groups of children act out each situation. Play "What If," using situations such as: "If you were an Indian alone in the woods, were lost with no food or water, what would you do?

Plan a visit to an Indian reservation. Decide on what information the campers will be seeking ahead of time and write down the interview questions. At the reservation tape the interviews. Return to camp and write up the interviews. Write or tape a play or story about the Indians of today. Talk about what the children observed while at the reservation. What would be their solutions to some of the problems? Mark Indian tribes on a map of North America.

Perhaps a group decides to use the theme "Early Settlers of America." They could listen to the stories, learn the songs, make the costumes and implements. Draw the early settlers' routes on the map with a magic marker or with wool strung between two pins. Hunt the woods for edible foods that were used by the settlers. Talk about how it felt to walk across America, how long it would take to walk from place to place without roads or bridges. Solve how a wagon train would cross a deep stream without a bridge, discuss how it would feel to have no neighbors. Talk about how people could be self-sufficient, functioning without stores. Discuss the extent to which we are dependent on others in our twentieth century society. Read one of the many current books on how to live off the land and have the campers make their own soap, candles, etc. Hold a settler day for the camp in which each group sets up booths, with some possible activities being apple bobbing, pancake making, log rolling, log chopping, and fire building. Close with a pioneer outdoor supper and pioneer stories around the campfire.

Some other theme ideas might be:

Circus	Shapes
Comic Book Characters	Hippies
Countries of the World	Transportation
States of U.S.A.	Communication
African Safari	Mythology
Sailors	Religions
Vikings	Wild Animals

"Shapes" can be an exciting theme for the entire camp. Each group can be a different shape. They could silk-screen the shape on their shirts, make large decorations for their cabin using the shape as the basic design, discuss the meaning of shapes and words denoting shape in communication, such as "You're a square," "The shape of things," "Let's look at this from another angle," and so on. They can plan a "Shape Day" in which each group cooks food in their shape (triangular turnovers, open-faced sandwiches, oval weiners, squiggly lasagna), and each group makes up a series of land and water games using their shapes. They must make up the rules of the games and teach them to the other campers.

LANGUAGE GAMES AND ACTIVITIES

Take polaroid pictures of a cabin program and describe the program in the dining hall using pictures in sequence. Or do as above and write a story below each picture.

Follow Indian trail signs, have a scavenger hunt, a treasure hunt (directionality and reading).

Read a recipe for cooking and then write up the recipe for other groups.

Have a library in each cabin.

Sing jingle songs in the dining room in which campers make up the verses, for example, "Quartermaster's Store."

Carry on a conversation in rhyme: "How are you?" "Feeling blue."

Make up rhymes around camper's and staff names.

Reach in the bag, pull out a word, and say a word that rhymes with it or make up a jingle around it.

Make catalogues and describe items in them. (Many l.d. children do not have a good store of adjectives.) Collect items in the woods, categorize and describe their shape, size, texture, and weight.

Roll a ball to each child and when he rolls it back he must say the name of an object in a predetermined category, such as fruits, vegetables, meats, countries, furniture, or transportation. Whenever there is doubt about a word, the children should discuss the attributes something has to have in order to belong in a specific category. If the children disagree about an object mentioned, it should be looked up in the dictionary. Whenever an object is mentioned with which a child is unfamiliar, have the cook order that fruit, vegetable, or meat, if possible, or show him that piece of furniture, or, failing that, show him a picture and describe it.

Look through magazines and catalogues. Name objects and describe.

Auditory Memory

The children sit in a circle. Each calls out his name. When "it" in the center calls out two names, those two players must change places while calling out their names. While they are doing this, "it" calls out his own name and tries to get one of the chairs of the two moving children. If he succeeds, the dispossessed player is "it." When "it" calls out "change," all the campers change seats.

The children stand in a circle and each calls out his name, going clockwise. Second time around, each camper must call out the name of the child on his right. Third time around, he must call out the name of the person two removed on his right. Then combine names with a simultaneous hand clap, hands on head, legs crossed, or foot tap.

The children stand in a circle and "it" in the center calls out a command to a specific camper, who must then do the opposite of the command.

Make two equal teams and give each player in a team a number from zero upwards, for example, first player is "zero," second is "one," and so on. One team colors their paper plates red and the other team colors theirs blue. They print their numbers on their plates and the two teams line up facing each other. "It" stands in the middle and calls out two-, three-, or four-digit numbers. Each team member with the appropriate number runs to the center and stands in proper order with his teammates so that the number reads correctly. The first team to get in place each time receives a point.

Each player is given the name of a part of a fireman's outfit or gear. Counselor keeps a list of the names he has given. Campers sit in a circle while the counselor tells a story about firemen. As he mentions an object assigned to a camper, that camper stands up and places his hand on the counselor's waist and walks after him. Next camper puts his hand on that camper's waist when his object is named, and so on. They walk around the circle and whenever the counselor calls out "fire," campers run back to sit in the circle. Can be varied by playing hunter, policeman, fisherman, cook, etc.

Play "I touched a table—I touched a table and then I touched a book." Each child touches and verbalizes all the objects that have been touched preceding his turn, touching and verbalizing them in the correct sequence, and then he adds an object to the list.

Categories. The children stand in a line with the leader facing them. Each thinks of an object in a predetermined category, telling one another the objects they have selected, but not telling the leader. "It" then names as many items as he can think of in that category. If he names an item that one of the campers has selected, that camper tries to run to the goal without being tagged by "it." If tagged, he becomes "it."

Tell a story and when children hear specific words they must do a corresponding action. Tell a story and whenever a child hears a word that starts with a certain sound he must clap, sit down, or stand up.

Auditory Discrimination

Peter Pan. Peter Pan sits in the middle of a circle of campers. He is wearing a blindfold. Each camper in the circle takes a turn being Captain Hook, who tries to sneak up on Pan to steal the treasure. If Pan hears a sound, he points in the direction of the sound he has heard and says, "Hook!" If he is pointing in the correct direction, the camper he is pointing at must go back to the circle. The camper who captures the treasure without being heard becomes "Pan." Vary using "Cat and Mouse."

Peter Pan, version 2. Pan and Hook each stand at opposite ends of the plank and both are blindfolded. Each tries to fool the other as to his whereabouts, for example, by making sounds, then running to another spot. When one is finally caught by the other, two other campers have a chance to be Pan and Hook.

Expressive Language

The children are all in a circle. "It" tries to make them say "good," "bad," "yes," or "no," asking all types of questions attempting to trick the children into saying these words. Each time a camper says one of the words, he is out and the last player left becomes "it." Vary using different words.

Body Concept

"It" walks around the circle whispering to each camper what he should make believe. "It" points to a camper who acts out his pantomime. The camper who guesses the other's pantomime acts his out next and then is "it."

The familiar game "Follow the Leader" can be done with an obstacle course, or with skipping and hopping, moving forwards and backwards.

All children except one sit in chairs in a circle, with one chair left vacant. "It" tries to sit down on the vacant chair while the other campers slide over to occupy the vacant seat. When "it" succeeds, the child left out is "it."

Two rows of children stand facing each other. "It" calls out commands such as "face to face," "side by side," "back to back," etc.

"It" leaves the room and the other players sit in a circle. They choose one player to be the leader, who makes a variety of motions which the other children imitate. The campers try not to look at the leader. "It" has to guess who the leader is. If he guesses correctly, he returns to the circle and another child has a turn.

Teach songs that have to do with body concept, such as: "One Finger, One Thumb," "Keep Moving," and "Dem Bones."

Directionality

Everyone in the circle says his name. "It" in the center points to a player and counts to five. Child to whom he is pointing must give the name of the child on his left before the count of five. If not, he becomes "it." Change to the right side, and then vary by having the children stand in a line and use "behind" and "in front of." When the campers become moderately proficient, the game can be made more sophisticated by having "it" call out "Right, 1-2-3-4-5," or "Left, 1-2-3-4-5." Finally he can substitute the words "dish" and "dash" for "right" and "left."

The campers sit on a chair in the circle. "It" calls out "shift right" or "shift left," sometimes several "shift rights" in a row or vice versa. During one shift, "it" tries to grab a chair and the child left out becomes "it."

MORE IDEAS FOR GAMES AND PROGRAMS

Body Image

Hang an old sheet or brown paper over the cabin door and make a hole in it. "It" stays outside and other players inside. Each camper puts part of his body through the hole (nose, feet, hand, etc.), and "it" guesses whose it is.

Sharp Eyes: "It" faces his cabin mates, then goes out of their view while he alters some item of his appearance, for example, changes his hair, undoes button, unties shirt. He returns and cabin mates have to spot the change.

Pantomime: With your body, show how you would climb stairs, cut meat, answer phone, put on pyjamas, brush teeth (don't forget steps such as turning tap off and putting paste on brush).

Pantomime: "Too hot, too cold, bitter, tastes good, peppery, oily, very sweet, very sour, something unfamiliar."

Pass around imaginary objects, changing objects frequently.

Marionettes: Thrust arm and index finger out. Child must touch your finger using the corresponding arm and finger. Do same with left arm, different fingers, thighs, forearms, etc.

Draw stick figures performing different movements. "It" must do movements with body. Then "it" draws figures and other camper must perform movements.

Imagery

Close your eyes and imagine your birthday party. Describe the day. Describe the birthday table.

Describe the camp in wintertime.

Describe the breakfast table at camp, the camp-wide program in correct sequence. Draw it (imagery and visual organization).

Guess what is in that bottle, medicine chest, drawer, etc.

Nature Games

Observe, smell, feel something with your eyes closed. Describe how things feel, compare, and taste. Describe shapes and sizes.

Make a terrarium, aquarium, or zoo. Study the natural habitat of animals that you wish to place there, and simulate it. Read which foods to feed them, the amounts and frequency.

Place a number of stones in a can and guess how much they weigh. Put different amounts of stones in several cans, discuss which is heavier, heaviest, lighter, and lightest.

Learn how to tie different knots. Cut lengths of a log and build a stool using knots instead of nails.

Learn to build a campfire. Find edible plants and go into the woods with no food, finding a meal from nature.

Make a barometer, weathervane, and sundial. Predict weather and broadcast over the camp radio station.

Learn to read a compass and take a hike following the compass.

Bird Watch: Look up the birds in an encyclopedia. Observe the different ways birds fly.

Nature Memory Test: Put a bunch of items found in the woods in a paper bag. Child closes his eyes, feels, and fishes them out, has to tell what he fished out in a sequential order. Or he closes his eyes and describes how the items in the bag feel.

Hide an object in the woods, such as a pine cone. Have a camper steer "it" to the hidden object by verbal commands. (Two steps forward, one to the right, etc.). This can also be done with "it" blindfolded.

Tell what event in your life smells and sounds remind you of, for example, smoke, bacon, fresh cut grass, hay, a bird singing, perfume, meat broiling. Walk around the campsite with eyes blindfolded. How many smells can you smell or sounds can you hear?

Nature Hike: How many items can you name? What items go into a bird's nest? Label trees with correct tags. Make a nature trail.

Category Games

Make a category chart for birds, mammals, trees, and fish.

Play a completion game: "Yellow reminds me of   ."
                        "The water is as rough as   ."
                        "Rushing water sounds like   ."
                        "How many words describe taste?"
                        "Describe this leaf, stone, etc."
                        "Describe the scene in front of you."

Repeat a four-line story, a three-line story, etc.

Tap a rhythm and use different tapping devices and surfaces. Child repeats using same devices and surfaces in same order.

Walk around camp and name objects. Many children do not know common words such as basin, bannister, teeth of a comb, bristles of brush, bottle cap, window sill or ledge, window pane. It is very important to repeat the game several days in a row and then come back to words a few days later. Learning-disabled children need to overlearn.

Gross-motor games

1. Roll downhill while grasping an object between your feet.

2. Child lies down on the edge of a blanket with his hands clasped over his head. Several children grasp the edge of the blanket and roll the child down a grassy incline, or roll the child out.

3. Conduct a grooming class which would include walking with a book on the head, then sitting with a book and a block on the head (or a book and a cup), then try walking with both on the head.

4. Crawl and push a potato or orange with your nose toward a target. Have a spoon relay (ball in spoon). Have a race blowing a ping-pong ball.

5. Frog race: children make a divided race track, measure out distances, mark distances, catch frogs, train and time them, and time the race.

6. Draw a circular course in the sand. Child crawls through it, then directs a blindfolded child how to crawl through it. For example, "Crawl one foot forward, turn left," etc. Walk through it blindfolded, crawl through it, and then draw an identical course in the sand from memory, or a picture of the course on paper. Draw a miniature course with your toes on wet and dry sand.

7. Children walk forwards, backwards, and sideways to and from a goal, up and down hills, up and down steps, through an obstacle course, and are timed by cabinmates. Repeat with crawling. Repeat with walking left foot over right. Reverse, walk on tiptoe, on knees.

8. Walk as different animals do. For example, a rooster—head and chest high, straight back with straight knees and hands at side of chest, wiggle elbows to flap wings. Bear—walk on all fours with legs stiff, keep head up, hands and feet plodding. Elephant—bend forward at waist, touch floor with hands, walk with big lumbering steps, swaying from side to side. Ostrich—bend forward at waist, grasp ankles, keep knees stiff while walking, stretch neck in and out. Duck—deep-knee bend, hands behind back with outsides together and fingers extended as tail of duck, walk forward one foot at a time, in bent knee position.

9. Assemble a number of objects of various heights. Children walk on top of them playing "follow the leader."

10. Arrange a crooked path of stones. Children walk on them without touching ground—turn like a dog, crab, horse.

11. Piggyback run.

12. Race blindfolded to a goal.

13. Walk along a fallen log holding a full glass of water. Have a relay game in which a player must walk the log and hand the full glass to the next person at the end of the log.

14. Relay race rolling tires to a goal while blindfolded.

15. Throw a crumpled paper into wastebasket.

16. Play "William Tell"—throw sponges at an apple on a child's head. Knock the apple off without hitting the child.

17. Throw a wet sponge at a counselor's face which is thrust through a hole in craft brown paper.

18. Knock down tin cans with rocks, throw rocks into cans.

19. Make a pyramid from empty milk cartons. Knock them down with a softball or a hardball. Throw a softball through an empty box.

20. Suspend a filled laundry bag or plastic garbage bag from the rafters of the cabin or from trees and throw a softball at it. Make a Mexican pinata and throw balls at it. When it falls and breaks, surprises are inside for the children.

21. Stand on one leg and throw balls at targets, then with one hand behind back.

22. Children go piggyback on other children's shoulders and one on piggyback throws a sponge at another on piggyback.

23. Jump from one seat of chair to the seat of another chair.

24. Jump over a candle.

25. Jump like a rabbit, kangaroo, frog. Slither like a snake.

26. Jump over natural hurdles—rocks, logs, etc. Jump over other children.

27. Jump rope, jump over a rope held by two children, skip along a rope held by two children. Make letters and numbers out of a piece of rope. Walk along the rope number or letter barefoot, then outside it, then inside.

28. Obstacle course—jump a box, jump rope ten times, jump a second box.

29. Have circle skip-games such as "go in and out windows." Skip shapes, figures, a large circle, a small circle. Skip to music, have skipping relays, skip up and down hill, in water, wet sand, dry sand, grass, along a line drawn on the beach, along a line of floor board. Skip to music fast, slow, and to drums. Skip while holding a child on your back. Imitate a crane or giraffe and skip. Skip backwards, skip while bouncing a ball, backwards, forwards, make into a relay.

30. Lighthouse: Camper holds a lighted flashlight in a dark room and turns around like a lighthouse. Campers are in a straight line facing him, some distance away. They have to wriggle to the goal without the light touching them. Vary with crawling forwards, backwards, crouching.

31. Indoor Hockey: Each camper is given a towel on which to skate. He uses a stick and plays indoor hockey using the stick, a puck, and the slippery towel under his feet.

Number Concept Games

Each camper has a paper plate on which a large colored number has been written. "It" calls out two-, three-, or four-digit numbers and campers have to run to a chalk line and stand in the correct left-to-right sequence to depict that number. Then make the game more difficult by calling out "two plus two" and "4" has to run up.

Write numbers on bingo cards and number facts on squares. The child matches number facts to the answer on the card.

Draw a hopscotch grid and print numbers in the squares. The child has to hop numbers adding up to ten or subtracting to four, etc.

Print numbers in the sand and the child does the same as above. Draw domino type numbers in the sand or make huge domino cards and do the same as above. Make a number line in the sand and the child walks along it to add and subtract. Use stones, sticks, leaves, etc., to teach concepts of one-to-one correspondence, amounts, addition, subtraction, and so on.

In the woods and on hikes match objects, talk about which objects go together, such as birds and nests, leaves and twigs. Count disarranged objects, count different objects, count objects visable but not touchable, count moving objects such as minnows in the lake, count objects just glimpsed such as pebbles in the sand, count missing objects such as petals of a flower, eggs in a carton, count events.

Sing sequence songs, such as: "The Smoke Went Up the Chimney Just the Same," "John Brown's Body," "Ninety-Nine Bottles of Beer on the Shelf."

Play dice games and dominoes.

Spatial Orientation

Play checkers, chess, dominoes, dice games. Copy pictures and patterns. Draw pictures, scenes, and patterns from memory. Copy cube designs and peg designs. Make a huge checker grid on the ground and use the children as human discs or as chess men.

Phonics

All the campers stand facing "it." He says, "I went to the store and bought a bottle of ketchup. I went to the store and bought a bottle of mustard," etc., whatever he decides to buy. However, when he says that he bought an item which starts with the sound that the group decided was the key sound, everyone has to run to the goal post. He can tease the group by saying, "I went to the store and bought a can of b-b-b-peas."

Make a lotto game in which "it" calls out "chair" and the campers have to find the card with a picture of a chair printed or drawn on it. They then tack it to the chair. Children can make their own lotto cards and it can become very amusing because they can make cards depicting campers and staff.

Bake cookies or cupcakes and print a letter on each with whipped topping spray. Arrange to make words.

Eye-Hand Coordination Games

Paint empty tin cans and paint a different number on each can. Children toss pebbles into the cans and add up their score. Tack hot-drink paper cups to the cabin wall, print a number on each with a magic marker and do the same as with the tin cans.

Fill plastic bottles or empty milk cartons with stones. Use them as bowling pins. Vary by painting numbers on the bottles.

Make life-size pictures of the staff on brown paper and throw darts at strategic points.

Organization, Conceptualization

Have the children make up their own games using the criteria of high interest, payoff, and logical consequences. They must decide the age range and the rules. Have them write the games for the other campers to follow. Make a game manual or make table games in the arts and crafts shop. Then tell them what you are trying to accomplish in remediation and have them make up games that are remedial in nature.